STUDIES IN ENGLISH LITERATURE

Volume XXVI

Ralph Waldo Emerson

THREE CHILDREN OF THE UNIVERSE

Emerson's View of
Shakespeare, Bacon, and Milton

by

WILLIAM M. WYNKOOP

Rutgers, The State University

1966

MOUTON & CO.

LONDON · THE HAGUE · PARIS

Printed in The Netherlands by Mouton & Co., Printers, The Hague.

To My Mother,
Margaret Magee Wynkoop

PREFACE

A brief description of the development of this study may be helpful in clarifying its purpose. Growth proceeded in three stages, oddly suggesting those Emerson found repeated in every cycle of development; the present form represents the completion of the third and final stage.

In the beginning, I had intended to show Emerson's relations with seventeenth-century English writers – to determine his attitude toward them and the extent of their influence on him. During the period of research, however, I became increasingly aware of what seemed to be significant habits of mind revealed primarily in his statements about Shakespeare, Bacon, and Milton. It became more and more apparent to me that he tended habitually to see these three writers as symbols of three levels of religious development corresponding with the beginning, the middle, and the end of every cycle of growth. Furthermore, I found that the meaning of many of his passages, in which apparent contradictions and inappropriateness of tone had been confusing, became suddenly clearer because of this discovery. Soon I was almost certain that the dialectical pattern of development, which he had apparently seen in Shakespeare, Bacon, and Milton, formed a circular design that, so far as Emerson's thought could be thus systematized, constituted its central symbol. Knowing that he would have regarded such a symbol as incapable of representing all truth and that he may not have been aware of the help it would seem to have given him, I became convinced that, whether or not he was conscious of the fact, it had probably served him as a guide in the development of his ideas about human experience in this world. Regarded not as a pattern to be imposed on his thought, but as a guide in his exploration of truth, this symbol, despite its limitations, seemed to me to offer considerable aid in the study of his ideas. So far as I could determine, its potential value for students of Emerson had never been recognized.

Having concluded most of my research and abandoned my original intention of showing Emerson's relations with all the seventeenth-century English writers he knew, I began to write. My purpose, in this second stage, was twofold. First, I wished to show that his thought had reached its fullest development as a result of the impetus it had received when he discovered that his "insights" were "arcs" of circles that would comprise, if completed, a symbol of universal truth. Next, I wanted to prove that his statements about Shakespeare, Bacon, and Milton reveal an habitual, though perhaps unconscious, tendency to be guided by that symbol of truth, whose circular form was indicated by those "arcs" he claimed to have seen. The result, however, was disappointing: the two aspects of my purpose were not sufficiently unified. I had emphasized the development of Emerson's philosophy with the intention of presenting his statements about the three figures as the final evidence. But there was little justification for giving those statements such marked emphasis in a study chiefly concerned with his ideas; and, since my research had been devoted largely to his relations with the seventeenth century, I was not sufficiently prepared to give the development of his thought the treatment it required.

The third stage entailed much rewriting in an effort to change emphasis, as it were, and thus to unify what had previously threatened to split into separate studies. Stressing, in this final version, Emerson's view of Shakespeare, Bacon, and Milton, I have tried to limit my treatment of his philosophy to an exposition of those ideas that shed direct light on the manner in which he would certainly seem to have regarded these writers. I have not attempted to trace their influence on Emerson's life and works, but I have indicated how each of them, in his own way, greatly inspired him. I have tried to show, moreover, that while he was original primarily in that quality, pervading all his works, which he called "tone", his ideas, closely resembling Coleridge's, were essentially part of the Neo-Platonic tradition. But my chief purpose throughout has been to demonstrate that Emerson was habitually inclined to regard Shakespeare, Bacon, and Milton as the men most representative, in the period we would call the English Renaissance, of the three stages of growth reflecting the divine trinity he found reappearing "under different names in every system of thought".

W. M. W.

ACKNOWLEDGMENTS

While my chief indebtedness in writing this book may be to the subject itself, which I found repeatedly invigorating and challenging, I am deeply grateful to Prof. Marjorie Hope Nicolson and Prof. Lewis Leary, of Columbia University, New York, for their invaluable criticism, suggestions, and encouragement. It was written first under their supervision as a doctoral dissertation. However, I am most indebted to them, and especially Miss Nicolson, who was my chief adviser, for what I learned while writing it.

I wish to thank the Research Council of Rutgers, The State University, whose generous financial assistance has enabled me to complete this study as a book.

My indebtedness extends also to the Emerson Memorial Association and the Houghton Library, Cambridge, Massachusetts, for permission to see the manuscripts of Emerson's lectures and to include a portrait of him.

I am sincerely grateful for the help I have received in various ways from Messrs. Mouton & Co., from colleagues and friends, especially Prof. David Lilien of University College, Rutgers, The State University.

TABLE OF CONTENTS

INTRODUCTION

> For the Universe has three children, born
> at one time, which reappear under different
> names in every system of thought. . . .
> Emerson, "The Poet".

For Ralph Waldo Emerson the period we would call the English Renaissance produced the greatest constellation of geniuses since the time of Pericles.[1] It was, he said, "the richest period of the English mind, with the chief men of action and of thought which that nation has produced".[2] Its books were those "in which the English language has its teeth and bones and muscles largest and strongest, . . .".[3] Its literary life was a most "complete circle of means & ends".[4] But Emerson felt that death entered that circle when, as he put it, "the Platonism died in the Elizabethans".[5] Afterward, the "sense of unity or the instinct of seeking resemblances" no longer "predominated in the mind of England". In fact, a splitting of perception had occurred, similar to what T. S. Eliot has described as a "dissociation of sensibility". A a result, the poetic impulse had suffered, had almost died. From then on,

---

[1] "Shakespeare; Or, The Poet", *The Complete Works of Ralph Waldo Emerson*, ed. Edward Waldo Emerson (Boston, 1903-1904), IV, 203. Cited hereafter as *Works*.

[2] "Books", *Works*, VII, 207.

[3] *Journals of Ralph Waldo Emerson,* ed. Edward Waldo Emerson and Waldo Emerson Forbes (Boston, 1909-1914), V, 22 (Aug. 21, 1838). Cited hereafter as *Journals*.

[4] "To Margaret Fuller, Concord, April 22, 1841", *The Letters of Ralph Waldo Emerson*, ed. Ralph L. Rusk (Columbia University Press, 1939), II, 395. Cited hereafter as *Letters*.

[5] *Journals*, VII, 438 (April 15, 1848).

Emerson claimed, although men would love the "fruit" of poets, they would "hate the tree", that is, "the tendency of their minds".[6] But, tending to convert this loss to moral gain and thus to complete the era's cycle of development, a spiritual redemption would seem to have occurred with "the piety and principle" of Milton's time.[7]

Believing that history is "the group of the types or representative men of any age",[8] Emerson shows clearly in his works that, for him, the chief group of representative men in this period were Shakespeare, Bacon, and Milton. In an 1835 lecture he declared: "If the English should lose all but Shakspear, Milton, and Bacon the concentrated attention given to those writers might atone for all."[9] He referred in his journal, in 1838, to "the glory of the name of Shakspear, Bacon, Milton".[10] The work of all three, taken together, he implied elsewhere, might comprise a Bible for the English.[11] Indeed, the conscience of Martin Luther, "animating sympathetically the conscience of millions", had produced a wave of thought which "ultimated itself", in this period, in the "Shakespeares, Bacons, and Miltons".[12] The moral history of the epoch was therefore reflected in this group of three persons; they most fully represented, respectively, the beginning, the middle, and the end of a wave-like cycle of growth that began

[6] *Ibid.*, VIII, 493 (1854).
[7] *Ibid.*, IV, 92 (Sept. 23, 1836).
[8] *Ibid.*, VII, 383 (Jan., 1848).
[9] "On the Best Mode of Inspiring a Correct Taste in English Literature", *The Early Lectures of Ralph Waldo Emerson*, ed. Stephen E. Whicher and Robert E. Spiller (Harvard University Press, 1959), I, 212-213. Cited hereafter as *Early Lectures*.
[10] *Journals*, V, 148 (Nov. 26, 1838). Emerson usually wrote Shakespeare's name as "Shakspear", but he was not consistent in this spelling.
[11] "Books", *Works*, VII, 194.
[12] *Journals*, V, 151 (Dec. 9, 1850). Emerson's view of the moral development of the age, culminating in Milton, resembles closely Coleridge's. See "Milton", *The Complete Works of Samuel Taylor Coleridge*, ed. Shedd (New York, 1853), IV, 298-300. Cited hereafter as *Complete Works*. Coleridge gave this lecture on Milton in 1818; it was published in 1836 in *Literary Remains*. In "Literature", *Works*, V (*English Traits*), 242-243, Emerson, tracing the intellectual and literary history of that age, gives 1625 as the approximate date of greatest expansion. Francis Bacon died in 1626.

not long before Shakespeare's first works appeared and that had ended, or was about to end, when Milton died, a period that lasted from about 1575 to about 1675 with its midpoint close to Bacon's death. Emerson's view of this era, his moral attitude toward it, his interpretation of its significance are found chiefly in his statements about these three representative figures.

Yet his treatment of history was affected significantly by certain other habits of mind. Emerson was accustomed, for example, to pay close attention to those facts which researchers had uncovered.[13] He acquired his knowledge of Shakespeare and his age by wide reading. But he was habitually suspicious of the scholar's method. According to his theory of knowledge, this was also the method of the scientist; though necessary and thus deserving high esteem, it proved inadequate, even misleading, if relied upon exclusively. More enlightening was the method of the poet, who saw each fact as a symbol with universal meaning. Emerson seems to have regarded seriously, therefore, not only those historical facts which could be "scientifically" verified, but also his own poetic insights which would convert them into symbols. Habitually, he sought to achieve a synthesis of thought and moral feeling which, he believed, would yield such insights and, consequently, a closer approach to historical truth.

Shakespeare's life, for example, could not be truly revealed by historical research alone:

I think, with all due respect to Aubrey, and Dyce, and Delia Bacon, and Judge Holmes, that it is not by discovery of contemporary documents, but by more cunning reading of the Book itself, that we shall at last eliminate the true biography of Shakespeare.[14]

The habitual distrust of mere "facts" which would seem to have prompted this assertion is evident in Emerson's earliest writings such as the following journal entry of 1824:

---

[13] Thomas A. Perry, "Emerson, the Historical Frame, and Shakespeare", *Modern Language Quarterly*, 9 (Dec., 1948), 440.
[14] *Journals*, X, 279-280 (1869). "As has been said before, Mr. Emerson always used eliminate as *bring out*, instead of *leave out*." *Ibid.*, editor's note 1.

Let no man flatter himself with the hope of true good or solid enjoyment from the *study* of Shakespeare or Scott. Enjoy them as recreation. You cannot please yourself by going to stare at the moon; 't is beautiful when in your *course* it comes.[15]

A similar distrust appears, much later, in the remark that ". . . nothing is of any value in books excepting the transcendental and extraordinary"[16] and in such statements in "The American Scholar" as the warning that books "are for nothing but to inspire".[17] These passages are not mere rationalizations of indolence, but expressions of sincere beliefs integral to his whole philosophy. As such, they indicate his mental "set"; and they prepare his readers for those references to historical subjects which arise chiefly from a poetic, rather than a scholarly, approach.

Closely related to this attitude toward the historical method of research was Emerson's habit of reading, not for facts alone, but for "lustres", by which he meant those passages which were "a mechanical help to the fancy and imagination".[18] He showed, significantly, that he used not only books, but men,[19] for "lustres" because they might thus inspire "new visions".[20] Hence, although he had delved deeply in the literature and history of the Elizabethan period and the seventeenth century, his reading consisted primarily of a quest for sources of inspiration.

Emerson's "new visions", however, were not always, or chiefly, the result of perusing what is commonly considered "inspirational" or mystical literature. While he implied, in his journal, that he was "disgusted", at times, with historical writing that was "precise, external, and indigent", he insisted that, at other times, he was equally dissatisfied with Böhme, Swedenborg, and Carlyle,

---

[15]   *Ibid.*, I, 394 (1824).

[16]   *Ibid.*, V, 496 (Dec. 20, 1840).

[17]   "The American Scholar", *Works*, I, 89.

[18]   "Nominalist and Realist", *Works*, III, 233. Emerson's "lustres" would seem to resemble, in their effect on him, the "hints" that were the sources of the Sublime for the early eighteenth-century critic John Dennis. See Marjorie Nicolson, *Mountain Gloom and Mountain Glory* (Cornell University Press, 1959), pp. 281-83.

[19]   "Fate", *Works*, VI, 344, editor's note 2 to p. 26.

[20]   "Friendship", *Works*, II, 215.

who wrote history mystically.[21] Thus, he was inclined to be guided by moods, finding "lustres" now in one type of writing, now in another.

Emerson's treatment of historical subjects in his own works was affected also by his concept of himself as a poet. In 1835 he explained to Lydia Jackson, before their marriage, why he so regarded himself:

I am born a poet, of a low class without doubt yet a poet. That is my nature & vocation. My singing be sure is very "husky," & is for the most part in prose. Still am I a poet in the sense of a perceiver & dear lover of the harmonies that are in the soul & in matter, & specially of the correspondences between these and those.[22]

As "a perceiver & dear lover of the harmonies" resulting from reconciliation of the opposites that compose the universe, without which there is no true being, a poet, in attempting to describe an historical figure, would try first to determine the extent to which the opposites in the subject's soul were in harmony and then the correspondence between this state of the soul and its reflection in the material conditions of the subject's life. The attention thus given to the presentation of opposite sides of a character frequently made Emerson's statements sound contradictory.[23]

This concept of himself as a poet had other consequences. It freed him from the task of explaining to his readers why he felt

---

[21] *Journals*, VII, 20 (1845).
[22] "To Lydia Jackson, Concord, Feb. 1, 1835", *Letters*, I, 435. " 'I am,' he [Emerson] said, 'in all my theory, ethics, and politics, a poet.' " Leslie Stephen, "Emerson", in *Studies of a Biographer* (London, 1902), IV, 134.
[23] In Walter Blair and Clarence Faust, "Emerson's Literary Method", *Modern Philology*, XLII (1944), 79-95, the authors have suggested that Emerson's use of opposites is a dialectical method derived from Plato's "twice-bisected line". Philip L. Nicoloff, in *Emerson on Race and History; An Examination of "English Traits"* (Columbia University Press, 1961), pp. 50-53, stresses the indebtedness of Emerson's theory of opposites not only to Plato, but also to Plotinus and to such Pre-Platonic thinkers as Heraclitus whom he had encountered in his reading of de Gérando's *Histoire Compareé des Systèmes de Philosophie* in 1830. Under the date October 27, 1830, Emerson noted in his journal what positions these early philosophers had taken on such subjects as idealism, unity, duality, God, the soul, virtue, the senses and reason. *Journals*, II, 330-345.

the way he did.[24] Similarly, it excused him from the obligation of arguing his point: he needed only to give conclusions.[25] Claiming that the poet "sees wholes, and avoids analysis",[26] Emerson, consequently, made statements that are often confusing because of the absence of the reasoning that led up to them. A related difficulty is caused sometimes by his tone. He believed that whatever language "the bard" uses, "the secret of tone is at the heart of the poem. ... The true inspiration always brings it." [27] As it comes with inspiration, that is, with the reception of the divine spirit [28] and therefore with the acquisition of the prophetic power to see "in the word or action of the man its yet untold results",[29] his tone sometimes baffles those readers who lack the inspiration and, consequently, the prophetic ability of the bard. Nevertheless, the poet's tone is always justified, however baffling, according to Emerson, because he is the "truer logician".[30] Finally, Emerson has created difficulties by his symbols. The poet, he said, "discovers that what men value as substances have a higher value as symbols. ... Your condition, your employment, is the fable of *you*." [31] Thus, his symbolic view of history was that which he believed a bard must take, regardless of the difficulties presented by the record.

The chief cause of his apparent contradictions and inappropriateness of tone was this habit of seeking the symbolic meaning in historical events and of attempting, not always consciously, perhaps, to find evidence in an historical period of a pattern of development which itself is a symbol of universal growth. The outlines of this symbolic design become clear when many of Emerson's statements about history are divided into three groups: those which emphasize the unity of history, those which point out

---

[24]   Norman A. Brittin, "Emerson and the Metaphysical Poets", *American Literature*, VIII (March, 1936), 16.
[25]   Stuart Gerry Brown, "Emerson's Platonism", *New England Quarterly*, XVIII (1945), 326.
[26]   *Journals*, X, 336 (1870).
[27]   "Preface", *Parnassus*, ed. Ralph Waldo Emerson (Boston, 1875), p. x.
[28]   "Inspiration", *Works*, VIII, 274.
[29]   "Poetry and Imagination", *Works*, VIII, 39.
[30]   *Ibid.*
[31]   *Ibid.*, 23.

the concurrence of two opposite movements, and those which indicate that historical development proceeds always in three stages. We shall try to show that recognition of this design helps to make his assertions about specific historical figures more meaningful, if not more accurate.

Considering all of history "a vanishing allegory" that "repeats itself to tediousness, a thousand and a million times",[32] Emerson revealed frequently that he saw in it a unified pattern symbolizing the whole of creation. The unity of this design is felt especially when the observer recognizes in events a reflection of his own life. "Every history in the world", Emerson declared, "is my history."[33] Conversely, the whole of history is to be found in that of one man.[34]

The effect of this theory on his method of reading is implied in his statement that the student is to approach the subject of history "actively and not passively; to esteem his own life the text, and books the commentary".[35] Furthermore, he is to prefer the history of individuals[36] because, properly speaking, there is "no history, only biography".[37] The student can find historical truth, therefore, only by recognizing reflections of his own life in the biographies of others: "Civil and natural history, the history of art and of literature, must be explained from individual his-

[32] *Journals*, VIII, 251-252 (Aug. 11, 1851).
[33] *Ibid.*, V, 448 (July 31, 1840). *Cf.* "Uses of Great Men", *Works*, IV, 5: "Other men are lenses through which we read our own minds"; and "History", *Works*, II, 10: "All history becomes subjective;..." Nicoloff has traced the probable influence on Emerson of Cousin, for whom "history was a reflection of the whole of human nature, and so the thought and action of all past ages was to be found summed up in the individual consciousness." *Op. cit.*, p. 72.
[34] "History", *Works*, II, 4. Since he believed that there is but one universal mind, Emerson could state emphatically that all historical events "are to be regarded as growths and off-shoots of the expanding mind of the race, ..." "Woman", *Works*, XI, 424.
[35] "History", *Works*, II, 7-8.
[36] "Books", *Works*, VII, 207.
[37] "History", *Works*, II, 10. *Cf.* "In like manner, all public facts are to be individualized, all private facts are to be generalized. Then at once History becomes fluid and true, and Biography deep and sublime." *Ibid.*, 21.

tory, or must remain words." [38] Hence, the "lustres" Emerson sought in his historical reading were obviously those passages which could inspire insights because they suggested the religious significance of his own personal experience.

The symbolic design represented, besides this unity, a persistent internal conflict between two opposite tendencies: "The history of mankind interests us only as it exhibits a steady gain of Truth and right, in the incessant conflict which it records between the material and the moral nature." [39] This "incessant conflict" is continually being resolved in a dialectical synthesis of the two natures, a process which includes emanation and evolution, the moral and religious experiences known as the Fall and the Redemption, apparent retrogression and real progress, time and eternity. While each historical tendency reflects its opposite, history that is "fluid and true" consists of both; they cannot be divided.

Yet there are two histories, or rather two in one – the apparently separate history of the material tendency and that of the moral. Neither represents the whole truth, according to Emerson, but those who perceive most clearly the history of the moral nature see more of the truth than those who can trace merely material development. Moreover, the vision of the ideal poet is most reliable, for he perceives not only the events recorded by the scholars, but also the moral truth which each event symbolizes; in fact, he sees the living truth which transcends both histories although its manifestation depends upon a recognition of their relation to each other.

"There are always two histories of man in literature contending for our faith." The first, that of the material tendency, traces an evolutionary process:

One is the scientific or skeptical, and derives his origin from the gradual composition, subsidence, and refining, – from the negro, from the ape, progressive from the animalcule savages of the water-

[38]   *Ibid.*, 17. While Emerson never repudiated nor abandoned this view, his later works emphasize the importance of historical studies because he had discovered the spiritual benefits to be derived from evidence of an ameliorating evolution. See Nicoloff, pp. 46-47.

[39]   "West India Emancipation", *Works*, XI, 101.

drop, from *volvox globator,* up to the wise man of the nineteenth century.

The second, that of the moral tendency, is "the history of the Fall":

The other is the believer's, the poet's, the faithful history, always testified by the mystic and the devout, the history of the Fall, of a descent from a superior and pure race, attested in actual history by the grand remains of elder ages, of a science in the East unintelligible to the existing population; Cyclopean architecture in all quarters of the world. In Swedenborg, it is called the "Most Ancient Church," and the nobilities of thought are called "Remains" from this. The height of this doctrine is that the entranced soul living in Eternity will carry all the arts, all art, *in power,* but will not cumber itself with superfluous realizations.

According to this "faithful dogma", the material, evolutionary history records merely "an optical show", for "the Universe was long already complete through law".[40] But, to the symbolic eye of Emerson's ideal poet, the "optical show" of material evolution reflects in the world of time the real moral progress that requires passage from eternity into time, culminating in a "Fall" which is "attested in actual history by the grand remains of elder ages", and back to eternity again by means of a Redemption. The first and third stages of this process of moral growth touch eternity, the "Foreworld": "Abide in the simple and noble regions of thy life, obey thy heart, and thou shalt reproduce the Foreworld again." [41] But the second, that of the Fall, is immersed in time. The ideal poet declares, therefore: " 'In the cycle of the universal man, from whom the known individuals proceed, centuries are points, and all history is but the epoch of one degradation.' " [42] In eternity, but "not in time is the race progressive".[43]

While Emerson's design represented both unity and duality,

---

[40]   *Journals,* VII, 80-81 (Aug. 19, 1945). *Cf.* "History", *Works,* II, 9: "The Garden of Eden, the sun standing still in Gibeon, is poetry thenceforward to all nations. Who cares what the fact was, when we have made a constellation of it to hang in heaven an immortal sign?"
[41]   "Self-Reliance", *Works,* II, 84.
[42]   "Nature", *Works,* I, 70.
[43]   "Self-Reliance", *Works,* II, 86.

it thus reflected a divine trinity manifested in the three stages – the beginning, middle, and end – of each cycle of growth. In the "faithful history", these three stages are, in fact, although he avoided the terms, the Age of Innocence, the Fall, and the Redemption. Thus adopting an old way of viewing the human experience, he described, according to the traditions he was following, the three corresponding ages in the history of western civilization:

1. *The Greek:* when men deified Nature, Jove was in the air, Neptune in the sea, Pluto in the earth, Naiads in the fountains, Dryads in the woods, Oreads on the mountains; happy, beautiful beatitude of Nature;
2. *The Christian:* when the soul became pronounced, and craved a heaven out of Nature and above it, – looking on Nature now as evil, – the world was a mere stage and school, a snare, and the powers that ruled here were devils, hostile to the soul; and now, lastly, –
3. *The Modern:* when the too idealistic tendencies of the Christian period running into the diseases of cant, monachism, and a church, demonstrating the impossibility of Christianity, have forced men to retrace their steps, and rally again on Nature; but now the tendency is to marry mind to Nature, and to put Nature under the mind, convert the world into the instrument of Right Reason.[44]

Later, in a lecture, Emerson included further details. According to a reporter's paraphrase, he claimed that the Grecian period occurred "when with little science man accepted nature as it lay before him". It was "the age of a healthy, vigorous well-developed sensuousness – the age of the gymnasium, the chariot-race, the wrestling-match, and of unrivaled sculpture and painting". The Christian period, a "reaction against the Grecian sensualism", was "the age of moral sentiment"; becoming exaggerated, it "gave birth to monkery, asceticism, superstition and a meager, barren, ungenial vein of life". The Modern Age, however, attempting to

<hr>

[44] *Journals*, VIII, 77-78 (Dec. 14, 1849). Emerson's friend Frederick Henry Hedge claimed that man develops in continuous fashion through three "realms": (1) The realm of nature; (2) the realm of morals; (3) the realm of "spirit", where man is "moved by love". Joseph L. Blau, *Men and Movements in American Philosophy* (New York, 1952), p. 117.

marry "ideal tendencies" with nature, is "the age of Commerce":
"Commerce governs education, and regards Arithmetic as the
most important of the sciences. Religion, too, is valued as it helps
to keep smooth the passages of trade." [45]

Emerson would not have claimed that such divisions were any
more original with him than his ideas of unity and duality. He
would have been the first to acknowledge their lack of originality;
but he would have contended that the persistence of such ideas,
especially in the history of Neoplatonic thought, and their cur-
rent popularity among his contemporaries, attested to their value
as guideposts to truth. Moreover, while the "word" always
shrouds, it nevertheless indicates – he would have claimed –
where the living body of truth lies. Such persistent smoke marks
the presence of eternal fire.

Thus echoing the words, if not the tunes, of old songs, Emerson tended to identify the first stage of historical development
with a state of unity – the material and moral natures so joined
as to produce health and genius; [46] the second stage with a splitting of the two natures and a conflict, felt as pain and reflected
in disease, between good and evil impulses; and the third stage
with regained unity, a marriage between opposite tendencies, and
the consequent predominance of Reason. This pattern is repeated
in the history of individuals; hence "every man passes personally
through a Grecian period".[47] It is repeated in the history of every
epoch, whose three most representative men correspond with its
three stages. It is repeated, as we have just seen, in the development of western civilization. And it is repeated in the whole story

[45] Lecture, 1850, "The Spirit of the Age", in Jeanne Kronman, ed.,
"Three Unpublished Lectures of Ralph Waldo Emerson", *New England
Quarterly*, XIX (March, 1946), 106-107.
[46] "The Grecian state is the era of the bodily nature, the perfection of
the senses, – of the spiritual nature unfolded in strict unity with the body."
"History," *Works*, II, 24.
[47] *Ibid.* H. D. Gray claims that "there is considerable point in making
the distinction that there are three stages in Emerson's optimism, corresponding to the three stages in the development of the individual: there
is the optimism of the senses, the pessimism of the understanding, and
the optimism of the reason". *Emerson: A Statement of New England
Transcendentalism as Expressed in the Philosophy of its Chief Exponent*
(Stanford University Press, 1917), pp. 78-79.

of man in this world while, in relation to that greatest history, man's present conflicts prove he has not yet recovered from his Fall. Never profane, but ever sacred,[48] the history "always testified by the mystic and the devout" includes these stages called, in the Christian tradition, Innocence, Fall, and Redemption, which are thus repeated again and again.

It was this "faithful", symbolic history, with its unified design, two opposite tendencies, and development in three stages, which Emerson felt that he, as a poet, must emphasize. The fact that its outlines were traditional seemed to him to testify to the validity of his vision of historical truth. "Faith" reproduced incessantly these old "forms"; but "soul" would always give them "new life":

I confess, all attempts to project and establish a Cultus with new rites and forms, seems to me vain. Faith makes us, and not we it, and faith makes its own forms. All attempts to contrive a system are as cold as the new worship introduced by the French to the goddess of Reason, – to-day, pasteboard and filigree, and ending to-morrow in madness and murder. Rather let the breath of new life be breathed by you through the forms already existing. For if once you are alive, you shall find they shall become plastic and new. The remedy to their deformity is first, soul, and second, soul, and evermore, soul.[49]

Thus "faith" provided the outlines, or "forms", of a coherent philosophy. These "forms", like the arcs of a stellar orbit, comprised a universal pattern reflected in criticism as in history.

Habitually inclined to rely on the guidance of "faith" and thus prepared to find the old "forms" reflected in literature as well as elsewhere in the universe, Emerson, in many of his utterances, reveals that his literary judgments, tending consistently to avoid the originality of a new "Cultus", were chiefly the result of a critical approach in harmony with this pattern. Hence, he adopted distinctions between *classic* and *romantic* which are applicable to the first two ages of man. As Norman Foerster has noted in *American Criticism*, these distinctions are closely related to Emerson's doctrine of organic art.[50] Believing, however, that all

---

[48] "The Over-Soul", *Works*, II, 297.
[49] "Address" (Divinity School), *Works*, I, 149-150.
[50] Norman Foerster, "Emerson", *American Criticism: A Study in Literary Theory from Poe to the Present* (Boston, 1928), p. 83.

of history is contained in every event, he recognized the futility of over-emphasizing these differences when they would seem to be manifested in the less significant developments of successive ages:

Historically, there is thought to be a difference in the ideas which predominate over successive epochs, and there are data for marking the genius of the Classic, of the Romantic, and now of the Reflective or Philosophical age. With the views I have intimated of the oneness or the identity of the mind through all individuals, I do not much dwell on these differences. In fact, I believe each individual passes through all three. The boy is a Greek; the youth, romantic; the adult, reflective.

He added, however, that "a revolution in the leading idea" of each age "may be distinctly enough traced",[51] thus implying that its chief human representative may be clearly distinguished among people who manifest less significant tendencies.

For Emerson, therefore, the terms *classic* and *romantic* refer properly to the first two stages of historical development. Classic art is unified and finished; a product of the creative instinct, which can best function only when thought and feeling, as opposite modes of perception, are focused and, consequently, in harmony, it appears when there is unified vision, which, in Emerson's opinion, means health. Romantic art, on the other hand, reveals the conflict between the material and moral natures which occurs when thought and feeling have been split, dissociated; hence, it reflects disease. Emerson declared, therefore, that "the Classic is creative and the Romantic is aggregative",[52] that is, the classic "unfolds", but the romantic "adds",[53] and, echoing Goethe and Sainte-Beuve,[54] he concluded: "The classic is healthy, the romantic sick." [55] When he stated that "classic art

[51] "The American Scholar", *Works*, I, 109.
[52] *Journals*, VI, 231 (Aug., 1842).
[53] *Ibid.*, IV, 25 (1856).
[54] "Wagner made music again classic. Goethe says, 'I call classic the sound, and romantic the sick.' Sainte-Beuve defines classic: '*Un auteur qui a fait faire un pas de plus, a découvert quelque vérité, qui a rendu sa pensée dans une forme large et grande, saine et belle en soi,*' etc. I abridge much. (See *Causeries*)." *Ibid.*, 24-25.
[55] "Art and Criticism", *Works*, XII, 304.

was the art of necessity: modern romantic art bears the stamp of caprice and chance",[56] he meant that the first, in contrast with the second, resulted when the artist permitted the universal spirit to guide his hand in the creation of works which would reflect by necessity the universal design. Such an artist, and none other, could be called a *genius*;[57] his "Imagination" creates images as "Nature makes flowers";[58] his method is truly "organic". By his vocabulary and tone, Emerson reveals that, as a poet-critic,[59] he tended to identify Shakespeare with the "classic" mode, Bacon with the "romantic", and Milton, in his perception and expression of the highest moral and religious truth, with a synthesis transcending both.

It may be argued that when, in his works, he presented this view of the three most representative figures of the English Renaissance, he was not always successful in achieving a synthesis of "faith" and "soul", thought and feeling, vocabulary and tone. Yet he did avoid the originality of a new "Cultus" while suggesting frequently, by his choice of words, the timelessness and universality of those truths he believed these men symbolized. More significantly, by so distributing his words as to give his meaning the appropriate emphasis, he often succeeded in creating what must have been the desired effect: a unique, distinctly personal tone that could awaken and inspire others to take a fresh look at old truths.

As a poet-preacher in need of a clarifying vocabulary, Emerson discovered an abundant source in the works of Platonists. Their words, like traffic lights on the road "faith" had paved for him, were shining "lustres". He described Cudworth, therefore, as "an armory for a poet to furnish himself withal".[60] He was

---

[56] *Journals*, IX, 24 (1856).
[57] "Works and Days", *Works*, VII, 181-182.
[58] *Journals*, VIII, 9 (March 19, 1849).
[59] "Art and Criticism", *Works*, XII, 305: "Criticism is an art when it does not stop at the words of the poet, but looks at the order of his thoughts and the essential quality of his mind. Then the critic is poet."
[60] *Journals*, IV, 8 (Jan. 24, 1836). "Emerson's chief guide to Plotinus and Neo-Platonic thought before 1837 was Ralph Cudworth's *The True Intellectual System of the Universe*, a copy of which (in four volumes) he seems to have acquired for his library sometime in 1834 or early in

"like a cow in June which breathes of nothing but clover and scent-grass. He has fed so entirely on ancient bards and sages that all his diction is redolent of their books." [61] His work is "a magazine of quotations".[62] There can be no doubt that the thoughts Emerson found glittering in those words increased self-trust and fortified faith, convincing him that the "high dogmas" he had supposed were "the rare and late fruit of a cumulative culture, and only now possible to some recent Kant or Fichte, were the prompt improvisations of the earliest inquirers; . . .". [63] Proclus, on the other hand, stimulated Emerson's "imagination" by his "Platonic rhetoric quoted as household words": "By all these and so many rare and brave words I am filled with hilarity and spring, my heart dances, my sight is quickened, I behold shining relations between all beings, and am impelled to write and almost to sing." [64] Hence, he could declare: "I read Proclus, and sometimes Plato, as I might read a dictionary, for a mechanical help to the fancy and the imagination. I read for the lustres, as if one should use a fine picture in a chromatic experiment, for its rich colors." [65]

The following passage, most of whose "words" Emerson encountered in reading Platonists, especially Proclus and Cudworth, has primary significance as a statement of his view of the universal trinity:

For the Universe has three children, born at one time, which reappear under different names in every system of thought, whether they be called cause, operation and effect; or, more poetically, Jove, Pluto,

---

1835." Kenneth W. Cameron, *Emerson the Essayist* (Raleigh, N. C., 1945), I, 56. According to Rusk, "A copy of Cudworth's *The True Intellectual System*, London, 1820, is still in Emerson's house, at Concord, and the first volume contains his signature." *Letters*, II, 451-52, n. 323. He used the four-volume London, 1820, edition. See Vivian C. Hopkins, "Emerson and Cudworth: Plastic Nature and Transcendental Art", *American Literature*, Vol. 23 (March, 1951), p. 80.
[61] *Journals*, III, 489 (June 10, 1835).
[62] *Ibid.*, VII, 95 (Sept., 1845).
[63] "Literary Etnics", *Works*, I, 160.
[64] *Journals*, VI, 375-76 (1843). Emerson owned *The Six Books of Proclus*, trans. Thomas Taylor, 2 vols. (London, A. J. Valpy, 1816). Rusk, ed., *Letters*, II, 430, n. 225.
[65] "Nominalist and Realist", *Works*, III, 233.

Neptune; or, theologically, the Father, the Spirit and the Son; but which we will call here the Knower, the Doer and the Sayer. These stand respectively for the love of truth, for the love of good, and for the love of beauty. These three are equal. Each is that which he is, essentially, and each of these three has the power of the other latent in him and his own patent.[66]

Describing the pagan trinity, Cudworth, among others, had claimed that they made up "one orderly and harmonious system of the whole":

One of those gods ruling only in the heavens, another in the sea, and another in the earth and hell; one being the god or goddess of learning and wisdom, another of speech and eloquence, another of justice and political order; . . .

Quoting Tyrius, Cudworth had said that the sea was assigned to Neptune, " 'the dark and subterraneous parts to Pluto, but the heaven to Jupiter' ", and that this trinity was therefore "sometimes called also the celestial, marine, and terrestrial Jupiter . . .".[67] The order of Cudworth's passage suggests that the god of the heavens was also the god of learning and wisdom; the god of the sea was, similarly, the god of speech and eloquence; and the god of the earth and hell was the god of justice and political order. This allocation of powers corresponds with Emerson's Knower, Sayer, and Doer. But Emerson has interchanged the position of the second and third persons of the trinity. Based on Proclus, a justification for this transposition also appears in Cudworth:

But besides this, there is another Platonic hypothesis . . . where the third hypostasis is made to be a certain middle betwixt the first and second. And this does Proclus also sometimes follow, calling the third in like manner . . . "a middle power" and "the relation of both the first and second to one another." Which agreeth exactly with that

---

[66] "The Poet", *Works*, III, 6-7. For this trinity, see also "The Transcendentalist", *Works*, I, 354-55, and "Art", *Works*, VII, 57.
[67] Ralph Cudworth, *The True Intellectual System of the Universe*, 3 vols. (London, 1845), I, 364. See John S. Harrison, *The Teachers of Emerson* (New York, 1910), pp. 200-202. According to Vivian C. Hopkins, "Cudworth's connection of the Platonic triad with the Christian trinity gives Emerson an opportunity to relate poetry to the religious and moral world". "Emerson and Cudworth", p. 96.

apprehension of some Christians that the third hypostasis is as it were the nexus betwixt the first and the second, and that love whereby the Father and Son love each other. Now, according to this latter Platonic hypothesis, there would seem to be not so much a gradation or descent, as a kind of circulation in the Trinity.[68]

Hence, Emerson's second person, called variously "operation", "Pluto", "the Spirit", "the Doer", and representing "the love of good", corresponds with the "certain middle betwixt the first and second". More significantly, as "operation" between "cause" and "effect", it corresponds with the second stage in every cycle of development. Thus denoting universal truths, such words, for Emerson, were like "coins of different countries ... they all represent the value of corn, wool, and labor, ...".[69]

Corresponding with these gods is "the eternal trinity of Truth, Goodness, and Beauty".[70] They are "but different faces of the same All".[71] Emerson indicated, however, that the "Goodness" of the second person is, specifically, justice and that the "Beauty" of the third is a reflection of love.[72] This would seem to imply, first, that the second person, the Doer and the lover of good, is also, as was apparently Cudworth's Pluto, the god of justice and political order; and, second, that the third person, the Sayer, identifiable with Cudworth's god of speech and eloquence, performs the function, as the lover of beauty, of the god of love. Supporting this interpretation is the fact that the specifically human faculties corresponding with the Knower, the Doer, and the Sayer are intellect, will, and affection, which become, when Emerson's Over-Soul breathes through them, genius, virtue, and love, respectively.[73]

---

[68] Cudworth, *op. cit.*, II, 429-31. Cudworth quotes St. Augustine's assertion (*De Civitate Dei*, Lib. 10, cap. 23) that Porphyrius put the Psyche (the Holy Ghost of the Christian trinity) between the Father and the Son. *Ibid.*, 462. In Proclus, *Theologia Platonica*, Lib. 3, cap. 11, this subject, according to Cudworth, is fully discussed. It is worth noting that the Spirit in Coleridge's "pentad" is in the middle. *Complete Works*, V, 574.
[69] *Journals*, V, 551 (1841).
[70] "The Transcendentalist", *Works*, I, 354.
[71] "Nature", *Works*, I, 24.
[72] "To truth, justice, love, the attributes of the soul, the idea of immutableness is essentially associated." "The Over-Soul", *Works*, II, 283.
[73] *Ibid.*, 271.

While Emerson may have regarded even the archangels Gabriel, Michael, and Uriel as reflections of this trinity in Christian angelology,[74] he tended to identify, on the human, historical level, the creative genius with an evolving Knower,[75] the virtuous hero with an evolving Doer,[76] and the poet inspired by divine love with an evolving Sayer. Hence, these three types are not static; they expand as a tree when the Over-Soul breathes through them. Emerson's statements about Shakespeare, Bacon, and Milton often suggest that, in reading their works, he was chiefly interested in evidence of their moral and religious development.

Consistent with his habits of thought, revealed in numerous passages in his works, each of these three types possesses opposing tendencies which are essentially modes of perception corresponding with the male and female principles, the universal centrifugal and centripetal forces, divine emanation and evolution, action and reaction. These opposites are similarly reflected in the polarity of thought and feeling, creative thought and passively receptive thought, action and thought, and many others deriving their distinctive value as reflections of the male or female principles by their relation to each other. The masculine tendency is centrifugal; it turns away from the spiritual center toward the world of matter. The feminine tendency is centripetal, turning back to the spiritual source.

While a synthesis of these opposites is ideal, one or the other tends to predominate as development proceeds along a spiral course from the beginning of the first to the conclusion of the third stage of each cycle of growth. Thus, creative thought tends increasingly to supersede the love of truth in the Knower type of person until, in the Doer, action predominates completely at the culmination of divine emanation when the Spirit, as Moral Sentiment, first turns the tide; thereafter, the tendency toward action subsides as its opposite, manifested in the Doer's concern for justice, gains increasing strength. Moral evolution is completed

[74]   Cf. *Journals*, VI, 394 (May 10, 1843) and the poem "Uriel", *Works*, IX, 13.
[75]   "The Over-Soul", *Works*, II, 271.
[76]   "The Poet", *Works*, III, 6.

in the Sayer, whose passive reception of truth as it flows upward from the source tends ever to supersede his function as a maker of poetry.

Hence, although Shakespeare's greatest achievement was his passive reception of truth, he preferred to devote himself primarily to its opposite, the creation of literary masterpieces. Bacon, experiencing the Fall that turned the tide, was more truly a man of action than Shakespeare, who preceded him, or Milton, who followed. And Milton gave himself more completely to the passive reception of truth than to its opposite, the enunciation of truth in his works.

The fact that Emerson viewed moral and spiritual development in the period these three writers represented as following this upward spiral course would reveal, according to his thinking, the position from which he viewed it, the "angle of vision" of a poet-priest. What he saw in that spiral course was not the "circulation in the Trinity" described by Cudworth, but its reflection. Marjorie Nicolson has shown, in regard to nineteenth-century writers, that then, "when the circle returned to literature, it tended, under the influence of the evolutionary theory and belief in progress, to be not the Circle of Perfection but a spiral, . . .".[77] This is certainly true of Emerson when he refers only to progress, or growth, in an attempt to assess moral character and development as would a priest. But, when he refers also to the deity or the divine laws, he indicates that the appearance of spiral upward motion in the created universe is due to the refraction of light when the "circulation in the Trinity" is observed, not directly, but indirectly, through its reflection in the world, by modes of perception that are not properly focused; the distortion results from his "bias" as a priest.

The horizontal and vertical dimensions of this figure, however, are both transient; absolute permanence is represented only by the area outside an inclosing, revolving sphere.[78] Emerson's

[77] Marjorie H. Nicolson, *The Breaking of the Circle*, revised edition (Columbia University Press, 1960), p. 8.
[78] I had intended originally to include in this study a long chapter attempting to develope the idea that Emerson's view of the English Renaissance revealed the influence of a circular figure that could be

"horizontal dimensions" mark the circular limits of moral a-
wareness on a "platform" where the Spirit, operating through the
law of compensation, reacts instantaneously to human actions
that have moral significance; and his "vertical dimension" is the
arc of a revolving circle indicating the direction of growth in a
process requiring time as men ascend the spiral stairs leading
from one level to the next, winding from the feminine side to the
masculine and back again to the feminine, in each cycle of development. His cycles, moreover, are not connected; each produces
an essentially new being, and his horizontal and vertical dimensions are both capable of infinite expansion and contraction. Like
the lines on a globe that can be blown up, as a balloon, to any
size, they suggest, by their elasticity, the rhythm of the growth
process which begins, on each cycle, with an explosion and ends
with an implosion corresponding with the pulsations of the universal heart.

Thus, the ideal Knower becomes, as he develops, a poet; and
the ideal Sayer becomes a philosopher. "The true philosopher
and the true poet are one, and a beauty which is truth, and a
truth, which is beauty, is the aim of both." [79] Moreover, since
the "true poet" represents the completion of a cycle of growth,
a synthesis of the fully developed powers symbolized by all three
pagan gods, Emerson, in addressing him, declared: "Thou true
land-lord! sea-lord! air-lord!" [80] But, when Emerson thus singled
out specific persons and types for praise or blame, he revealed,
by his own admission, the limitations of his "angle of vision".

These limitations indicate, not the perception of truth in the
"circulation of the Trinity", but the perception of truth's reflec-

---

called, perhaps, the central symbol in his philosophy. Consisting of three
circles revolving at right angles to each other, and constantly changing
in size, it would appear, two-dimensionally, as a cross in a circle. But,
as a sensible investigation of this subject would require giving more
attention to his psychological development and his philosophy than is
desirable here, it has been omitted.

[79] "Nature", *Works*, I, 55.
[80] "The Poet", *Works*, III, 42. "The poet contemplates the central identity,
sees it undulate and roll this way and that, with divine flowings, through
remotest things; ..." "Poetry and Imagination", *Works*, VIII, 21.

tion in the spiral upward movement of a dialectical process of development. Emerson found that mythology helped him to transcend these limitations and to perceive the unity of truth itself. Referring, for example, to "the types or representative men of any age", he claimed that mythology provided examples of "the same group at another remove".[81] He woud seem to have found these mythological associations helpful as hints of historical truth, for, in speaking of the history of the "genius of humanity ... whose biography is written in our annals", he declared that we must "infer much, and supply many chasms in the record". Then, recalling the unified design of history and its power as a guide to the divine truth it symbolized, he exclaimed, "Could we one day complete the "immense figure which these flagrant points compose!" [82] That "immense figure" would be the time-transcending image of Universal Man now divided chiefly into the three most representative men of every epoch.

When, with the limitations of his own "bias" and "angle of vision", Emerson made pronouncements about those men whom he regarded as representative of the three stages in the unfolding of the "leading idea" of the English Renaissance, he intended to present portraits that "would evoke the spirit of each" [83] and that would inspire others to see, from their own respective positions, the extent to which each of these three men reflected or refracted the light streaming from the universal image of "the virtuous man", "the central figure in the visible sphere".[84] As creations of a poet-preacher who found it necessary to "infer much, and supply many chasms in the record", these portraits, designed primarily to inspire, were essentially moral "characters".[85]

---

[81]   *Journals*, VII, 383 (Jan., 1848).
[82]   "Uses of Great Men", *Works*, IV, 32-33.
[83]   *Journals*, II, 504 (Aug. 12, 1832).
[84]   "Nature", *Works*, I, 22.
[85]   F. O. Matthiessen has shown how Emerson "profited from his fondness for the seventeenth-century's mode of presenting type-characters" while failing to equal Carlyle in this genre because of "the long Puritan conditioning in habits of inward scrutiny". *American Renaissance* (Oxford University Press, 1941), pp. 71-72. In Emerson's defense, it may be said, however, that, as a preacher addressing those he hoped to inspire with a vision of religious truth, his purpose was not the same as Carlyle's.

Revealing, early in his career, that his "bias" and "angle of vision" were not those of an historian, Emerson expressed his desire to "draw characters, not write lives":

The British Plutarch and the modern Plutarch is yet to be written. They that have writ the lives of great men have not written them from love and from seeing the beauty that was to be desired in them. But what would operate such gracious motions upon the spirit as the death of Lord Cobham and of Sir Thomas More, and a censure of Bacon, and a picture of George Fox and Hampden, and the chivalrous integrity of Walter Scott, and a true portrait of Sir Harry Vane, and Falkland, and Andrew Marvell? I would draw characters, not write lives. I would evoke the spirit of each, and their relics might rot. Luther, Milton, Newton, Shakespeare, Alfred, a light of the world, – Adams ... I would make Milton shine. I would mourn for Bacon. I would fly in the face of every cockered prejudice, feudal or vulgar, and speak as Christ of their good and evil.[86]

A religious poet, a dedicated preacher, Emerson was not a true critic or historian. When he wrote the lives of great men, he aimed chiefly to write "from love and from seeing the beauty that was to be desired in them". While the following chapters, presenting his view of Shakespeare, Bacon, and Milton, are not intended to emphasize the development of his attitudes toward these figures or to trace their influence on his own work and thought, they should reveal that Emerson habitually regarded these writers as moral types most representative of the three stages of the English Renaissance – its beginning, middle, and end – and that the position from which he viewed them, the "angle of vision" of a poet-priest, impelled him to "speak as Christ of their good and evil".

[86]   *Journals*, II, 503-504 (Aug. 12, 1832).

I. SHAKESPEARE AS THE KNOWER

The title of Emerson's essay "Shakspeare; Or, The Poet",[1] in the Representative Men Series, indicates that he had then intended, in 1845, a portrayal that would emphasize Shakespeare's significance as "the type of the poet" [2] rather than as a dramatist. In the essay itself, he not only makes this purpose clear, but reveals also his intention to create an image that would give special emphasis to those powers of perception which made this poet a "philosopher".[3] And he had still another purpose in this essay. At the end, where, as he avers, he seeks "to strike the balance",[4] he attempts to show that, while this philosopher may be like "some saint" in the universal truth of what he has to say, he is also like many saints, priests, and prophets in that he shares "the halfness and imperfection of humanity"; the religious thoughts and feelings they express in their lives and works are

---

[1] This essay was one of seven lectures presented before the Boston Lyceum in the winter of 1845-46, and elsewhere in New England. During the winter of 1847-48, Emerson made use of the same material in lecturing on Shakespeare in the British Isles. Ralph L. Rusk, *The Life of Ralph Waldo Emerson* (New York, 1949), pp. 309-310, 335 ff. The entire series was published in a volume entitled *Representative Men* on Jan. 1, 1850. *Ibid.*, p. 374.

[2] Shakespeare was "the type of the poet" because of his "power of expression, or of transferring the inmost truth of things into music and verse". "Shakspeare; Or, The Poet", *Works,* IV, 213.

[3] "Shakspeare; Or, The Poet", *Works*, IV, 210-211. Emerson concluded the passage with the following words: "And the importance of this wisdom of life sinks the form, as of Drama or Epic, out of notice. 'T is like making a question concerning the paper on which a king's message is written." *Ibid.*, 211.

[4] *Ibid.*, 216.

like the "half-views of half-men". In this respect, he is no more "whole" than they. But, while he and they are thus alike in their "halfness", his angle of vision, when compared with theirs, appears to lie opposite: on the one hand, "Swedenborg the mourner", representing the saints, must "grope in graves", and, on the other, this philosopher, "Shakespeare the player", must "trifle", "using his genius for the public amusement".[5]

While this essay contains Emerson's best known words on Shakespeare, it presents a view of the poet which requires for its clarification the light often provided by statements in his other writings: his journals, essays, letters, and other lectures, especially the two early lectures on Shakespeare first given in 1835 and the Tercentenary Address, written but possibly not delivered in 1864.[6]

The second of the two earliest lectures consists chiefly of "remarks, necessarily somewhat miscellaneous, upon his Rhythm; his Language; upon his characters; and upon his sentences and maxims",[7] but it begins with a summary of the first lecture which provides a brief description of his general view of the poet:

In my last lecture I attempted to distinguish the leading elements of Shakespeare's Genius. It was shown chiefly from his earlier poems that he possessed in prodigious degree the Imaginative power, the primary talent of a poet.

It was then shown that the dangers incident to the mind from the preponderance of this faculty were averted from him both by the

---

[5] *Ibid.*, 218-19.

[6] The two earliest lectures on Shakespeare were the fifth and the sixth in a series of ten on "English Literature", given before the Society for the Diffusion of Useful Knowledge at the Masonic Temple in Boston, December, 1835. The Shakespeare Tercentenary Address, prepared for delivery before the Saturday Club at Revere House, Boston, April 23, 1864, appears, greatly condensed from the extant MS, in "Shakspeare", *Works*, XI, 447-53. Emerson gave also a reading of favorite passages from Shakespeare, with a short introduction, as the fourth in a series of ten "Readings on English Poetry and Prose" at Chickering's Hall, Boston, a series that began Jan. 2, 1869. Among the more valuable references to the poet in his letters are the remarks contained in the 1841 letter to his young cousin, Christopher Gore Ripley, and, in his journals, those that appear under the date April 24, 1864, the day following the Tercentenary celebration.

[7] "Shakspear" (second lecture), *Early Lectures*, I, 305.

natural check of a clear Reason, or the state of the mind when its faculties are in equipoise and admit all impressions with equal freedom, and also by the extra-ordinary activity of his reflective powers, which had they been alone, would have made him the extremest of Skeptics.

It was then shown that to this double faculty of Imagination and of Philosophy was added a third in quite equal energy, that of Common sense, a clear perception of and a strong interest in the ongoings of the actual world. So that he was by these three rarely united gifts, the imaginative, the spiritual, and the practical faculties, at once a poet, a philosopher, and a man.[8]

His chief purpose, then, in his first lecture on Shakespeare, was to emphasize his significance as "a poet, a philosopher, and a man". Consequently, it resembled his purpose ten years later, in "Shakspeare; Or, The Poet", in that, in both the 1835 and the 1845 lectures, he tried to stress Shakespeare's importance as a poet and as a philosopher; but he emphasized in 1835 what he called the "practical man" as well as the poet and the philosopher, and he contrasted in 1845 this poet and this philosopher with the type of religious man represented by Swedenborg.

Emerson's view of Shakespeare is most clearly presented in these two works. Other references tend to clarify, to complete the picture; but the essential outlines are here. They indicate that he habitually compared and contrasted him with four universal types: the "practical man", the poet, the philosopher, and the saint-prophet-priest. Such an approach invites speculation as to its relations with the three-fold division of universal types, reflecting the deity, which he presented in "The Poet" in 1844.[9] Since these three types are reflected in cause, operation, and effect, or three stages of development occurring in time, the type which Shakespeare most nearly represents would tend to be identified with one of these stages as they are reflected in the history of the "Greek", "Christian", and "Modern" eras.[10] According to Emerson's descriptions of these eras, the Knower would be iden-

[8] *Ibid.*
[9] "The Poet", *Works*, III, 67. First published, in 1844, in Emerson's second book of essays, this work includes a few paragraphs from another lecture, "The Poet", given in Boston in the winter of 1841-42.
[10] *Journals*, VIII, 77-78 (Dec. 14, 1849).

tified with the Greek stage, the Doer with the Christian, the Sayer with the Modern; and the Sayer would be the ideal poet, representing a new synthesis of mind, or soul, and Nature, and, consequently, the culmination of a dialectical process of growth. But Shakespeare, as Emerson makes clear in his 1845 lecture, does not have the prerequisites of the Sayer, although he was the greatest poet that ever lived.

As a type, he seemed more "masculine" than the Sayer, more even, at times, than the Doer, who, experiencing the Fall, strives actively to reconcile his centrifugal and centripetal tendencies. The second, or Christian, stage, that of the Doer, was apparently visualized by Emerson as consisting chiefly of two segments representing the masculine (centrifugal) and feminine (centripetal) principles in conflict. The saints, prophets, and priests, like Swedenborg, were on the feminine side.

When compared with theirs, Shakespeare's perception of, and personal reaction to, moral and religious truth would seem to be of an opposite kind; his moral and religious perceptions included those of the skeptical philosopher on the masculine side of the second level; yet, complicating the problem for Emerson, these perceptions included also those of a person who could represent the whole first stage, the level of Innocence of the player who used his genius merely "for the public amusement". When, on the other hand, the stage of his religious development is not being measured by such comparisons with saints, those "reflective powers", which make him a philosopher, are seen to be prevented, "by the natural check of a clear Reason", from converting him into "the extremest of Skeptics". Hence his "halfness" is an aspect of his nature which, though real, does not become visible until the level of his own religious growth is compared with that of those who have progressed beyond it; and it does not detract at all from the appearance, or the reality, of his wholeness, the essential unity of his life and work, when such comparisons are not intended.

But Emerson, although he would seem to have intermittently thought only of the wholeness or the "halfness" of Shakespeare, tended usually to hold in his mind an image of the poet which, although it failed to satisfy what was truly an insatiable yearning for more specific knowledge about the divine element in the poet's life, rendered both aspects simultaneously visible, thus indicating, despite the outward appearance of a contradiction, the inner reality of a harmonious co-existence. Hence, as if one image had been superimposed upon the other, the result was a portrait in depth.

When thus viewed, Shakespeare, because of his "halfness", could not represent the Sayer, or the Doer, and, because of his wholeness, could not represent either half of the second stage, the level of the split between mind and Nature. Emerson tended, therefore, to identify him with the Knower and the Father, the Greek, or first, stage of development. His "halfness" reflected the level of religious consciousness of his age. This chapter will show how such an image of the poet emerges when Emerson's comments on the biographical and critical materials he used are considered in the light of his own philosophy and opinions of Shakespeare's life and works.

I

In a letter to his brother William in 1849, Emerson, after describing his present task of reprinting *Nature*, closed with the following pasage:

When I get through with this, I hope to go to printing "Representative Men," if I dare. But who dare print, being unlearned, an account of Plato, or of Swedenborg, or, being uninspired, of Shakespeare? Yet there is no telling what we rowdy Americans, whose name is Dare, may do! [11]

This reference to the publication of his "Representative Men" series of lectures, which he had often made use of on the platform in recent years, would at first seem to imply that only adequate inspiration was needed, an inspiration he felt the lack of, for publishing an "account" of Shakespeare. However, his brother would have understood his meaning: inspiration was needed, now,

---

[11]   "To William Emerson, Concord, May 29, 1849", *Letters*, IV, 149.

to fuse the facts gathered from many sources with his own thoughts and feelings about them into a satisfying image of the poet. His references to Shakespeare's works and to the biographical research and criticism of more than two hundred years prove that, for Emerson, any effective "account" would demand, first, not inspiration alone, but knowledge.[12]

It is difficult to determine precisely the extent of his reading of the works, but his references and quotations would seem to indicate that he was familiar with all of the poems and most of the plays.[13] He had begun to read Shakespeare early in life. John Hill, a college classmate, claimed – wildly – that Emerson knew Shakespeare almost by heart in his freshman year.[14] But Rusk believes that "significant first-hand acquaintance" did not begin much earlier than 1822, the year after his graduation.[15] Although his letters lack evidence of noteworthy interest during his college

[12] In "Emerson, the Historical Frame, and Shakespeare", Thomas A. Perry rightly claims that Emerson has been misjudged as a purely "romantic critic", a practitioner of the merely intuitive method. "Instead, one may think of Emerson as meeting intermittently in historical research a compelling, though perhaps to him unattractive, force which he cannot ignore, and which ultimately he comes to desire to utilize. The historical method becomes one more approach to a work he seeks to understand, a method perhaps not inconsistent with other approaches." *Op. cit.*, p. 440. He was, Perry concludes, "intermittently concerned with the artist in his historical frame, even to the point of recognizing the usefulness of the historical approach for a more nearly complete understanding of the artist and his work". *Ibid.*, p. 447. Early evidence of a respect for "facts" appears in a letter to Withington, a Harvard classmate, written in Boston, Nov. 21, 1822: "Gibbon values himself upon knowing thoroughly whatever he touches, and this, it seems to me, is the prime value of an historian." "Early Letters of Emerson", ed. Mary S. Withington, *The Century*, XXVI, 457 (July, 1883).
[13] According to Vivian C. Hopkins, "His reading covers the *Sonnets, Venus and Adonis*, and some twenty plays, including a few that are still caviar to the general – *Coriolanus, Troilus and Cressida, Measure for Measure*". *Spires of Form*, pp. 241-42. But his references show that he knew well *The Rape of Lucrece* and *The Phoenix and the Turtle* and that he had at least some familiarity with considerably more than twenty of the plays.
[14] Rusk, *Life*, p. 67. Born May 25, 1803, Emerson entered Harvard College in 1817 and graduated in 1821. In 1811, when he was eight years old, an eight-volume set of Shakespeare's works from his father's library was sold at auction. Cameron, *Emerson the Essayist*, II, 137.
[15] "Introduction", *Letters*, I. xxxiii.

years, from about 1824 "quotations and allusions show a familiarity with many works by the same author". Throughout his life, he relied more upon the words of Shakespeare than those of any other writer to express his meaning in his letters, which alone contain quotations from and references to some twenty of the plays.[16]

But Emerson admitted, in answer to an inquiry in 1865, that he was "not much an expert in editions". He had contented himself "these forty years with the plain duodecimos of the Isaac Reed Edition, London, 1820".[17] When he bought a new one, he added, it would be Richard Grant White's.[18] While he apparently did rely chiefly on Reed's edition of the plays, his obvious familiarity with the poems in his 1835 lectures was derived from other sources,[19] and his knowledge of historical and critical matters was certainly augmented, for those lectures, by the three

---

[16] *Ibid.*, xxxii-xxxiii.

[17] "To – Russell, Concord, Nov. 6, 1865", *Letters*, V, 432. The copy of Isaac Reed's *The Dramatic Works of William Shakespeare* which Emerson probably used is still in his library at the Antiquarian House, Concord. It bears the signature of his brother Charles and the date July, 1822. *Ibid.*, 432-33, editor's note. This may be the Isaac Reed, London, 1820 edition in twelve volumes listed in the catalogue of Emerson's books in the Houghton Library.

[18] *Ibid.*, 432. The first volume of White's *The Works of William Shakespeare,* which was the last to appear, was published in Boston in August, 1865. *Ibid.*, editor's note. Emerson apparently did not purchase a Grant White edition. At least, it is not listed in the Houghton Library catalogue. He would have hailed the presen availability of paperbacks: "The only mechanical means of importance which we have not, is cheap editions in good type but on cheapest paper of the best authors: Bacon, Milton, Shakspeare, Taylor." "On the Best Mode of Inspiring a Correct Taste in English Literature", *Early Lectures, p.* 215.

[19] On Sept. 5, 1816, before entering Harvard, he withdrew from the Boston Library Society *The Poems of Shakespeare* (Boston, 1807). Cameron, *Emerson the Essayist,* II, 153, 182. And, in 1817 and 1823, he withdrew from the Harvard College Library volumes of an unidentified edition of Shakespeare. Kenneth W. Cameron, *Ralph Waldo Emerson's Reading* (Raleigh, 1941), pp. 44, 45, 104. According to Whicher and Spiller, eds., *Early Lectures,* p. 287, Emerson's library contained at least three editions of Shakespeare in 1835. The Houghton Library catalogue of his books includes *The Beauties of Shakespeare; selected from his works* (London, Kearsley, Rivington, etc., ca. 1800), and *The Poems and Songs of William Shakespeare* (London, W. Strange, 1830).

volumes of "Prolegomena" of "Boswell's Malone".[20] In regard
to those volumes, Emerson declared, while directing a young
cousin in 1841 to "the few volumes which contain the few material facts": "The three volumes of Prolegomena to Malone's S.
hold the little all we knew of our Thaumaturgus, until very lately
– I mean of personal history." [21] But, apart from this familiarity
with Reed and with Malone, his knowledge of editions was apparently not extensive.

He was comparatively well informed, however, in other parts
of Shakespeare scholarship – in biographical research and criticism. And his interest in them was intense. "I am inquisitive of
all possible knowledge concerning Shakspeare, and of all opinions", he wrote in 1864.[22] Indeed, he knew the value of facts as
well as inspiration.

As to biography, his knowledge is apparent in those passages
in which he tries to evaluate sources and evidence. Such passages
not only reveal what Emerson knew about Shakespeare's life, but
also contribute to an understanding of his view of the poet because they present evaluations of biographical materials which
are ultimately based on significant assumptions regarding his
character.

These assumptions provided him with such guiding principles
as the following: First, the most important biographical facts are
those that point to the divine origin of Shakespeare's genius and

[20] Edmund Malone's *The Plays and Poems of William Shakspeare*, 21
vols., ed. James Boswell (London, F. C. and J. Rivington, 1821). Emerson
withdrew Vol. I (containing the prefaces of eighteenth century and early
nineteenth century editions, essays on the learning and style of Shakespeare, Rowe's "Life", additional anecdotes, etc.) from the Harvard
College Library on July 20, 1835. *Ralph Waldo Emerson's Reading*, pp.
48, 104. He withdrew Vol. II (containing Malone's "Life") from the Boston Athenaeum on Nov. 19, 1835 and Vol. III (containing Malone's
"Enlarged History of the Stage" and the "Genealogical Table of Ardens,
Grants, Wills", etc.) on Dec. 10, 1835. *Ibid.*, pp. 22, 104. Some of this
material he already had access to in the Isaac Reed edition. On June 30,
1835, he withdrew from the Boston Athenaeum Vol. XX (containing the
non-dramatic verse and the "Memoirs of Southampton"). *Ibid.*, pp. 24,
104.
[21] "To Christopher Gore Ripley, Nantasket Beach, Massachusetts, July
14, 1841", *Letters*, II, 424.
[22] *Journals*, X, 31 (April 24, 1864).

thus to the ultimate source of his greatness. Second, verification of such facts must be found in the hearts of readers of the works. Third, the chief source of these most important facts will ever remain the works themselves. Fourth, much more historical information than that which has thus far been produced by scholars is needed to illuminate the poet's meaning. Fifth, much more inspiration than that which has thus far been provided by the combined activity of hearts and brains of poet-critics is needed to further illuminate the poet's meaning, on the one hand, and to evoke, on the other, a response in the hearts of readers sufficient for the verification of its truth. In other words, the facts pertaining to the divine source of Shakespeare's powers, what Emerson regarded as the most significant biographical information, are all reflected in his works and may some day be verified by his readers because the same facts comprise a living truth in every heart. But the reflection of this truth in the works is now obscured by our inability to understand all the meaning the words conveyed to his society – hence the need for historical research. Yet even more than this is needed: we must find him in ourselves to comprehend all the truth reflected in his works – hence the necessity for poet-critics whose inspiring insights can strike within us a responding chord that will make us more fully aware of the presence in our own hearts of the same divine truth. Guided by these principles in evaluating biographical materials, Emerson reveals an undeniable familiarity with the evidence available to him.

In any attempt to determine the extent of this knowledge, it is first necessary, however, to recognize the influence on his evaluations not only of these principles, but also of his religious emotions. For him, as for many of his contemporaries, Shakespeare's life contained an extremely unusual amount of divine mystery. Because of his intensely religious nature, moreover, Emerson's quest for the kind of biographical facts he regarded as most significant was part of the preacher's lifelong search for divine truth. The influence of these emotions is apparent in the following passage from his journals, written in January, 1837:

I either read or inferred to-day, in the Westminster Review, that Shakespeare was not a popular man in his day. How true and wise. He sat alone and walked alone, a visionary poet, and came with his piece, modest but discerning, to the players, and was too glad to get it received, whilst he was too superior not to see its transcendent claims.[23]

Another passage, similar in tone, appeared in his journals the following October:

We are eager to know what Shakespeare said at the Boar's Head in Eastcheap. We should like to see him bring wood to his fire, or walking in his yard, but rather would we see what book he chose to entertain a solitary evening, or, refusing all books, what he did. Rather would I know how he looked at the Supreme Being in some lonely hour of fear or gratitude, hear what he said, or know what he forbore to say.[24]

Such passages indicate that he was seeking facts that would be significant not just because they could illuminate what was, for him, the dark, yet inspiring subject of Shakespeare's religious life, but because the light produced by that illumination would provide him with a personal revelation of religious truth and enhance his power as a preacher.

Searching chiefly for such facts, he seems to have depended mostly, while preparing his 1835 lectures, on Malone. Although he found in Aubrey some "traditions" that were not included in the notes of this edition, Malone provided him with a convenient, though not always reliable, treasury of biographical lore. By 1838, if not before, he was well aware of the modern researches of "Messrs Collyer & Dyce".[25] But it was probably not until

---

[23] *Ibid.*, IV, 186 (Jan. 21, 1837). *Cf. Ibid.*, X, 29 (1864): "He neglected his works, perchance he did not know their value? Ay, but he did; witness the sonnets. He went into company as a listener, hiding himself ... was only remembered by all as a delightful companion." The *Westminster Review* article may refer to the note which E. K. Chambers thought Aubrey got from William Beeston, the actor, a probable reference to Shakespeare: " 'The more to be admired quod he was not a company keeper, lived in Shoreditch, wouldn't be debauched, & if invited to court; he was in paine.' "

[24] *Journals*, IV, 332 (Oct. 20, 1837).

[25] "To Christopher Gore Ripley, Nantasket Beach, Massachusetts, July 14, 1841", *Letters*, II, 424-25. Referring to Collier and Dyce, Emerson says, in this letter, "I have never seen these books except in the possession

December, 1845, when Longfellow lent him nine volumes published by the Shakespeare Society, that he obtained, while preparing his lecture for the *Representative Men* series, a comprehensive view of modern research.[26] Despite his avid interest in what he hoped these external sources of biographical information might produce, he was usually disappointed by what he found; it often seemed to him that he would never discover more than "mere fables", "tavern stories", and other kinds of insignificant data. In February, 1835, therefore, ten months before he delivered his first lectures on the poet, he was inclined, in a lecture on Milton whose kind of superiority to Homer and Shakespeare he was trying to point out, to dismiss, under the guidance of feelings rather than knowledge, as "mere fables" the tales indicating that Shakespeare was "content with a mean and jocular way of life".[27] Emerson's feelings guided him here – his "admiration and joy", his "feeling of regret", among others. Such feelings contributed, ten years later, to the conclusion of his 1845 lecture. Like the "unpleasing dualism" and "double consciousness" referred to in this passage of 1835, the "halfness" he described there in 1845 evoked, despite his "admiration and joy", a similar "feeling of regret". By that time, however, his knowledge had grown; and his view of the poet had consequently been clarified.

---

of G. W. Haven at Portsmouth, but all that you want of them you will find in either the London Quarterly or the Westminster Reviews (of I should say 1838 or 1839)." *Ibid.*, 424. On a visit to Portsmouth in November, 1838, "Emerson seems to have been much impressed by his host's reading to him from Sir Thomas Browne and by a collection of works on Shakespeare (*Journals*, V, 146; and the letters of July 8, 1839, and July 14, 1841)." *Ibid.*, 173, editor's note. Rusk, in the following note, indicates the source Emerson was referring to: "*The London and Westminster Review*, IV, 30-57 (Oct., 1836), discusses several works on Shakespeare, including J. Payne Collier's *New Facts* (letter to Amyot), 1835, and *New Particulars* (letter to Dyce), 1836; also notices the Aldine edition of that poet, with Dyce's memoir." *Ibid.*, 424.

[26] "To Henry Wadsworth Longfellow, Concord, Dec. 2, 1845", *Letters*, III, 313. In a letter to Emerson written four days earlier, Longfellow had said: " 'I here send you a specimen of the books of the Shakespear Society, nine volumes in all, and the only ones of the series, which seem to contain much about the great bard and his times.' " *Ibid.*, editor's note.

[27] "John Milton", *Early Lectures*, p. 161. This lecture was given in February, 1835.

Meanwhile, this problem of the "unpleasing dualism" referred to in the Milton lecture in 1835 had developed into two problems, both of which he solved, or at least illuminated, while regretting the results. The first problem concerned Shakespeare's intellectual powers; the second, his moral and religious feelings. The problem caused by his intellectual powers was how to account for the fact that his works showed that he eminently possessed them while his personal history not only contained virtually no evidence of their existence, but did contain plenty of evidence of paltry interests which would seem to be completely incompatible with them. Emerson approached this problem by showing, first, that the evidence of such interests was also evidence of the divine instinct and therefore not incompatible with the existence of intellectual powers, and, second, that the lack of evidence of such powers in his personal life had two causes: the "obscurity" of a genius in his own age and the mystery ever accompanying poetic creation. The "obscurity" can be penetrated by gaining more historical information about the poet's age, which he represented because he had absorbed, and influenced the development of, its mind and soul. The mystery of poetic creation, on the other hand, can be at least partly dispelled by experiencing it as the Shakespeare in every heart is awakened by an inspired reading of his works. This way of viewing the first problem was accompanied by regret because, in the first place, scholars, fascinated by the insignificant details of the poet's personal life, have not yet sufficiently concentrated on that which could be truly revealing, historical research; and, in the second, critics, until recently, have failed to respond sufficiently to the poet's influence to become his "sons" and thus to develop the power to awaken, by their inspired and inspiring insights, the Shakespeare in the hearts of others. Similarly, the problem concerning his moral and religious feelings was how to account for what, in 1845, Emerson called his "halfness": while his intellectual powers were unsurpassed, both internal and external evidence indicated that these feelings failed to represent a comparable development. Emerson clarified this problem by indicating, first, that it was a problem in the history of the English race and would therefore be solved only when the whole of English history is known, and, second, that it revealed the relative inferiority of Shakespeare's level of religious development to that of the prophets, priests, and saints who were immediately above him in the scale of religious and moral feeling, and especially to that of the reconciler, Sayer, or ideal poet whose level was above theirs. This way of viewing the second problem was also accompanied by regret for two reasons – the lack of sufficient historical knowledge and the fact that the world's best poet fell short of the ideal.

In the month following his reference to the "unpleasing dualism" that made Shakespeare's level of growth inferior to Milton's, it was Emerson's knowledge of the works as well as his feelings that led him to dismiss as untrue the early "tavern stories" about the poet's want of education and "total unconsciousness":

We have made a miracle of Shakespeare, a haze of light instead of a guiding torch, by accepting unquestioned all the tavern stories about his want of education and total unconciousness. The internal evidence all the time is irresistible that he was no such person.[28]

---

[28] *Journals*, III, 452-53 (March 19, 1835). Indebted to this passage is the following from the first lecture on Shakespeare, given in December of the same year: "It needs then in order to any just understanding of this shining genius that we dismiss from the mind at once all the tavern stories that circulate, as if he were an untutored boy who without books or discipline or reflection wrote he knew not what, and see in him what he was, a Catholic or Universal mind of very great cultivation and one who by books, by discourse, and by thought formed his own opinions, who wrote with intention and who knew that his record was true and in every line he penned has left his silent appeal to the most cultivated mind." *Early Lectures*, p. 304. A comparable passage in the second lecture comments on the internal evidence of "thought": "The plays of Shakspear are works of art altogether of too great and grave a cast to be supposed to have been thrown off at a heat or as little men wish to think in the fumes of wines and youth. There is no juggle of this sort in Nature, least of all in her costliest productions. The laws of the mind are never eluded. It takes an ounce to balance an ounce, and deep thought and the most keen insight into all parts of society and all the acts of life cannot be evinced by a profligate and buffoon." *Early Lectures*, p. 319. *Cf.* "Culture", *Works*, VI, 141: "The best heads that ever existed, Pericles, Plato, Julius Caesar, Shakspear, Goethe, Milton, were well-read, universally educated men, and quite too wise to undervalue letters." Emerson may have been at least partly indebted, in 1835, to Shakespeare's German translator, August Wilhelm von Schlegel, for his assurance that these

Furthermore, in his first lecture on the poet, given in December
of the same year, he revaled that, since the previous February,
presumably, he had learned the futility of suggesting, chiefly on
the basis of feelings, that the evidence indicating Shakespeare
was "content with a mean and jocular way of life" consisted only
of "mere fables". He attempted, in this lecture, to present a view
of the poet which, taking account of such evidence, accepted it
not as entirely true but as containing proof of the presence of
"instinct". As such, it did not conflict with the internal evidence
of vast intellectual powers. But, Emerson implied, it did indicate
the absence of the deeper kinds of religious and moral experience
and thus justified the feelings which had led him earlier to doubt
its validity.

Drawing at random on his sources, he sketched a portrait of
the poet in this first lecture to show that both external and internal evidence indicated the presence of that divine power, "instinct", which he later defined as "at all points a god".[29] Thus,
while the works reveal he can soar to a "heaven of thought"
where he "poises himself as if it were his natural element", they
also show "he returns instantly to the ground and walks and
plays and rolls himself in hearty frolic with his humble mates".
And "all the little that we know of his personal history" and even
"the fables and traditions about him" testify to his delight "in

traditional anecdotes were baseless. In 1841, he declared that "Schlegel
(in his Dramatic Literature) very rightly treats all the common traditions
about his youth as tavern gossip entitled to no credit. And indeed there
was always a [strange] incompatibility between the roysterer [of the]
anecdotes & the gentle & all accomplished sage who wrote the plays."
"To Christopher Gore Ripley, Nantasket Beach, Massachusetts, July,
1841", *Letters*, II, 424-25. According to Rusk, "An American edition
available at this time was *A Course of Lectures on Dramatic Art and
Literature*, tr. John Black, Philadelphia, 1833". *Letters*, II, 424, note 201.
The following passage in this work is probably the one Emerson had in
mind: "It is true we know very little of the poet's life; and what we do
know consists for the most part of raked-up and chiefly suspicious anecdotes, of such a description nearly as those which are told at inns to
inquisitive strangers, who visit the birthplace or neighborhood of a celebrated man." *A Course of Lectures on Dramatic Art and Literature,* tr.
John Black, rev. by A. J. W. Morrison (London, 1861), pp. 351-52.
[29] *Journals*, VII, 99 (1845).

the earth and earthly things".[30] Both kinds of evidence, internal and external, reveal, therefore, the presence of "instinct".

Explaining this particular manifestation of deity, Emerson, in this section of his first lecture, implied that its occurrence depends upon the harmonious co-existence and unified activity of two opposites. The first is "Common Sense". This he defined as the perception of "the relations of the outward or apparent world", the physical world that is "the natural discipline which God has fastened upon the human spirit".[31] He, doubtless, regarded it as a masculine type of perception. Paralleling Common Sense, on a superior level, is another masculine, but deeper kind of perception, that of the philosopher, the perception of "truth". Opposite to Common Sense, on its own level, is "humanity". This Emerson defined as "a conformity of the spirit to this condition of its being", that is, "a conformity of the spirit" to its condition of being subjected to the "natural discipline" imposed by the physical world.[32] In Shakespeare, humanity is seen in "the overflowing love of life, the hearty sympathy of this great man with every pulse and sensation of flesh and blood, with the sweet and bitter lot of mortal man".[33] This love, or sympathy, Emerson regarded as a feminine type of perception. Paralleling humanity, on a superior level, is another feminine, but deeper kind of feeling: the sympathy, or love, imparted by the Moral Sentiment. While, apparently, not developed in Shakespeare, it is the deeper love of the saints, prophets, and priests; and it includes what Emerson referred to here as "the divine aspirations of the soul". While the unification of the types of perception of the philosopher, on the one hand, and of the saint, on the other, would seem to indicate, if the first were still dominant, an embattled Doer, and, if the second were dominant, a Sayer, the harmonious unity of Common Sense and humanity reveals the presence of the Father as a predominating instinct in a Knower. Hence, this poet pre-

---

[30] "Shakspear" (first lecture), *Early Lectures*, pp. 300-301. Emerson substituted "Much Ado About Nothing" for Aubrey's "Midsomernight's Dreame".

[31] *Ibid.*, p. 300.

[32] *Ibid.*

[33] *Ibid.*, p. 302.

ferred entertaining the public in the theater rather than moral action of the heroic kind or the announcing and interpreting of higher truth. "It was", Emerson declared, "this overpowering instinct of Nature, this fitness for and pleasure in the common social world in business and society and amusement that drew Shakspear to the drama." [34]

Having thus accepted as fundamentally valid that kind of evidence which he chose to interpret as revealing the presence of the divine power, instinct, Emerson apparently could see more clearly "the grand elements of his genius": those three "elements" that made him, respectively, "a poet, a philosopher, and a man".[35] They were "the three great intellectual faculties of man, the Imaginative, the Reflective, and the Practical".[36] What their great power in Shakespeare revealed about man's potential abilities stimulated Emerson's quest of their sources:

His immense and evergrowing influence over the human mind places him alone among poets. The silence and steadiness with which this kingdom of the intellect has been reared, a stone cut out from the mountain without hands to form the most great and durable of edifices, add to the interest of the event, and stimulate our inquiry into the sources of his power. It is not without cause, this irresistible dominion. It proceeds from a structure of mind as remarkable. To analyze the powers of such an individual is to analyze the powers of the human mind.

Thus, "this irresistible dominion", "this kingdom of the intellect" and "most great and durable of edifices" – which has resulted from Shakespeare's "immense and evergrowing influence over the human mind" – makes him "alone among poets". In other words, his uniqueness lies chiefly in his intellectual influence; he sowed seeds of thought in his works, which have given rise to a new "kingdom of the intellect". Yet he was not, as Emerson would make clear in 1845, the ideal poet, although, as he said here in the earlier lecture: "He possessed above all men the essential gift of the Poet, namely, the Imaginative Power."

This "Imaginative Power" "depends on the fact that the mate-

[34]   *Ibid.*
[35]   *Ibid.*
[36]   *Ibid.*, p. 303.

rial world is a symbol or expression of the human mind and part for part. Every natural fact is a symbol of some spiritual fact." [37] By means of this power, the poet dominates nature; [38] he acquires it "by sharing the ethereal currents".[39] As a mode of perception, Imagination perceives truth in images and seizes "beauty", which is "the moment of transition, as if the form were just ready to flow into other forms".[40]

In this first lecture on the poet, Emerson attempted to show – significantly, since Shakespeare would later be described as lacking in religious and moral zeal – that great passion as well as "intensity of thought" can generate this intellectual "Imaginative Power": [41] The sonnets, he claimed, "form perhaps as striking an example of this intellectual function as any book in the history of literature".[42] Although their "wonderful merit has been thrown into the shade by the splendor of his plays", he did not know where "in English or in foreign poetry more remarkable examples can be found of the tyranny of the imagination or the perfect control assumed of all nature by the poet".[43] But "this intellectual function" would be, if "untempered by other elements", a mental disease. It has "this vice that it leaves us without any measure or standard for comparing thought with thought".[44]

There is, however, an antidote, guaranteeing sanity:

The antidote provided in nature against the influence of any part is in the influence of the whole. There is a state of repose, an integrity to the mind, in which all objects are thrown back to stand in their due proportion. This vision of all being we call Reason. We speak of it generally as the mind's Eye. It is the Reason which affirms the laws of moral nature and thereby raises us to a region above the intellect.[45]

[37] *Ibid.*, pp. 288-89.
[38] *Ibid.*, p. 291.
[39] "Poetry and Imagination", *Works*, VIII, 21.
[40] "Beauty", *Works*, VI, 292.
[41] "Shakspear" (first lecture), *Early Lectures,* p. 291.
[42] *Ibid.*, p. 296.
[43] *Ibid.*, p. 293.
[44] *Ibid.*, p. 296.
[45] *Ibid.*, pp. 296-97. In his 1845 lecture, Emerson described how his works testified to Shakespeare's "healthful mind": "But Shakspeare has

The Reason, therefore, this "vision of all being", the "mind's eye", curbs the imagination and thus prevents the excesses that would lead to mental disease; since it "affirms the laws of moral nature", it can control such purely intellectual powers as the imagination. But, to maintain the presence of "Reason", there must be a desire, or "appetite", for truth, which, as an "influence of the whole", can help prevent excess and guarantee balance. This desire would seem to have been regarded by Emerson as an expression of the universal, feminine, centripetal tendency, the opposite, therefore, of the universal, masculine, centrifugal tendency expressed by the imagination and other intellectual faculties. In other words, it was apparently that aspect of universal love which is found ideally in the Knower's love of truth.

Moreover the special check to the excess of imagination is the appetite which leads man to introvert his eye, to explore the grounds of his own being, to compare his own faculties. This is philosophy when applied to man, criticism when applied to his works, and of all faculties esteemed the most fatal to the triumphs of the poetic art, because it seems necessary that the poet should believe his own fable and be the first convert to his own inspiration.

Shakespeare added to this towering Imagination this self-recovering, self-collecting force. Universality is the trait that all men remark in him.[46]

This "Universality" explains why "it is exceedingly difficult to extract an autobiography from his works, so impartial and devoid of all favorite moods and topics are his works". Shakespeare recognized "the spiritual truths which are the basis and fountain of our being", and he possessed "a habit of the most subtile and searching speculation into the cause and foundation of man's being and faculties". Hence, he not only had the "appetite", which led him "to introvert his eye" and thus counteract the "excess of imagination", but also the philosopher's "reflective powers". "The questions are ever starting up in his mind as in

---

no peculiarity, no importunate topic; but all is duly given; no veins, no curiosities; no cow-painter, no bird-fancier, no mannerist is he: he has no discoverable egotism: the great he tells greatly; the small subordinately." "Shakspeare; Or, The Poet", *Works*, IV, 212-213.

[46] "Shakspear" (first lecture), *Early Lectures*, p. 297.

that of one of the most resolute skeptics concerning life and death and man and nature." [47]

Besides imagination, the intellectual faculty characteristic of the poet, with its love of beauty, and the reflective power, the intellectual faculty characteristic of the philosopher, with its love of truth, Shakespeare possessed also a third intellectual faculty, the "Practical".[48] Without it, he might have been "thrust by the derision of the world into the class of mere contemplators and visionaries", not, significantly, with saints, prophets, and priests like Swedenborg, whom Emerson contrasted with Shakespeare in his 1845 lecture, but "with Pyrrho, Plato, Plotinus, Kant, with students and philosophers, . . .".[49] This saving "practical" faculty was his "Common Sense". It enabled him to give us "truth, clear, wholesome, and practical"; men are therefore drawn to him for his wisdom. But the "secret of his transcendent superiority as a writer", Emerson claimed, "lies in the joint activity and never ceasing presence" of all three intellectual faculties – those of the "Poet", the "Philosopher", and the "man".[50] However, it is noteworthy that, while his imagination and reflective power balanced each other, the combined weight of these intellectual faculties would seem to have been equalled by the third, Common Sense, which, in union with humanity, permitted the domination of instinct.

When Emerson composed his 1845 lecture, he clarified further the important role played by Shakespeare's humanity: "An omnipresent humanity", he said, "co-ordinates all his faculties." [51] Thus, it would seem to have been a feeling of love which, in its relation to the love of beauty Shakespeare felt as a poet and the love of truth he felt as a philosopher, corresponded in the superiority of its force with the superiority of his Common Sense, with which it was allied under the domination of instinct. By co-ordinating all his faculties, it gave a unique form to his vision of

[47] *Ibid.*
[48] *Ibid.*, p. 303.
[49] *Ibid.*, p. 299.
[50] *Ibid.*, p. 303.
[51] "Shakspeare; Or, The Poet", *Works*, IV, 212.

life, yet guaranteed a balanced and harmonious approach while being chiefly concerned with the physical world.

According to this view of the poet, the evidence indicated, on his intellectual side, the unsurpassed power of a "towering" imagination balanced by the reflective power of the philosopher's introverted eye and, offsetting the combined power of these, his level Common Sense, which, together with humanity, the love that co-ordinated all his faculties, provided a circular bridge uniting the side of intellectual powers with that of feelings and containing, in its center, the fountain of the divine instinct. But the evidence did not indicate the presence of a co-ordinating love deeper than this humanity.

This deeper love, Emerson implied in his first lecture, was that which gave Milton "the purity and religious elevation of his life".[52] Referring to Common Sense, he said, "Shakspear possessed this quality of clear perception of the relations of the actual world in at least as remarkable a manner as he had the perception of truth"; [53] but he did not add that the poet possessed a humanity that could be similarly compared to "the divine aspirations of the soul" which characterize the love of good. The implication is that he, in contrast with Milton and with saints like Swedenborg, was relatively lacking in this deeper religious feeling.

Both external and internal evidence indicated to Emerson the absence of this deeper feeling, the love of good, and the presence of a predominating instinct. Therefore, he would seem to have already concluded, as he certainly had by 1845, that, so far as religious development was concerned, Shakespeare's level was, relative to that of men like Swedenborg, the lower, and that, since the deity was most fully experienced by him as instinct, rather than as the Moral Sentiment, he felt religious love chiefly in the form of humanity. But the external and internal evidence were not similarly in agreement as to the presence of the superior intellectual powers. Although they were obvious in his works, the external evidence had so far failed to indicate that, in his life as

[52]   "Shakspear" (first lecture), *Early Lectures,* p. 303.
[53]   *Ibid.,* p. 300.

well, he could soar to a "heaven of thought" and poise himself there "as if it were his natural element". Yet Emerson was convinced that, in his personal life, Shakespeare had received in a "heaven of thought" the seeds that would give rise to his future "kingdom of the intellect" Hence, while the unity he found in the poet's works was the result of the divine power of instinct, and the external, as well as internal, evidence attested to its presence, thus solving one problem arising from the impression of what he had earlier called an "unpleasing dualism", the fact that his works manifested the greatest of intellectual powers while they remained concealed in his personal life, presented a second problem which, without more facts that would illuminate his personal history and more insights that would reveal his life in his works, could not be entirely solved. It also was a problem that was essentially religious because it involved Shakespeare's relations with the divine "intellect" that created the world. The difficulties it apparently caused Emerson in his attempts to account for the poet contributed to his interest in contemporary scholars and critics.

This interest is revealed in the 1841 letter to his young cousin, Christopher Gore Ripley, written from Nantasket Beach. Surprisingly informative, considering that he was denied access to his own library at the time, it shows that Emerson's desire to learn more about the poet's personal life had thus far been largely unsatisfied. Modern scholars had made only one significant contribution:

The most important probability they established, if I remember, on very slender external evidence, was, that on his early marriage he left Stratford & kept a school for years in the country . . . Now this hypothesis of the schoolkeeping gives us some external ground for all his contemplation & philosophy to stand upon, and is so natural a story, that I wish you may find it to be something more than a guess.[54]

The "schoolkeeping" hypothesis, based on "very slender evidence", provided the only "external ground for all his contemplation & philosophy to stand upon". By "contemplation &

[54] "To Christopher Gore Ripley, Nantasket Beach, Massachusetts, July 14, 1841", *Letters*, II, 424-25.

philosophy" Emerson meant the reception and love of higher truth; it referred to Shakespeare's greatest achievement, and the intellectual influence of his works indicated that he had been capable of it; but there was virtually nothing in his personal history to show that his contemporaries had been aware of this transcendent ability. At least so far, scholars had not produced such significant evidence.

But Emerson, in 1845, as in his second 1835 lecture, praised modern scholars who were accumulating information about Shakespeare's era and the history of the stage, because they were thus casting light upon the representative nature of his powers and his manner of employing them in his work. His irony, however, reveals his disdain of their failure to produce the facts that he wanted about the poet's personal life:

> Elated with success and piqued by the growing interest of the problem, they have left no bookstall unsearched, no chest in a garret unopened, no file of old yellow accounts to decompose in damp and worms, so keen was the hope to discover whether the boy Shakspeare poached or not, whether he held horses at the theatre door, whether he kept school, and why he left in his will only his second-best bed to Ann Hathaway, his wife.[55]

Probably because it testified to the presence of a predominating instinct, Emerson did acknowledge the importance of this information: "It was well worth the pains that have been taken to procure it."[56] Yet what he obviously wanted was not further evidence of the poet's instinct, but historical information illuminating those occasions when he received the influxes of the divine mind that manifested itself in him as instinct.

Such information, however, could never cast a light strong enough to penetrate the heart of the mystery of poetic creation. While it could help reveal the presence of conditions necessary for the creative act – the harmonious conjunction of the poet's feelings of love and his intellectual powers – it could not illuminate the act itself, dependent chiefly on the infusions of the divine creative energy from beyond the world of time and space:

[55]   "Shakspeare; Or, The Poet", *Works*, IV, 201-202.
[56]   *Ibid.*, 204-205.

But whatever scraps of information concerning his condition these researches may have rescued, they can shed no light upon that infinite invention which is the concealed magnet of his attraction for us. We are very clumsy writers of history. We tell the chronicle of parentage, birth, birth-place, schooling, school-mates, earning of money, marriage, publication of books, celebrity, death; and when we have come to an end of this gossip, no ray of relation appears between it and the goddess-born; and it seems as if, had we dipped at random into the 'Modern Plutarch,' and read any other life there, it would have fitted the poems as well. It is the essence of poetry to spring, like the rainbow daughter of Wonder, from the invisible, to abolish the past and refuse all history. Malone, Warburton, Dyce and Collier have wasted their oil. The famed theatres, Covent Garden, Drury Lane, the Park and Tremont have vainly assisted. Betterton, Garrick, Kemble, Kean and Macready dedicate their lives to this genius; him they crown, elucidate, obey and express. The genius knows them not. The recitation begins; one golden word leaps out immortal from all this painted pedantry and sweetly torments us with invitations to its own inaccessible homes.[57]

Thus, "the Genius draws up the ladder after him, when the creative age goes up to heaven, and gives way to a new age, which sees the works and asks in vain for a history".[58] As the heart of the mystery of poetic creation lies in eternity, Emerson would seem to imply, it has no history; one must experience creative power like Shakespeare's to know what happened.

The most complete body of evidence, and the most satisfying, is therefore found only in the works themselves and by those who are prepared by inspiration to receive it. The reader must find the Shakespeare in himself to know what should be contained in "anecdotes of his inspirations" – how he received truth and how he endeavored to express it under the compelling force of the creative energy that came from the same divine source. But he

---

[57] *Ibid.*, 205-206.
[58] *Ibid.*, 207-208. "Can any biography shed light on the localities into which the Midsummer Night's Dream admits me? Did Shakspeare confide to any notary or parish recorder, sacristan, or surrogate in Stratford, the genesis of that delicate creation? The forest of Arden, the nimble air of Scone Castle, the moonlight of Portia's villa, 'the antres vast and desarts idle' of Othello's captivity, where is the third cousin, or grand-nephew, the chancellor's file of accounts, or private letter, that has kept one word of those transcendent secrets?" *Ibid.*, 207.

can find the poet in himself only in his "most apprehensive and sympathetic hour", that is, only when, in reading the works, his own intellectual faculties, on the one hand, and his own feelings, on the other, are most actively aroused so that he may receive the poet's influence.[59] Hence, "with all due respect to Aubrey, and Dyce, and Delia Bacon, and Judge Holmes", as Emerson expressed it many years later, "it is not by discovery of contemporary documents, but more cunning reading of the Book itself, that we shall at last eliminate the true biography of Shakspeare." [60]

The word *cunning* would seem to refer here to a reading that is especially "apprehensive and sympathetic", in all ways knowledgeable and deft. Although historical information and scholarly skills alone, without the knowledge and facility produced by feeling and spiritual insight, would fail to elicit the significant facts, they too are requisite to a *cunning* reading. A discovery of the intellectual and the poetic history in the works requires, in other words, a knowledge of time and place as well as sympathetic feeling and an experiencing of divine infusions from the infinite. This historical knowledge is especially necessary in reading those passages which at present conceal the biographical information Emerson was most eager for – information that could reveal how Shakespeare experienced the receiving of higher truth.

Such passages – and they are the best in the work of any writer – demand an awareness of historical facts because the reader must

---

[59]   *Ibid.*, 208. In his poem "The Enchanter", Emerson wrote: "The little Shakspeare in the maiden's heart Makes Romeo of a ploughboy on his cart." *Works*, IX, 373. In an early lecture, he cautioned against "passive" reading: "The pupil must conspire with the Teachers. It needs Shakspear, it needs a Bacon, to read Shakspear and Bacon in the best manner." "On the Best Mode of Inspiring a Correct Taste in English Literature", *Early Lectures*, p. 214. But to be a Shakespeare requires a "passive" acceptance of his influence, which would enable the pupil to read creatively.

[60]   *Journals*, X, 279-80 (1869). Delia Bacon and Judge Nathaniel Holmes were early supporters of the theory that Shakespeare was really Bacon. Although the editors announce that "Mr. Emerson always used eliminate as *bring out*, instead of *leave out*" (*ibid.*, 280), the presence of two "Baconians" in this list of four, and Emerson's theory of the obscurity of genius suggest deliberate ambiguity.

be able to recognize the evidence of thoughts which were then most potent in order to determine the extent to which the poet was able to represent and influence his people's contemporary level and direction of development and therefore the extent and nature of his reception of truth. Like seeds portending the possible directions of future growth, the thoughts thus received and expressed were then so widely distributed that the poet, although he influenced the course of their development, gave them utterance without fully realizing it.[61] The "highest criticism", therefore, needs the help of those scholars who are chiefly concerned, not with gossip and "scraps of information" about the poet's life, but with the history of his influence and of his intellectual and religious milieu. Only that kind of historical research, Emerson would seem to imply in the following journal entry, can ultimately hope to explain, first, the "protective coloration" that made his intellectual "proportions" indistinguishable from others in that age of genius he represented; and, second, the fact that his works reveal both wholeness of vision and halfness of moral and religious development, for his "problem" was England's:

English Poetry. Yet it is fair (is it not?) to say that the ideal of any poeple is in their best writers, sculptors, painters, and builders, in their greatest heroes and creators in any and every kind. In Hamlet, in Othello, in Coriolanus, in Troilus and Cressida, we shall pick up the scattered bones of the English Osiris, as they haunted the mind of the greatest poet of the world; and he was English. But we pause expectant before the genius of Shakespeare as if his biography were not yet written and cannot be written until the problem of the whole English race is solved.

The English genius never parts with its materialistic tendency, and even in its inspirations is materialistic. Milton, Shakespeare, Chaucer, Spenser, Herbert, who have carried it to its great height, are bound to satisfy the senses and the understanding, as well as the Reason.[62]

Hence, although "a school-boy can read Hamlet and can detect secrets of highest concernment yet unpublished therein",[63] only

[61]   "Compensation", *Works*, II, 108.
[62]   *Journals*, VIII, 359-60 (January, 1853).
[63]   "Experience", *Works*, III, 63.

the most *cunning* reader will have sufficient knowledge to recognize and fully apprehend the reflection, in the works, of the history of the poet's mind.

Since all the facts in that history are already there, Shakespeare is "the only biographer of Shakespeare". Even now, we have gleaned so much "material" information about him from his works that he is the only person in modern history we know:

> Hence, though our external history is so meagre, yet, with Shakespeare for biographer, instead of Aubrey and Rowe, we have really the information which is material; that which describes character and fortune, that which, if we were about to meet the man and deal with him, would most import us to know.[64]

Then Emerson summarized, in his 1845 lecture, the significant "material" information about the poet's mind which we have been able to receive, up till now, from his own pen.

In his conclusion to that lecture, he turned to the subject of the poet's "halfness". When assessed morally and religiously, he proves, despite his intellectual comprehension of truth, to have been but the "master of the revels to mankind".[65] Shakespeare could perceive the higher truth – he "knew that a tree had another use than for apples" – but he lacked the deeper religious and moral feeling that would have motivated him to pursue a different purpose in life, that would have provided the means of seeing, at closer range, the moral and religious aspects of truth, magnified,[66] as it were, by experiencing them, and that would have enabled him thus "to explore the virtue which resides in these symbols and imparts this power". He failed, therefore, to take "the step which seemed inevitable to such genius". That step, the exploration of "the virtue which resides in these symbols", would have made him a true poet, an interpreter of the higher truth.

Such a failure indicates a lack of development of the kind of

---

[64] "Shakspeare; Or, The Poet", *Works*, IV, 208-210.
[65] *Ibid.*, 216-18.
[66] "Poetry and Imagination", *Works*, VIII, 10: "Passion adds eyes; is a magnifying glass. Sonnets of lovers are made enough, but are valuable to the philosopher, as are prayers of saints, for their potent symbolism."

perception which results from deeper moral feeling and a corresponding lack of a kind of knowledge which Emerson could not "marry" with the "talent and mental power" demonstrated by his verse.[67] Hence, the problem is how he, who possessed such great intellectual powers, "should not be wise for himself", that is, should not have sufficiently matured to know that the benefit to be derived from dedicating his efforts to interpreting and teaching the higher truth would be greater than the benefit to be derived from merely using the truth as he saw it for the purpose of dramatic entertainment.

This failure reflects a "halfness" in development which is opposite to that of the priest and prophets. In his lecture on Swedenborg, Emerson stressed the importance of noting "the line of relation that subsists" between him and Shakespeare, between his sanctity and the poet's intellect.[68] The "kingdom of the intellect" which Shakespeare established lies opposite and below, in the scale of development, the "kingdom of the will" established in the "atmosphere of moral sentiment". The true poet, who will unite these two kingdoms by means of an inspired will, has not yet appeared.

Swedenborg, the saint, experienced infusions of deity in the form of moral sentiment rather than instinct and thus represents a higher level of religious growth. Since the moral sentiment "inspires the will", furthermore, this saint's "region of grandeur" possesses more freedom than Shakespeare's "city of refuge", which tends to be dominated by fate. But Swedenborg lacked Shakespeare's "royal trait" of "cheerfulness, without which no man can be a poet".[69] Hence, he could not represent the Sayer:

Well, other men, priest and prophet, Israelite, German and Swede, beheld the same objects: they also saw through them that which was contained. And to what purpose? The beauty straightway vanished; they read commandments, all-excluding mountainous duty; and obligation, a sadness, as of piled mountains, fell on them, and life be-

---

[67] "Shakspeare; Or, The Poet", *Works*, IV, 218.
[68] "Swedenborg; Or, The Mystic", *Works*, IV, 94-95.
[69] "Shakspeare; Or, The Poet", *Works*, IV, 215.

came ghastly, joyless, a pilgrim's progress, a probation, beleaguered round with doleful histories of Adam's fall and curse behind us; with doomsdays and purgatorial and penal fires before us; and the heart of the seer and the heart of the listener sank in them.[70]

While Shakespeare, beholding the things which were the emblems of the mind's thoughts, "rested in their beauty", although he "saw through them that which was contained", these saints, also seeing through them, ignored the beauty, which therefore "straightway vanished". The consequent result, in reporting what they saw, had to be "half-views of half-men".[71]

When Shakespeare is thus compared with the saints, he too is seen to share "the halfness and imperfection of humanity".[72] Although he was the world's best poet, "the world still wants its poet-priest, a reconciler, who shall not trifle, with Shakespeare the player, nor shall grope in graves, with Swedenborg the mourner; but who shall see, speak, and act, with equal inspiration".[73]

Thus, Emerson, with the biographical evidence available to him, evaluated according to his own characteristic principles, developed an image of the poet that included both wholeness and "halfness", the unified vision of the whole of truth that produced the universality in his works and the limitations of perception by moral feeling that produced the "halfness" in the growth of his capacity to fully experience and therefore truly know what he saw. There was no paradox here, no essential contradiction: a representative of the Creator and Knower would cast such a reflection in depth when viewed from two levels: his own level of instinct, when a reading of the works is aided by the Shakespeare in the heart, and the higher level of the Doer, when his acts are judged in the "atmosphere of moral sentiment".

But Emerson was apparently not satisfied with such an image although he would seem, even in his later years, to have still contemplated its outlines with wonder as he saw them in his

[70]   *Ibid.*, 218-19.
[71]   *Ibid.*, 219.
[72]   *Ibid.*, 216.
[73]   *Ibid.*, 219.

mind. The reason for this dissatisfaction may have been the difficulty of keeping the image of Shakespeare at a "true focal distance", with the opposition between wholeness and halfness resolved as it is, by implication at least, in Emerson's writings on the poet, when the evidence of a divine mystery remained so obvious. He felt, certainly, a religious reluctance to insisting he had penetrated that mystery.

In his Tercentenary Address of 1864, Emerson repeated what, in substance, he had said before. Shakespeare's "fame is settled on the foundations of the moral and intellectual world".[74] So far as intellect is concerned, he was "the most robust and potent thinker that ever was". He "unites the extremes" of thought.[75] Then, writing in his journal the day after the tercentenary celebration, Emerson identified the poet's intellect with the source of a steady, unbroken light like the sun, on the one hand, and with the earth and its creation, on the other.[76] Referring to his art, he declared that his "point of praise" was "the pure poetic power".[77] Hence, "he was rhetorician, as was never one before, but also had more thoughts than ever any had".[78]

But, as in his earlier comments on "the first poet of the world",[79] Emerson, in these 1864 passages of praise, did not attribute to him the moral sentiment. Instead, he praised Shakespeare's "humanity", which made him "king of men".[80] Like the "earthly" Franklin and the others listed here, Shakespeare perceived higher truth and stated it; but his emotional response to it was no more than "humanity". He remained a "man", though "king of men". It was this humanity, this "appetite" for truth, that "unites the extremes" of thought, enabling him to speak "the pure sense of humanity on each occasion" in works whose form reflects his own personal "bias". Furthermore, its shaping influence upon the activity of his intellectual powers made possible

[74] "Shakspeare", *Works*, XI, 448.
[75] *Ibid.*, 449-50.
[76] *Journals*, X, 34-35 (April 24, 1864).
[77] *Ibid.*, 27.
[78] *Ibid.*, 29.
[79] "Shakspeare", *Works*, XI, 448.
[80] *Ibid.*, 452-53.

his "great heart of equity". It did not impel him to forsake unity by "pulpiting" as would the saints, but to speak with the balanced, controlled tone of a Greek oracle, the "level tone" [81] characteristic of a state of innocence.[82] Therefore, he was "the greatest master of language, who could say the thing finer, nearer to the purity of thought itself than any other; and with the security of children playing, who talk without knowing it".[83] According to Emerson's habitual pattern of thought, those things the poet stated "nearer to the purity of thought itself" were seeds of thoughts sown more or less unconsciously in his works but revealing a capacity of receiving truth superior even to his creativity. But, if he had strongly felt the presence of the moral sentiment, which inspires the will, he would not thus have been able to speak "the pure sense of humanity" with the spontaneous directness of an oracle.

Thus Emerson retained, in his later life, the essential outlines of that image of the poet he had earlier formed, but it did not satisfy him: there was too much mystery surrounding "the sources of his power" which he had referred to in his first Shakespeare lecture. Believing that there are always two histories, the scientific and the poetic,[84] he looked to scholars for new light on the first and to critics for inspiring insights into the second. Too little knowledge had already caused Shakespeare's readers, dazzled by the "incessant" light of his works, to regard him as mythical, like the Greek Orpheus and Homer.[85] A problem remained – that which had to do, apparently, with the contrast between vast intellectual powers and comparatively undeveloped religious feeling – for the scholars to solve with the "problem of the whole English race".[86] But even the solution of that problem could not dispel the sense of divine mystery. True poet-critics could inspire a reader of the poet's works to feel what he felt and thus learn more about his religious life; but too much theorizing about what would ever remain essentially mysterious was somehow, for

[81] *Journals*, X, 31 (April 24, 1864).
[82] "Shakspeare", *Works*, XI, 451.
[83] *Journals*, X, 29 (April 24, 1864).
[84] *Ibid.*, VII, 80-81 (Aug. 19, 1845).
[85] "Shakspeare", *Works*, XI, 449.
[86] *Ibid.*

Emerson, "profane". Hence, he confessed in his journal, in 1864: "Shakespeare puts us all out. No theory will account for him." [87]

II

In making these comments about the biography, Emerson showed that he was well acquainted with the available facts, traditions, and sources of information. His knowledge of the criticism seems also to have been substantial; and it, too, is most clearly revealed in his evaluations of it. These evaluations, furthermore, serve the additional, and more important purpose, in this study, of clarifying his view of Shakespeare. They are generally based upon assumptions which are consistent with his position in regard to the biographical materials: no adequate criticism of the poet has appeared until recently; the truly satisfying critic, like the ideal biographer to come, has yet to make his appearance; and the best criticism, like the best biography, will always be found in the works themselves, for Shakespeare is his own best critic as well as biographer.

In his letter to Ripley in 1841, Emerson declared: "All the criticism that contents us in the least, has been written – though not quite all since you were born, – yet at least since this Century came in." [88] Later, in his "Shakspeare; Or, The Poet", he held that "not until two centuries had passed, after his death, did any criticism which we think adequate begin to appear". It had taken one century to make the true nature of his greatness even suspected.[89] Then, after Addison's time, Emerson said in his second lecture on the poet, he became "the wonder of the world".[90] But anything approaching satisfactory criticism had to wait until the coming of Coleridge and Goethe, whom he described in his 1845 lecture as "the only critics who have expressed our convictions with an adequate fidelity".[91]

[87] *Journals*, X, 29 (April 24, 1864).
[88] *Letters*, II, 425.
[89] "Shakspeare; Or, The Poet", *Works*, IV, 204.
[90] "Shakspear" (second lecture), *Early Lectures*, p. 306.
[91] "Shakspeare; Or, The Poet", *Works*, IV, 204.

The fundamental cause of this delay is implied in such defini-
tions of criticism as the following:

Criticism is an art when it does not stop at the words of the poet, but
looks at the order of his thoughts and the essential quality of his
mind. Then the critic is a poet. 'Tis a question not of talents but of
tone; and not particular merits, but the mood of mind into which
one and another can bring us.[92]

Earlier critics had tended, on the one hand, to stress "the words
of the poet", which Emerson believed had been provided by
Shakespeare's imagination, and, on the other, to ignore what was
always more significant, "the order of his thoughts and the essential quality of his mind", which depended on powers greater
than the imagination; the resulting criticism had been something
less than poetry. Furthermore, while "the highest criticism should
be written in poetry",[93] and while this poetry should supersede,
"as every new thought does, all foregone thoughts", "making a
new light on the whole world",[94] these earlier commentators had
largely failed because such poetry cannot be composed except
by those who, inspired by the poet's tone and subjected to moods
induced by his "particular merits", are rendered sufficiently receptive to his influence to perceive the changes it has wrought in
their own creative power and to measure, accordingly, the magnitude of his spirit. For his criticism to be just and illuminating,
in other words, the critic must be able to permit the awakening
of the Shakespeare in his own heart; and he must also be able to
perceive, under its influence, the changes it has wrought and to
express inspiringly what he thus sees.

The true critic, therefore, is not chiefly concerned with the
poet's "words" and talents, but with the tone and the moods he
is subjected to, for these tend to reproduce in himself the "order"
of the poet's thoughts and "the essential quality of his mind",

[92]   "Art and Criticism", *Works*, XII, 305.
[93]   *Journals*, VI, 249 (September, 1842).
[94]   "The Editors to the Reader", *The Dial*, I (July, 1840), 3: "All criticism
should be poetic; unpredictable; superseding, as every new thought does,
all foregone thoughts, and making a new light on the whole world. Its
brow is not wrinkled with circumspection, but serene, cheerful, adoring.
It has all things to say, and no less than all the world for its final
audience."

thus casting light upon the shaping power that produced this
"order" and the way in which the deity, the essence of his mind,
affected its quality. The "fundamental law of criticism", Emerson
declared, is that "every scripture is to be interpreted by the same
spirit which gave it forth".[95] That spirit, in the poet, reproduces
itself, in the critic, as a characteristic "frame of mind" which
provides the critic with a measuring-stick for his evaluations:

We can only judge safely of a discipline, of a book, of a man, or
other influence, by the frame of mind it induces, as whether that be
large and serene, or dispiriting and degrading.[96]

Older critics had been chiefly concerned with "words" and talents
because, having been first subjected to influences other than
Shakespeare's, they were not inclined to be receptive to, or at
least conscious of, his. They had lacked the opportunity, moreover, to be influenced by others who, coming later, were his
progeny:

It seems as if the Shakspear could not be admired, could not even
be seen until his living, conversing and writing had diffused his
spirit into the young and acquiring class so that he had multiplied
himself into a thousand sons, a thousand Shakspears and so under-
stands himself.[97]

Even now, Emerson wrote in 1864, the "criticism and study of
him" are in their infancy.[98] Neither his own age, as he expressed
it in a poem, nor "sequent centuries could hit Orbit and sum of
SHAKSPEARE'S wit".[99] But, with the poets Goethe and Coleridge, true criticism had begun, finally, to appear.

[95] "Nature", *Works*, I, 35.
[96] "Natural History of Intellect", *Works*, XII, 67.
[97] *Journals*, V, 104 (Oct. 27, 1838). In 1874, Emerson wrote that "mankind have required the three hundred and ten years since his birth to
familiarize themselves with his supreme genius". "Preface", *Parnassus*,
p. v. But, in "The American Scholar", he had declared: "The English
dramatic poets have Shakspearized now for two hundred years." *Works*,
I, 91.
[98] *Journals*, X, 28 (April 24, 1864).
[99] "Solution", *Works*, IX, 222. Where this poem is printed as the epigraph to "Shakspeare", *Works*, XI, 446, the lines quoted are replaced by
the following: "And centuries brood, nor can attain The sense and bound
of Shakspeare's brain." *Cf.* "Shakspeare", *Works*, IX, 296: "Unmeasured
still my Shakspeare sits, Lone as the blessed Jew"; and "The Harp",
ibid., 239: "Or Shakspeare, whom no mind can measure."

The failure of the poet's contemporaries to make more of Shakespeare than they did was always, for Emerson, a cause of wonder even though he believed that "obscurity" was characteristic of genius. In various passages commenting on this supposed blindness to the poet's real stature, Emerson attempted to evoke scenes of a magnificent age of genius and of a brilliant society which, as it underwent the changes of time, tended, more or less unknowingly, to follow paths of thought illuminated by Shakespeare's "incessant light", whose source they could not easily recognize as he was not clearly distinguishable from themselves.

Throughout the major part of his life, Emerson retained in his mind this view of Shakespeare's relations with his age. On May 16, 1835, for example, he noted in his journal that Herrick had never mentioned the poet:

Robert Herrick delights in praising Ben Jonson, and has many panegyrical pieces to others, and in one copy of verses praising many, Beaumont and Fletcher and others, yet never drops the name of Shakspear. 'T is like the want of the statues of Cassius and Brutus in the funeral of Junia, *"Eo ipso praefulgebant, quod non visebantur."* [100]

In his first lecture on Shakespeare, given the following December, he made this daring assertion: "He was so much like other men that his genius was not suspected in his own time." [101] Drawing on Malone and other sources available to him, Emerson composed a description of the age that would demonstrate "the neglect of Shakspear by his contemporaries".[102] Two years later, he drew in his journal an imaginary portrait of Shakespeare showing that he was essentially alone among the players: "He sat alone and walked alone, a visionary poet, and came with his piece, modest but discerning, to the players, and was too glad to get it received, whilst he was too superior not to see its transcendent claims." [103] Writing to Ripley from Nantasket Beach in 1841, he included a rough sketch of the description presented

[100] *Journals*, III, 483 (May 16, 1835).
[101] "Shakspear" (first lecture), *Early Lectures*, p. 300.
[102] "Shakspear" (second lecture), *Early Lectures*, pp. 305-306.
[103] *Journals*, IV, 186 (Jan. 21, 1837).

earlier in his second lecture.[104] Yet the fullest description of this kind, whose chief value, perhaps, with that of similar passages, is what it reveals about Emerson's knowledge of the biographical materials, appears in his 1845 lecture. Thus, Shakespeare, according to Emerson, was "the founder of another dynasty, which alone will cause the Tudor dynasty to be remembered"; this dynasty he had referred to, in his first lecture on the poet, as the "kingdom of the intellect" established by Shakespeare's influence. He will nourish by his thoughts "for some ages" "the foremost people of the world". He "carries the Saxon race in him by the inspiration which feeds him"; that is, the nature of his inspiration was such that it led him to absorb, represent, and express the characteristics of the Saxon race – to identify himself, as a poet, with that race as well as all mankind. And, finally, the "minds" of his "sons" not only will be nourished for some ages on his thoughts, but will "receive this and not another bias"; in other words, their minds will receive as food for growth his thoughts ordered, emphasized, and slanted in the manner which was uniquely his. Yet, so it seemed to Emerson, nobody in his own day could recognize him as "the poet of the human race", "the best head in the universe".[105]

"Egotism" was the cause of that failure of recognition. In his tercentenary address, in 1864, Emerson, thinking in terms of his circular wave theory of history, pictured Shakespeare as dwarfing the giants in one of the "great wine years".[106] The chief reason for this ability to dwarf giants was his lack of the "egotism" that obscured their vision of truth: "He dwarfs all writers without a solitary exception. No egotism. The egotism of men is immense. It concealed Shakespeare for a century." [107] The word *egotism*, Emerson implied in his journal the day after the tercentenary, refers to a writer's unwillingness to see clearly, objectively, fully, to submit to the vision of all truth.[108] Shakespeare, alone among his contemporaries, had the clarity and fullness of vision neces-

[104]   *Letters*, II, 425.
[105]   "Shakspeare; Or, The Poet", *Works*, IV, 202-203.
[106]   "Shakspeare", *Works*, XI, 452.
[107]   *Ibid.*, 451.
[108]   *Journals*, X, 29 (April 24, 1864).

sary to recognize the true value of his genius. "He neglected his works. Perchance he did not know their value? Aye, but he did; witness the Sonnets." Emerson visualized him, therefore, as being truly alone among his companions and colleagues in the theater; he went into company "as a listener, hiding himself", moving like Night. Consequently, he was "only remembered by all as a delightful companion".[109]

Yet, from the poet's own day, certain receptive, and therefore more perceptive, men had at least glimpsed the outlines of "his colossal proportions". After claiming in 1835, for example, that Shakespeare "lived among a cloud of intelligent witnesses un-praised, unmentioned", Emerson admitted there were significant exceptions:

It is pleasant to observe that from the first a very small number of sensible persons have selected Shakspear with very significant com-mendation, viz. Jasper Mayne, the author of some fine lines prefixed to the first edition of his Plays; Southampton; and Essex; the Ever Memorable John Hales; Lord Falkland; Selden; Milton; Dryden; Addison, since whose time he became the wonder of the world.[110]

---

[109] *Ibid.*

[110] "Shakspear" (second lecture), *Early Lectures*, p. 306. The "fine lines" Emerson attributes to Jasper Mayne are apparently those signed "I.M." in the *First Folio*:

> Wee wondred (Shake-speare) that thou went'st so soone
> From the Worlds-Stage, to the Graves-Tyring-roome.
> Wee thought thee dead, but this thy printed worth,
> Tells thy Spectators, that thou went'st but forth
> To enter with applause. An Actors Art,
> Can dye, and live, to acte a second part.
> That's but an Exit of Mortalitie;
> This, a Re-entrance to a Plaudite.

Mr. William Shakespeares Comedies, Histories, & Tragedies, a facsimile edition prepared by Helge Kökeritz (Yale University Press, 1954). In his lecture "Ben Jonson, Herrick, Herbert", *Early Lectures*, p. 353, Emerson refers to "the ever memorable John Hales" as the friend of Essex. A note included in the manuscript of the second 1835 lecture on Shakespeare says: "Rowe's Life appeared 1709 Gildons letters & Essays with the ac-count of John Hales 1694." Houghton 1957. This note suggests that, when he referred to Hales in this lecture, he had in mind the anecdote that appears in Malone, I, 445-46. In a note to the passage containing Rowe's version in his "account of the Life, & c. of Mr. William Shakspeare", Malone gives the longer version from Charles Gildon's *Reflections on Mr. Rymer's Short View of Tragedy,* quotes Tate's preface to *The Loyal*

Others, however, had observed his ability to turn a phrase, to improve the harmony of the expressions he had borrowed: "Jonson compliments him on his 'true torned and well filed lines' and Meres thinks the soul of Ovid has revived in this melodist." [111] Such observations, according to Emerson's view, were concerned merely with "the words of the poet" and his "talents", not with "the order of his thoughts and the essential quality of his mind". Hence, criticism of this kind was not poetry.

Significantly, Jonson, the "President of that brilliant society of men of letters which illuminated England in Elizabeth and James's reign", [112] had failed to be sufficiently influenced by the spirit of Shakespeare to create the "highest criticism" when speaking or

---

General, 1680, on the same subject, and states that these writers were indebted, for this information, to Dryden, who gave his own version in the *Essay of Dramatic Poesy*, 1667: "'The consideration of this made Mr. Hales of Eton say, *that there was no subject of which any poet ever writ, but he would produce it* MUCH BETTER *done by Shakespeare*; ...'" According to D. Nicholl Smith, ed., *Shakespeare Criticism* (Oxford University Press, 1916), p. 18, note, the conversation in which Hales thus defended Shakespeare appears to have taken place between 1633 and 1637, and Dryden probably derived his knowledge of it from Sir William Davenant, who, according to Rowe, was one of the company. The manuscript of Emerson's lecture also indicates that Selden's name was inserted after the passage was written. *Early Lectures*, p. 504, note to lines 24-25 on p. 306. Selden's inclusion, with that of Southampton and Essex, suggests that, when Emerson claimed they had "selected Shakspear with very significant commendation," he was merely following Malone.

[111] "Shakspear" (second lecture), *Early Lectures*, pp. 309-310. Jonson's compliment appeared in his poem "To the Memory of My Beloved the Author Mr. William Shakespeare: and what he hath left us," which was included in the introductory material of the *First Folio*:

Looke how the fathers face
Liues in his issue, euen so, the race
Of *Shakespeares mind*, and manners brightly shines
In his well torned, and true-filed lines:
In each of which, he seemes to shake a Lance,
As brandish't at the eyes of Ignorance.

In *Palladis Tamia: Wit's Treasury*, Francis Meres had said: "As the soule of *Euphorbus* was thought to liue in Pythagoras: so the sweete wittie soule of Ouid liues in mellifluous & hony-tongued *Shakespeare*, witnes his *Venus* and *Adonis*; his *Lucrece*, his sugred Sonnets among his priuate friends, & c." In the same passage, Meres referred to "*Shakespeares* fine filed phrase".

[112] "Ben Jonson, Herrick, Herbert, Wotton", *Early Lectures*, p. 338.

writing about him. Apparently, Jonson's couplets in the *First Folio,* to the "Soul of the age, The applause, delight, the wonder of our stage", possessed at least a tone indicating the author's mind had been molded by an influence other than Shakespeare's and were therefore not deserving of more than a brief reference to his comment on the "true torned and well filed lines". The passage in the Discoveries, furthermore, "which at the first reading seems to be something fit & interesting", turned out to be but "remote & inadequate".[113] Moreover, instead of concluding with a judgment revealing a true apprehension of the poet's mind, "Jonson sums up his praise of his friend with the frugal encomium that there was ever in him more to be praised than to be pardoned".[114] To Emerson, such praise no doubt sounded condescending and thus helped to provoke the assertion that Jonson "esteemed himself, out of all question, the better poet of the two".[115] Because of the predominating strength of earlier influences, he was probably regarded by Emerson as incapable of having the Shakespeare in his own heart sufficiently awakened to make him truly aware of its superiority to his usual "frame of mind".

Jonson's usual "frame of mind" was characteristic, not of "the height of the human soul in that hour",[116] but of the "brilliant society" over which he presided, whose vision of truth still dominated that larger vision in the process of being created in men's minds by the deity as reflected in Shakespeare's "transcendent reach of thought" and "humanity". Hence, although Emerson had read Dryden's later statement to the contrary,[117] he adhered

[113]   "To Christopher Gore Ripley, Nantasket Beach, Massachusetts, July 14, 1841", *Letters*, II, 425.
[114]   "Shakspear" (second lecture), *Early Lectures*, p. 306.
[115]   "Shakspeare; Or, The Poet", *Works*, IV, 202-203.
[116]   "Art", *Works*, II, 353.
[117]   ". . . however others are now generally preferred before him, yet the age wherein he lived, which had contemporaries with him Fletcher and Jonson, never equalled them to him in their esteem: And in the last King's court, when Ben's reputation was at highest, Sir John Suckling, and with him the greater part of the courtiers, set our Shakespeare far above him." "Of Dramatick Poesie, An Essay", *Essays of John Dryden* ed. W. P. Ker (Oxford, 1900), I, 80.

to the view that, among their contemporaries, "Beaumont and Jonson were evidently thought the true poets".[118] In that age, only Milton, presumably on account of his youth, had been able to say "the first sensible word" on Shakespeare; and even he was lacking in appreciation.[119]

[118] "Shakspear" (first lecture), *Early Lectures*, p. 300.
[119] "To Christopher Gore Ripley, Nantasket Beach, Massachusetts, July 14, 1841", *Letters*, II, 415. The "first sensible word" appeared, according to Emerson, whose books were unavailable when he wrote this letter, in the "sonnet" and the "Penseroso". The lines from "L'Allegro" (not "Il Penseroso" – "Or sweetest *Shakspear* fancies childe, Warble his native Wood-notes wilde" – may have appealed to Emerson because they suggested what he had referred to in 1835 as the poet's "overpowering instinct of Nature". "Shakspear" (first lecture), *Early Lectures*, p. 301. But Emerson would not have approved Milton's implication that Shakespeare wanted learning. It is likely, because of its possible influence on Emerson's own attitudes toward the poet, that the "first sensible word" appeared more specifically in the other poem (not a sonnet), Milton's 16-line epitaph, dated 1630 by the author but first appearing in 1632 in the Second Folio of Shakespeare's plays:

> What needs my *Shakespeare* for his honor'd Bones
> The labor of an age in piled Stones,
> Or that his hallow'd relics should be hid
> Under a Star-ypointing *Pyramid*?
> Dear son of memory, great heir of Fame,
> What need'st thou such weak witness of thy name?
> Thou in our wonder and astonishment
> Hast built thyself a livelong Monument.
> For whilst to th' shame of slow-endeavoring art,
> Thy easy numbers flow, and that each heart
> Hath from the leaves of thy unvalu'd Book
> Those Delphic lines with deep impression took,
> Then thou our fancy of itself bereaving,
> Dost make us Marble with too much conceiving;
> And so Sepulcher'd in such pomp dost lie,
> That Kings for such a Tomb would wish to die.

It is not hard to imagine that, since Emerson tended to visualize the unfolding of life in any period as proceeding according to a dialectical pattern, Milton's reference to the "Star-ypointing *Pyramid*" helped to suggest to him the position of Shakespeare in relation to the subsequent developments of the English Renaissance. He may have been indebted to Milton also for the idea expressed by the words "shame of slow-endeavouring art" when he referred, in "The Snow-Storm", to the contrast between the speed of nature's organic creative processes and the relative slowness of art's:

> And when his hours are numbered, and the world
> Is all his own, retiring, as he were not,

Of the three critics Dryden, Addison, and Johnson, the first two were included in the list of earlier writers that had "selected Shakspear with very significant commendation", and the third had put "fine things" into his "Preface".[120] While one proof that Dryden's contemporaries seemed not to have read the poet was, according to Emerson, their failure to perceive the truth of his female characters,[121] the "very significant commendation" by Dryden himself must have included his epithets "the Divine Shakespeare",[122] "that Divine Poet",[123] "the Homer, or father of our dramatic poets"; [124] and his commendation must have seemed, to Emerson, to have at least foreshadowed the "highest criticism" because of his perception of the poet's "Universal Mind" [125] and his declaration that Shakespeare was "the man who of all modern and perhaps ancient poets, had the largest and most comprehensive soul".[126]

Similar foreshadowings must have appeared also in the "very significant commendation" of Addison, whose influence, according to Emerson, has been "undoubtedly beneficent" and whose

---

Leaves, when the sun appears, astonished Art
To mimic in slow structures, stone by stone,
Built in an age, the mad wind's night-work,
The frolic architecture of the snow.

Works, IX, 42. But he would not have agreed with Milton that Shakespeare's "numbers" flowed swiftly and easily, although their creation was governed by the organic principle. Similarly, Milton's choice of the words "Delphick lines" is reminiscent of his own tendency to identify Shakespeare's lines with the pronouncements of a Greek oracle ("The American Scholar", *Works*, I, 93, for example), and their impression on the heart at least suggests Emerson's references to the Shakespeare in every heart.
[120]   "To Christopher Gore Ripley, Nantasket Beach, Massachusetts, July 14, 1841", *Letters*, II, 425.
[121]   "In Dryden's time they were wont to commend Shakspear for his men and to suppose he did not draw women.... It seems to show that he was little read, or they would have found the truth of Imogen, Isabel (purity), Juliet, Cato's daughter Portia (heroism), Desdemona, Cordelia (piety), Cleopatra (luxury), Lady Macbeth (ambition), Beatrice (satire)." "Shakspear" (second lecture), *Early Lectures*, p. 313.
[122]   Preface to *All for Love; or, the World Well Lost.*
[123]   *Containing the Grounds of Criticism in Tragedy.*
[124]   "Essay of Dramatic Poesy", *Essays of John Dryden*, ed. Ker, I, 82.
[125]   *Containing the Grounds of Criticism in Tragedy.*
[126]   "Essay of Dramatic Poesy", *Essays of John Dryden*, ed. Ker, I, 79.

heart, although his mind was "not very original", was "in the right place".[127] When he declared that Shakespeare was "born with all the seeds of poetry",[128] that, like Homer, he was a "great natural Genius", a description which, so far as it suggested how his genius compared with that of later poets, Emerson would have accepted as accurate,[129] and that his supernatural characters, like Caliban, reveal the power of his imagination to create wholly new beings not patterned after anything already present in nature,[130] Addison was no doubt earning the place Emerson gave him among earlier writers with exceptional perceptive ability. Certainly his "beneficent" influence, by making the poet's "colossal proportions" at least suspected, helped Shakespeare to become later "the wonder of the world".

But Dr. Johnson was undoubtedly the better critic. In 1838 Emerson wrote Margaret Fuller: "Except something in Johnson's Preface; and Lamb; Coleridge's seems to me the first English criticism on Shakspear that was at all adequate – and now it seems only introductory." [131] Three years later, in his letter to Ripley, he declared that the "Preface" "certainly contains fine things" although its tone was different from that of "Schlegel, Goethe Coleridge & Lamb & their associates & friends",[132] thus implying that this difference of tone revealed a relatively inferior

---

[127] "Ethical Writers", *Early Lectures*, p. 366.
[128] "Spectator", No. 592.
[129] "Among great Genius's, those few draw the Admiration of all the World upon them, and stand up as the Prodigies of Mankind, who by the meer Strength of natural Parts, and without any Assistance of Art or Learning, have produced Works that were the Delight of their own Times and the Wonder of Posterity. There appears something nobly wild and extravagant in these great natural Genius's, ... Many of these great natural Genius's that were never disciplined and broken by Rules of Art, are to be found among the Ancients, and in particular among those of the more Eastern Parts of the World. *Homer* has innumerable Flights that Virgil was not able to reach, ... Our Countryman *Shakespear* was a remarkable Instance of this first kind of great Genius's." *Spectator*, No. 160. Although Emerson would not have agreed that Shakespeare lacked the "Assistance of Art or Learning", he did tend to believe that, compared with later poets, he was a great "natural" genius.
[130] *Spectator*, Nos. 279, 419.
[131] "To Margaret Fuller, Concord, November 9, 1838", *Letters*, II, 173.
[132] *Letters*, II, 425-26.

response to the poet's influence and a consequently inferior apprehension. But, despite this weakness, Johnson's criticism in the "Preface" apparently contained, in contrast to that of earlier writers, genuine "lustres", passages which Emerson would have described as lying "close to my own soul, that which I also had well-nigh thought and said".[133]

Indeed, the following passage, unconcerned as it is with mere "words" and "talents", attempts the "highest criticism" in describing the poet's greatest defect in terms suggesting Emerson's conclusion to his lecture on Shakespeare in the "Representative Men" series:

His first defect is that to which may be imputed most of the evil in books or in men. He sacrifices virtue to convenience, and is so much more careful to please than to instruct, that he seems to write without any moral purpose. From his writings indeed a system of social duty may be selected, for he that thinks reasonably must think morally; but his precepts and axioms drop casually from him; he makes no just distribution of good or evil, nor is always careful to shew in the virtuous a disapprobation of the wicked; he carries his persons indifferently through right and wrong, and at the close dismisses them without further care, and leaves their examples to operate by chance. This fault the barbarity of his age cannot extenuate; for it is always a writer's duty to make the world better, and justice is a virtue independent on time or place.[134]

Since this passage casts light on the nature of the poet's moral feelings, and since his own view of Shakespeare's "first defect" closely resembled Johnson's, Emerson may well have had this negative criticism in mind when, in his letter to Margaret Fuller, he referred to "something in Johnson's Preface" that had the honor of being "the first English criticism on Shakspear that was at all adequate". If so, it may be worth noting that, when English Shakespearean criticism first approached the level of poetry, it was negative in its treatment of the poet and, therefore, though "adequate", not satisfying. In any case, in his letter to Ripley, Emerson declared: "All the criticism that contents us in the least, has been written – though not quite all since you were born, –

[133]   "The American Scholar", *Works*, I, 92.
[134]   Samuel Johnson's "Preface" to his edition of Shakespeare, 1765.

yet at least since this Century came in." [135] When compared with what he had earlier told Margaret Fuller, this statement would seem to imply that, however successful Johnson had been in elucidating Shakespeare's "first defect", the tone of his criticism had betrayed him. Unlike that of more recent critics,[136] the tone, at least, had been inadequate.

In 1837 Emerson wrote in his journal that "it is as hard to get the right tone as to say good things. One indicates character, the other intellect." [137] But, since "character is higher than intellect",[138] it is really more important for the poet-critic to get his tone right than to say "good things".[139] When he declared that "tone, rather than lines, marks a genuine poem",[140] he must have included in his meaning of *poem* the "highest criticism", which is poetry. Hence, while the best critics are more concerned with tone than with "words" and "talents", in making their evaluations, their competence, resulting chiefly from their receptivity to the poet's influence, is revealed more by their own tone than by the "good things" they say. The character of Dr. Johnson, who, for Emerson, was "an unleavened lump at least on which a genial unfolding had only begun",[141] had presumably not sufficiently unfolded, or developed, under Shakespeare's influence, to have been able to adopt an appropriate tone. His criticism, therefore, could not satisfy.

Where Johnson had failed, the Germans had been relatively successful. Advising Ripley that "Schlegel, Goethe [sic] Coleridge & Lamb & their associates & friends speak in quite another tone", Emerson wrote "2" under "Schlegel" and "1" under "Goethe", thus indicating his order of preference.[142] Goethe and,

---

[135] *Letters*, II, 425.
[136] *Ibid.*, 425-26.
[137] *Journals*, IV, 364 (Nov. 23, 1837). *Cf.* "The tone a man takes indicates his right ascension", *Ibid.*, V, 110 (Oct. 30, 1838).
[138] "The American Scholar", *Works*, I, 99.
[139] "It is not the proposition, but the tone that signifies. Is it a man that speaks, or the mimic of a man?", *Journals,* VI, 88 (Oct. 14, 1841).
[140] *Journals*, X, 277 (1869).
[141] *Ibid.*, IV, 357 (Nov. 8, 1837).
[142] *Letters*, II, 425, editor's note 210.

after him, Schlegel, led even the best English critics in this matter of tone, because they were, presumably, more outstanding representatives of that "young and acquiring class" in whom Shakespeare's spirit had first been so widely "diffused" that "he had multiplied himself into a thousand sons, a thousand Shakspears and so *undertsands himself*".[143] In the following passage, Emerson offered such an explanation.

It was not possible to write the history of Shakspeare till now; for he is the father of German literature: it was with the introduction of Shakspeare into German, by Lessing, and the translation of his works by Wieland and Schlegel, that the rapid burst of German literature was most intimately connected. It was not until the nineteenth century, whose speculative genius is a sort of living Hamlet, that the tragedy of Hamlet could find such wondering readers. Now, literature, philosophy and thought are Shakspearized. His mind is the horizon beyond which, at present, we do not see. Our ears are educated to music by his rhythm. Coleridge and Goethe are the only critics who have expressed our convictions with an adequate fidelity: but there is in all cultivated minds a silent appreciation of his superlative power and beauty, which, like Christianity, qualifies the period.[144]

It is obvious from this passage that Goethe not only got the right tone; he also said "good things". Hence he is coupled [145] with Coleridge: they alone expressed Emerson's convictions "with an adequate fidelity". Although German criticism was merely "adequate", it was included in the best of the modern age; and, significantly, in the following list of the best critics to date, three are Germans, but only two are Englishmen and one an American: "Shakspear has for the first time in our time found adequate criticism, if indeed ye have yet found it. Coleridge, Lamb, Schlegel, Goethe, Very, Herder." [146]

---

[143] *Journals*, V, 104 (Oct. 27, 1838).
[144] "Shakspeare; Or, The Poet", *Works*, IV, 204. Christoph Martin Wieland's prose translations of twenty-two of Shakespeare's plays appeared from 1762 to 1766. August Wilhelm Schlegel's translations appeared from 1797 to 1810.
[145] "Even Shakspeare, of whom we can believe everything, we think indebted to Goethe and to Coleridge for the wisdom they detect in his Hamlet and Antony." "Art", *Works*, VII, 47.
[146] *Journals*, V, 133 (Nov. 12, 1838). *Cf.* "Shakspear" (second lecture),

While Emerson was certainly inspired by the tone of Schlegel [147] and stimulated, in a similar way, by Herder,[148] Goethe was, for him, the greatest of the German poet-critics. "You know Goethe's critique on Hamlet in Wilhelm Meister", he wrote Ripley. "There is an essay called 'Shakspeare & no end' in one volume of his Posthumous Works which is well worth seeing." [149] In these writings, Emerson must have found much that he himself had "well-nigh thought and said". A passage in *Wilhelm Meister*, for example, comes close to expressing what would seem to have been his own feeling as to the divine origin of the poet's

---

Early Lectures, I, pp. 306-307: "The commendation which was withholden at first has been given in the present age without stint, and often without wisdom, until it seems useless to add to his eulogy: but it may be pleaded there is reason for our panegyrics on Shakspear because it is just now that his preeminent merit is breaking into light. He is of that merit that needs a long perspective to show it truly and the judgments of men could not be trusted which had assigned a contemporary the superlative praise we have awarded him. We indulge our admiration at first timidly, until we see that a man who has been dead in England two hundred and twenty years is no longer aided by any accidental advantages at all adequate to the [witchcraft] which he exercises over our minds. And that influence reaches not over one faculty, but over all."

[147] In the following passage on Shakespeare's uniting of the opposites, Schlegel expressed a point of view resembling Emerson's, in a tone that would have contented him: "He unites in his soul the utmost elevation and the utmost depth; and the most opposite and even apparently irreconcilable properties subsist in him peaceably together. The world of spirits and nature have laid all their treasures at his feet: in strength a demi-god, in profundity of view a prophet, in all-seeing wisdom a guardian spirit of a higher order, he lowers himself to mortals as if unconscious of his superiority, and is as open and unassuming as a child," *A Course of Lectures on Dramatic Art and Literature* (London, 1861), p. 368.

[148] "William Emerson wrote Aug. 27, 1824 (MS owned by Dr. Haven Emerson): 'Read all of Herder you can get...'" Rusk, ed., *Letters*, I, 153, note 62. The inclusion of Herder's name with those of his favorite modern Shakespearean critics suggests that Emerson had followed his elder brother's advice. His view of the poet as representative of his age and race may be owing, at least in part, to his reading of Herder.

[149] *Letters*, II, 426. Emerson was reading *Wilhelm Meister* in June, 1834, more than a year before he gave his first lectures on Shakespeare. *Journals*, III, 309. Rusk believes he probably used the following edition: *Wilhelm Meisters Lehrjahre*, Vol. XIX of Goethe's *Werke*, ed. Cotta (1828). *Letters*, II, 426, note 211.

works.[150] Another indicates the kind of effect likely to be produced by Shakespeare's beneficial influence: [151]

The few glances I have cast over Shakspeare's world incite me, more than anything beside, to quicken my footsteps forward into the actual world, to mingle in the flood of destinies that is suspended over it; and at length, if I shall prosper, to draw a few cups from the great ocean of true nature, and to distribute them from off the stage among the thirsting people of my native land.

A third, containing a comment on Shakespeare's characters, employs imagery suggesting Emerson's own.[152] Similarly, the "Shakspeare & no end" essay he had recommended to young Ripley is replete with passages that nearly express Emerson's own feelings and thoughts. Goethe claimed here, for example, that the poet's works "contain much more of spiritual truth than of spectacular action", that he "gets his effect by means of the living word" and is therefore better read than played on the attention-distracting stage, that he "associates himself with the World-Spirit", and that he truly represents his nation and age, their glory and deficiencies.[153] He "belongs by necessity", Goethe declared, "in the annals of poetry; in the annals of the theatre he appears only by accident". As he was essentially a poet, and therefore a "universal interpreter of Nature", the stage was not "a worthy field for his genius". Unlike other poets, however, he, in his works, "puts an idea at the centre, and to it relates the world and the universe".[154] At the same time, he was "a true child of nature".[155] This view of him as "a true child of nature" who, though essentially a poet, was different from others because he put ideas at the center corresponds closely with Emerson's.

As a representative of the Knower, Emerson's Shakespeare,

---

[150] *Goethe on Shakespeare, being Selections from Carlyle's translation of Wilhelm Meister* (London, 1904), p. 5.
[151] *Ibid.*, p. 6.
[152] *Ibid.*
[153] "Shakespeare ad Infinitum", tr. Randolph S. Bourne, *Goethe's Literary Essays*, ed. J. E. Spingarn (New York, 1921), pp. 175-77. According to Rusk, *Letters*, II, 426, note 212, Emerson had purchased a large number of "*Goethe's nachgelassene Werke*".
[154] *Op. cit.*, pp. 185-87.
[155] *Ibid.*, pp. 183-84.

although he allowed himself to become concerned primarily with beauty in his works, was more a lover of truth than of good or even of beauty. Hence, what he saw chiefly as central in life was intellectual truth; that vision was, moreover, uncomplicated by the deeper moral and religious feelings, on the one hand, and the love of the beauty of higher truth, on the other.

Goethe's tendency to see Shakespeare involved with fate also resembles Emerson's. As a representative of the Greek stage of innocence, Emerson's Shakespeare symbolized the power of Fate while it still maintained its dominance over Freedom, a power which would ultimately be overthrown by instinct as that manifestation of deity evolved into a higher form of the divine, creative force at work in the world. Emerson made the following comment on this subject in his journal:

Fate and Instinct. Fatalism the right formula to be holden: but by a clever person who knows to allow the living instinct. For, though that force be infinitely small, infinitesimal against the Universal Chemistry, it is of that subtlety that it homoeopathically doses the system.[156]

Since instinct represents a growing freedom on a stage of development still dominated by fate, the works of a poet who symbolized that stage would suggest both the "voice of instinct" and the still dominant power of fate. Shakespeare's works, as the reflection of both his mind and his age, would seem to have suggested such a world to Emerson. Goethe's view was strikingly similar: "In his plays Will and Necessity struggle to maintain an equilibrium; both contend powerfully, yet always so that Will remains at a disadvantage." Throughout the discussion of this subject in his essay, Goethe compares Shakespeare with the Greek dramatists and concludes that, since his Necessity is a "moral necessity", he has succeeded in combining "in such a remarkable fashion the old and the new".[157] Emerson would have given the term Fate to Goethe's Necessity as Goethe applied it to the Greek drama; and he would have included, by the term Necessity or Beautiful Necessity, more than Goethe meant by

---

156   Journals, VIII, 391 (July 21, 1853).
157   "Shakespeare ad Infinitum", pp. 182-83.

the "moral necessity" found in Shakespeare; but he would have agreed that Shakespeare's works, like the Greek drama, depicted a world in which freedom, or will, always "remains at a disadvantage" in the struggle with fate. There seemed, to him, to be little evidence, in the poet's life and works, of the freedom bestowed by the Moral Sentiment on the will of the Doer engaged in moral action.

As a critic, Goethe had thus reached a level of apprehension and sympathy which, though no more than "adequate", had not yet been surpassed. But also "adequate", in Emerson's estimation, was the level attained by Lamb, Very, and Coleridge. It is obvious why he included Lamb in this favored group. As to the acting of Shakespeare's plays, Lamb's opinion was similar to Goethe's and Emerson's: they were "less calculated for performance on a stage, than those of almost any other dramatist whatever" because "there is so much in them, which comes not under the province of acting, with which eye, and tone, and gesture, have nothing to do".[158] Lamb pointed out also "how much Hamlet is made another thing by being acted" [159] and contended that "the Lear of Shakspeare cannot be acted . . . They might more easily propose to personate the Satan of Milton upon a stage, or one of Michael Angelo's terrible figures" because "the greatness of Lear is not in corporal dimension, but in intellectual".[160] Lamb

[158]   Charles Lamb, "On the Tragedies of Shakespeare, Considered with Reference to Their Fitness for Stage Representation", in D. Nichol Smith, ed., *Shakespeare Criticism*, p. 219. Emerson said, in his conversation with Edwin P. Whipple: " 'I see you are one of the happy mortals who are capable of being carried away by an actor of Shakspeare. Now whenever I visit the theatre to witness the performance of one of his dramas, I am carried away by the poet. I went last Tuesday to see Macready in Hamlet. I got along very well until he came to the passage:
    "thou, dead corse, again, in complete steel,
    Revisit'st thus the glimpses of the moon;"
and then actor, theatre, all vanished in view of that solving and dissolving imagination, which could reduce this big globe and all it inherits into mere "glimpses of the moon". The play went on, but, absorbed in this one thought of the mighty master, I paid no heed to it.' " "Some Recollections of Ralph Waldo Emerson", *Harper's New Monthly Magazine*, Vol. 65 (Sept., 1882), 580.
[159]   Lamb, *op. cit.*, p. 222.
[160]   *Ibid.*, p. 232.

claimed, furthermore, that the manner of speaking was "only a medium" for permitting the audience to comprehend a character's psychology.[161] Similarly, the characters themselves, considered more or less apart from their actions, were true "objects of meditation".[162] Lamb, finally, with a tone like Emerson's when he regretted that "the best poet" had been "a jovial actor and manager" who "led an obscure and profane life, using his genius for the public amusement",[163] compared Shakespeare with Garrick, but found it inconceivable that the two men, just because they were both actors and managers, could have had similar moral characters. After citing passages in the sonnets which would seem to reveal the poet's feelings of shame for his theatrical activities, Lamb asked the following rhetorical question:

Who can read these instances of jealous self-watchfulness in our sweet Shakspeare, and dream of any congeniality between him and one that, by every tradition of him, appears to have been as mere a player as ever existed; to have had his mind tainted with the lowest players' vices, – envy and jealousy, and miserable cravings after applause; ... a manager full of managerial tricks and stratagems and finesse ...[164]

While Emerson obviously approved the tone and many of these "good things" Lamb said about Shakespeare, he would not have agreed with this argument that the moral dispositions of the "jovial actor and manager" and David Garrick were perforce so uncongenial.

The only American critic that approached the level of these writers was Jones Very. On September 1, 1838, Emerson wrote to his aunt, Mary Moody Emerson: "There is a young man at Cambridge named Jones Very who I think would interest you. He studies Shakspear now & will presently finish & probably publish an Essay on S. and from a point of view quite novel & religious." [165] Later that month, after reading the essay, he described it in a letter to Margaret Fuller as "a noble production:

---

161 *Ibid.*, pp. 219-20.
162 *Ibid.*, p. 230.
163 "Shakspeare; Or, The Poet", *Works*, IV, 218.
164 Lamb, *op. cit.*, p. 228.
165 "To Mary Moody Emerson, Concord, September 1, 1838", *Letters*, II, 154.

not consecutive, filled with one thought; but that so deep & true & illustrated so happily & even grandly, that I account it an addition to our really scanty stock of adequate criticism on Shakspear." [166] When he wrote again to Margaret Fuller, on November 9, he said: "When you come here I will show you Very's two dissertations, – one on the general subject, & the other on Hamlet, – which are pretty great criticism." [167]

Very had earned this praise pursuing an aim that lay at the heart of the mystery blurring Emerson's image of the poet: "What led him to study Shakspear", Emerson said, "was the fact that all young men say, Shakspear was no saint, – yet see what genius! He wished to solve that problem." [168] Thus, endeavoring to explain how "the best poet" could be "content with a mean and jocular way of life", Very, in Emerson's opinion, had succeeded in reaching the level of criticism that was at least "adequate". His two pieces, "Shakespeare" and "Hamlet", appeared in 1839 in *Essays and Poems*, a volume of his works edited by Emerson.

In "Shakespeare" Very attempted to show, in analyzing the

[166] "To Margaret Fuller, Concord, September 28 and 29, 1838", *Letters*, II, 164-65.
[167] "To Margaret Fuller, Concord, November 9, 1838", *Letters*, II, 173. In his letter to Margaret Fuller of Sept. 28 and 29, Emerson informed her that "poor Very, the tutor at Cambridge", was "at the Charlestown Asylum & his case tho't a very unpromising one". He concluded: "Such a mind cannot be lost." *Ibid.*, II, 164-65. On October 24, Very began a visit with the Emersons. Two days later, Emerson wrote: "His position accuses society as much as society names it false and morbid; and much of his discourse concerning society, the church, and the college was perfectly just." As Very was "one of these monotones", "the partial action of his mind in one direction is a telescope for the objects on which it is pointed". *Journals*, V, 98-99 (Oct. 26, 1838). After Very departed on October 29, Emerson diagnosed his mental condition in a letter to Miss Peabody: "I have been very happy in his visit as soon as I came to understand his vocabulary. I wish the whole world were as mad as he. He discredits himself I think by a certain violence I may say of thought & speech; but it is quite superficial; he is profoundly sane, & as soon as his thoughts subside from their present excited to a more natural state, I think he will make all men sensible of it. If it shall prove that his peculiarities are fixed, it can never alter the value of the truth & illumination he communicates, if you deal with him with perfect sincerity." "To Elizabeth Palmer Peabody, Concord, October 30, 1838", *Letters*, II, 171.
[168] *Journals*, V, 105 (Oct. 28, 1838).

character of the poet, "that a desire of action was the ruling impulse of his mind; and consequently a sense of existence its permanent state". He claimed that "this condition was natural; not the result felt from a submission of the will to it, but bearing the will along with it". The poet's mind was therefore, he claimed, "phenomenal and unconscious, and almost as much a passive instrument as the material world", and he was himself "the unconscious work of God". But he would have been even greater, Very declared, if he had also represented "conscious nature", that is, if his will, not "borne down and drawn along by the mind's original impulse", had but yielded flexibly, "though capable of resistance", to all the mind's "natural movements". These movements of the human mind that he called "natural" were those that harmonized with the operations of God's will on two levels: unconscious and conscious nature. Shakespeare did not need to submit his will to God's on the level of unconscious nature; his will moved with God's on that level almost as if he were a passive material object. His will obeyed, therefore, its "original impulse", which resulted in those "natural movements" that corresponded with the activity of God's will in unconscious nature, but it did not respond to higher impulses that could have produced just as natural actions on the higher level where God's will operates in conscious nature. By thus failing to develop "conscious nature", he could not grow into "that higher phenomenon which genius and revelation were meant to forward in all men".

Shakespeare's "desire of action ("the ruling impulse of his mind") and his "sense of existence" (his mind's consequent "permanent state") were, Very declared, the manifestation of childish innocence. His "desire of action" had two results: "involuntary activity" and "a sense of existence" or "sense of life" which, producing, in turn, his "childlike love of variety and joyous sympathy with all things", was that "consciousness of being" which "by most of us is known but in youth".

This life of his in all objects and scenes was the simple result of the movements of a mind which found only in all it saw around it something to correspond with its own condition. Its own activity was its possession; circumstances and things seemed to be, because it was; these were accidents, and not, as with other men, realities. His power, while exerted on every thing, seems independent of its objects.[169]

This "sense of life", Very implied, existed before the Fall. "We all feel at first that life is more than the meat, but from the corrupt world around us we soon learn to prize the meat more than our spiritual life." In our fallen state only love can redeem us.

Perhaps Emerson would have substituted "humanity" for what Very called "a desire of action", "the ruling impulse of his mind". And for his mind's consequent "permanent state", "a sense of existence", Emerson might have substituted "instinct". Moreover, he would have said, with Very, that the poet's mind was merely "phenomenal and unconscious, and almost as much a passive instrument as the material world". Emerson's position was that, because of his instinct, Shakespeare's mind was becoming supremely "conscious" though it remained less so, and less free, than if, with its vast intellectual powers, it had had the deeper moral consciousness imparted by the Moral Sentiment. This deeper moral consciousness, moreover, with its "divine aspirations", took the place, in Emerson's thought, of "conscious nature".

Believing in the unification of opposites represented by the Sayer, the Doer, and the Knower, he would have approved this assertion:

From what has been said we may perceive that universality is not a gift of Shakespeare alone, but natural to the mind of man; and that whenever we unburthen ourselves of that load of selfishness under which what is natural in us lies distorted, it will resume as its own estate that diversity of being in which he delighted. That which in the poet, the philosopher, or the warrior, therefore affects us is this higher natural action of the mind, which, though exhibited in one, is felt to be harmonious with all; which imparts to us, as it were, their own universality, and makes us for a while companions of their various life.

[169] Jones Very, "Shakespeare", in Perry Miller, ed., *The Transcendentalists* (Harvard University Press, 1950), p. 347.

And Emerson would have accepted Very's statement that, if Shakespeare had had the "higher motives" of one "who is by duty becoming consciously natural",[170] he would have been more successful than he was in showing us the good; and he would have approved his argument that the poet's success in this respect, such as it was, had resulted from his innocence.[171] The moral benefit we derive from him results, according to Very, from the innocence that enabled him to hold "a pure and untarnished mirror up to Nature". But his weakness, as a moral and religious influence, results from the absence of a deeper feeling, what Emerson meant when he referred to the Doer's "love of good".[172] When Very refers here to "feeling more deeply that all things are ours", "that love which knew what was in man", and "a sense of duty", he is employing terms that Emerson himself might have used to explain the same deficiency.

Furthermore, since Emerson believed that feeling was a form of perception, a means of knowing, he would have agreed with Very that Shakespeare, if he had not been lacking in this respect, not only would have exerted a greater moral and religious influence, but also would have created truer art. "It is that the poet should represent things as they are, for which we contend",[173] Very declared. "Shakespeare's characters are true and natural indeed; but they are not the truest and most natural which the world will yet see." [174] What he lacked was "the spiritual eye":

We need not substitute our ideals of virtue and vice for the living

---

[170] *Ibid.*, p. 348. "This natural action of the mind, in whatever direction applied, is ever revealing to us more than we have before known; for this alone unconsciously moves in its appointed path; the only human actor in the drama of existence, save him who is by duty becoming consciously natural, that can show us any good. In its equable and uninterrupted movements, it harmonizes ever with Nature, giving the spiritual interpretation to her silent and sublime growth. In the movements of Shakespeare's mind, we are permitted to see an explanation of that strange phenomenon in the government of Him who made us, by which that which is most universal appears to be coincident with that which is most particular."

[171] *Ibid.*, pp. 349-350.

[172] *Ibid.*, p. 350.

[173] *Ibid.*

[174] *Ibid.*, p. 351.

forms around us; we need not brighten the one, nor darken the other; to the spiritual eye, even here, will the just begin to appear as angels of light; and as the sun of Divine Favor sets on the wicked, their lengthening shadows, ever here, are seen to blacken and dilate into more gigantic and awful proportions.[175]

The "spiritual eye" necessary to create such characters resembled Emerson't "love of the good". But when Emerson first read the following words of a youth supposed to be crazy, Jesus rather than the "Doer" must have come to mind: "No one can enter more entirely into the lives of others than Shakespeare has done, until he has laid down his own life and gone forth to seek and to save that which is lost." [176]

The theory of art Very adumbrates here includes, besides the idea that strong moral feelings and profoundly religious experience increase the amount of truth conveyed in a literary work, thereby improving it, the related belief that the will, too, is involved. The problem of Shakespeare, as Very sees it, is essentially one of consciousness, which implies will. While Emerson saw the poet as a great voice of instinct creating and representing a world which only tends to be dominated by fate, Very saw virtually no evidence of any kind of freedom. For him, Shakespeare was a poet whose will conformed with that of God only as it manifested itself in material, or unconscious, nature, and not with the Divine will as it manifested itself, on a higher level of feeling, in "him who is by duty becoming consciously natural". Consequently, the characterizations of Hamlet and Macbeth would have contained more of the truth, he contended, if their creator had been growing by a sense of duty into a more "consciously natural" artist: "From the states of mind of a Hamlet and Macbeth rise tones of which the words he has made them utter bear but faint intelligence; and which will find a stronger and yet stronger utterance as the will of the poet conforms to that of his Maker." [177] Thus, Shakespeare, because of his lack of "that sense of responsibility" which would have improved his creations, had no more consciousness, or freedom, than a natural phenome-

175   *Ibid.*
176   *Ibid.*, p. 350.
177   *Ibid.*, p. 351.

non.[178] Emerson had always rejected such an extreme position.
Although Very did not regard the poet as representative of an
archetypal Knower and his love of truth, he did contend that
Shakespeare could have been a greater artist if he had had what
Emerson called the "love of good" and that his "master passion"
was "the love of intellectual activity for its own sake". Hence,
he believed that the poet lacked "that assurance of eternal existence which Christ alone can give, – which alone robs the grave
of victory, and takes from death its sting. . . . From the wrestling
of his own soul with the great enemy come that depth and mystery
which startle us in 'Hamlet.' " [179] While Emerson would not have
accepted the idea that Shakespeare's "master passion" was as
Very had described it, since he believed that "passion" was his
love of truth as it was chiefly manifested in his "humanity", he
would have admired the tone of this passage; and, because Very
here emphasized those tendencies which Emerson had seen also
and regarded as being of the highest significance, he must have
applauded this statement as one of the best of the "good things"
in Very's "pretty great criticism".

In the letter to Margaret Fuller in which Emerson had given
Very this extraordinary praise, he announced he was sending her
a volume of Coleridge, one which would seem to have contained
Shakespeare's criticism; [180] and after stating that, except "something in Johnson's Preface; and Lamb; Coleridge's seems to me
the first English criticism on Shakspear that was at all adequate",
he added, significantly, "and now it seems only introductory.
Shakspeare has not done growing yet: and a great day it will be
for any mind when it has come to put Shakspeare at a true focal
distance." [181] Although, as he stated elsewhere, Coleridge "wrote
and spoke the only high criticism in his time",[182] Emerson was

178 *Ibid.*
179 Jones Very, "Hamlet", in Perry Miller, ed., *The Transcendentalists*,
p. 354.
180 "Vols. I-II of *The Literary Remains of Samuel Taylor Coleridge*, ed.
H. N. Coleridge, had appeared at London in 1836. Vol. III followed in
1838 and IV in 1839. The Shakespeare criticism is in Vol. II." *Letters*,
II, 173, n. 268.
181 "To Margaret Fuller, Concord, November 9, 1838", *Letters*, II, 137.
182 "Literature", *Works*, V, 248.

unwilling to grant that his remarks on the great poet were more than "introductory" or that even he had "put Shakspeare at a true focal distance".

This opinion was based upon Emerson's familiarity with the criticism contained in the second volume of Coleridge's *Literary Remains*, which he presumably sent to Margaret Fuller in 1838, and with that contained in *Biographia Literaria*, which he was reading at least as early as 1826,[183] *The Friend*, which he apparently first read in 1829,[184] and the *Table Talk*, which, in 1835, he described as "good as Spence's or Selden's or Luther's; better".[185] After reading, over a period of at least twelve years, most of what Coleridge had said about Shakespeare, he felt sufficiently familiar with his criticism of that poet to express such an opinion.

Coleridge made many statements concerning the order of the poet's thoughts and "the essential quality of his mind" [186] which express views closely resembling, or easily identifiable with, those Emerson later made his own. Frequently, however, a fairly wide disparity becomes apparent when their terms are defined and their judgments are interpreted in the light of their respective philosophical positions. A fundamental cause of this difference, for example, is Emerson's belief that the "self" is God and that Shakespeare, consequently, stands above most men because he revealed better than they the universal "self" of all men.

In *Biographia Literaria*, apparently the first book by Coleridge that Emerson read, he found the author commenting on Shakespeare's powers as a philosopher in terms suggesting those he later used himself.[187] Another passage in the same work brings to mind Emerson's distrust of "the tavern stories about his want

183   "Introduction", *Letters*, I, xxxvi.
184   *Journals*, II, 277 (letter to his aunt, "Boston, *December* 10, 1829"). Emerson possessed then, or later, the three volumes of the 1818 edition of *The Friend*. *Letters*, I, 291, note 2.
185   "To William Emerson, Concord, July 27, 1835", *Letters*, I, 448. "At least the first volume of *Specimens of the Table Talk of the Late Samuel Taylor Coleridge* (New York, 1835), (the first American edition), is still in Emerson's library at the Antiquarian House, Concord." *Ibid.*, n. 65.
186   "Art and Criticism", *Works*, XII, 305.
187   *Complete Works*, III, 381.

of education and total unconsciousness",[188] on the one hand, and
his own manner of contrasting Shakespeare and Milton, on the
other:

What then shall we say? even this; that Shakspeare, no mere child
of nature; no *automaton* of genius; no passive vehicle of inspiration
possessed by the spirit, not possessing it; first studied patiently,
meditated deeply, understood minutely, till knowledge, become habitual and intuitive, wedded itself to his habitual feelings, and at
length gave birth to that stupendous power, by which he stands
alone, with no equal or second in his own class; to that power,
which seated him on one of the two glory-smitten summits of the
poetic mountain, with Milton as his compeer not rival. While the
former darts himself forth, and passes into all the forms of human
character and passion, the one Proteus of the fire and the flood;
the other attracts all forms and things to himself, into the unity of
his own ideal. All things and modes of action shape themselves
anew in the being of Milton; while Shakspeare becomes all things,
yet forever remaining himself. O what great men hast thou not
produced, England, my country! [189]

Moreover, Coleridge uses the example of Shakespeare in an attempt to disprove the theory of the "Supposed Irritability of Men
of Genius".[190] This passage in *Biographia Literaria* suggests the
picture Emerson drew in his journal, in 1837, of the "visionary
poet" who "came with his piece, modest but discerning, to the
players, and was too glad to get it received, whilst he was too
superior not to see its transcendent claims".[191] It also suggests
the similar picture, drawn in Emerson's journal more than a
quarter of a century later, of the poet who, though neglecting his
works, knew their value, as the sonnets show, and "went into
company as a listener, hiding himself", moving like Night, "only
remembered by all as a delightful companion".[192]

But a more significant example of Coleridge's "high criticism"
is his description of what he called the poet's "peculiar excellence" in the essay on method in thought in *The Friend*.[193] For

188   *Journals*, III, 452-53 (March 19, 1835).
189   Coleridge, *op. cit.*, 381-82.
190   *Ibid.*, 166.
191   *Journals*, IV, 186 (Jan. 21, 1837).
192   *Ibid.*, X, 29 (April 24, 1864).
193   *Complete Works*, II, 416.

Emerson, however, Shakespeare's "peculiar excellence" was his "point of praise . . . the pure poetic power".[194] Yet both Coleridge, when he referred to that excellence as the method of the poet's works, "consisting in that just proportion, that union and inter-penetration, of the universal and the particular", and Emerson, when he referred to "the pure poetic power", were attempting to draw attention to those elements in the works which illustrate the application of the organic principle.[195]

Emerson, however, seeing a reflection and manifestation of the deity in every kind of human experience, found it necessary to make distinctions and define terms in a quite different manner. For example, toward the end of his second lecture on the poet in 1835, he described the power which enabled Shakespeare to pursue the organic method Coleridge had referred to; this power, according to Emerson, was "Composition", "methodical union", "this instrument of Synthesis".[196] Like all human powers, it is an aspect of deity and a mode of perception. But such powers may

---

[194] *Journals*, X, 27 (April 24, 1864).

[195] According to Henry A. Pochmann, Schlegel was the first to describe the "organic principle": the "Schlegelian interpretation of Aristotelian organic unity, first applied to Shakespeare, soon received a wider applica-tion, and in the thought of an Emerson or a Thoreau became the basis of all art and life". *German Culture in America: Philosophical and Liter-ary Influences, 1600-1900* (University of Wisconsin Press, 1957), p. 795, note 647. Schlegel contrasted "mechanical" and "organical" form in a passage which Emerson undoubtedly read: "Form is mechanical when, through external force, it is imparted to any material merely as an acci-dental addition without reference to its quality; as, for example, when we give a particular shape to a soft mass that it may retain the same after its induration. Organical form, again, is innate; it unfolds itself from within, and acpuires its determination contemporaneously with the perfect development of the germ. We everywhere discover such forms in nature throughout the whole range of living powers, from the crystallization of salts and minerals to plants and flowers, and from these again to the human body. In the fine arts, as well as in the domain of nature – the supreme artist, all genuine forms are organical, that is, determined by the quality of the work. In a word, the form is nothing but a significant exterior, the speaking physiognomy of each thing, which, as long as it is not disfigured by any destructive accident, gives a true evidence of its hidden essence." *A Course of Lectures on Dramatic Art and Literature*, p. 340.

[196] "Shakspear" (second lecture), *Early Lectures*, pp. 317-319.

be divided into those purer aspects of deity which, as modes of perception, transcend symbolic expression, and those which convey truth by means of images and form. "Composition", like "Imagination", in Emerson's terminology, is one of these more specifically human powers.

In his second lecture on the poet, Emerson listed those qualities – "habits of wisdom and goodness, a mind beyond experience candid and open to all impressions with the utmost tenacity in hoarding its observation, the most daring flights of imagination, the most gentle and magnanimous spirit" – [197] that made possible the utilization, in the works of Shakespeare, of this "Composition", which he defined also as "a law that lies at the foundation of literature" and "the most powerful secret of Nature's workmanship".[198] These qualities thus included, by implication at least, the Common Sense and humanity providing the conditions necessary for the manifestation of the divine instinct, which, like the "vegetable sap" in Coleridge's description of the "same nature" that is revealed everywhere in the poet's method, pervades all his work.

In Emerson's view of man, this divine instinct is the knowledge of all truth as it is first received in the mind. Shakespeare's humanity co-ordinated all his faculties, his powers of perception, so that he might perceive and experience truth in a form that was uniquely his. But it would seem that, during those intermittent periods when he was in the process of creating his work, his humanity required the assistance of another formative power, his Composition, which functioned in harmony with its opposite, imagination, as did humanity with its opposite, Common Sense. Since this whole subject remained for Emerson a profound mystery, he woud have regarded the appearance of a too perfect symmetry as a probable distortion of truth. But, with a recognition of the inevitability of error, one could find amusement, perhaps, and acquire, at the same time, a clearer picture if he tried to visualize these powers as eyes that are facets of one great composite eye.

[197] *Ibid.*, 319.
[198] *Ibid.*, p. 317.

When Emerson's ideal poet is creating, this one great composite eye comes under the control of two of its facets, imagination, representing, as it were, the intellectual hemisphere, and Composition, representing the opposite hemisphere of feeling. In the center is the eye of God, in whose depths lies the central, universal self. Below the outer rim of the coneshaped passage which permits the deity to rise to the surface is the section which is the eye of the will, that which is reflected in the "military eye" of the hero.[199] Flanking it on the surface, on either side of the total sphere, is the eye of the philosopher, on one side, and the eye of the saint, on the other. Yet deeper in the central cone is the eye of instinct, "the brain of the brain".[200] This eye is, and therefore perceives, the whole of truth; but it is too sluggish to express vividly what it sees.[201] The eye of the philosopher and the eye of the saint can better express what they see, one by logic, the other by moral tone, but each tends to see only half. The philosopher, who is "a failed poet",[202] but in whom ideally "the love of truth predominates",[203] lacks sympathetic understanding. The saint, or prophet, in whom ideally "the moral sentiment predominates",[204] lacks objectivity. Hence, the philosopher, because "the fact of intellectual perception severs once for all the man from the things with which he converses", has "this vice ... that you cannot quite trust" him;[205] the prophet, or saint, on the other hand, because he lacks objectivity, is subject to illusions. The eye of the hero, or will, lying in the center between these two outer eyes, is, when compared with them, an "advance to that which rightly belongs to us", conveying "the presence of God to men"[206] in the form of the Spirit. But, although it sees truth whole, as the good, it cannot communicate

---

[199]   "Fate", *Works*, VI, 29-30; "Immortality", *Works*, VIII, 342; "Education", *Works*, X, 157.
[200]   "Natural History of Intellect", *Works*, XII, 65.
[201]   "And what is Inspiration? It is this Instinct, whose normal state is passive, at last put in action." *Ibid.*, 68.
[202]   "Poetry and Imagination", *Works*, VIII, 56.
[203]   "The Comic", *Works*, VIII, 159.
[204]   *Ibid.*
[205]   "Natural History of Intellect", *Works*, XII, 44-45.
[206]   *Ibid.*, 46.

its beauty because it is too far below, in the central cone, the level of imagination and Composition. The result is heroic action, but not poetry. Unlike the hero, the poet, who also sees truth whole, can express it inspiringly, interpreting it so that others will see its beauty and therefore desire to possess it. But, to do this, the poet must see truth both whole and beautiful. He must see it, in other words, more vividly than does the sluggish instinct, more accurately than does the eye of the philosopher or the eye of the saint, and more as a thing of beauty than does the eye of the hero. Yet all these facets of the composite eye contribute to the poet's vision of truth; and when he is creating, they are so co-ordinated that he is able to see the beauty of truth in the flowing of an infinite succession of changing images each of which is perceived by means of his imagination while the oppositions and syntheses of these forms in the flowing are perceived by means of his Composition.

Both Coleridge and Emerson saw the same pattern in this flowing, or unfolding of truth, and found it reproduced in the works of Shakespeare. But Coleridge attributed its presence, in the poet's writings, to the God-inspired ability and willingness to follow the divine method of creating that would result in "that just proportion, that union and interpenetration, of the universal and the particular", while Emerson attributed this pattern in the poet's works to "Composition", a mode of perceiving truth which includes all the poet's formative powers and which can only function when these powers are working in harmony with the imagination when it includes all the poet's intellectual powers. It would seem, therefore, as if Emerson, earlier in life, had caught Coleridge's vision of this process in nature and in art and had then divided and subdivided its various parts while retaining the essential outlines and differing chiefly in his belief that the poet not only follows God's will and his method in creating, but is God himself in his role as the Son.

While all men are incarnations of God, the poet, according to Emerson, is superior as an incarnation because he thus reveals more fully and more accurately than do the others the various aspects of God as he is manifested in the material world. When the deity first enters the mind by that means of knowing which Emerson called "instinct", the result is an incarnation of God as the first member of the trinity. The instinct, therefore, is "the spirit creative",[207] "the same mind that built the world".[208] In "its lower function, when it deals with the apparent world, it is common sense. It requires the performance of all that is needful to the animal life and health." But it also "requires", or is reflected in, the shaping influence of "humanity":

> Then it requires a proportion between a man's acts and his condition, requires all that is called humanity; that symmetry and connection which is imperative in all healthily constituted men, and the want of which the rare and brilliant sallies of irregular genius cannot excuse.[209]

As an incarnation, it then evolves from the level of instinct, that is, of common sense and humanity, to the second level, that of intellectual and moral laws:

> The Instinct begins at this low point, at the surface of the earth, and works for the necessities of the human being; then ascends step by step to suggestions which are when expressed the intellectual and moral laws.[210]

Entering the mind as the Spirit on the second level, the deity is first experienced partially, either as Intellect or as Moral Sense, when each is viewed apart from the other, and then is perceived whole again by the eye of the will. On the third level, it is the Son, with whom Emerson tended to identify Milton as he tended to identify Shakespeare with the Father.

With other opposites, that which is particular and that which is universal are thus united as divine truth on both the levels of religious development these two poets would seem to have represented. But, although both of them saw this truth whole, it is chiefly reflected in Shakespeare's works as the Creator and in Milton's as the Sayer, or Interpreter. This difference, resulting from Milton's greater development of the will, would have led

207   "Art", *Works*, VII, 39.
208   "Natural History of Intellect", *Works*, XII, 34.
209   *Ibid.*, 36-37.
210   *Ibid.*, 35.

Emerson to approve Coleridge's effort to contrast these poets as they are reflected in their works:

SHAKESPEARE is the Spinozistic deity – an omnipresent creativeness. Milton is the deity of prescience; he stands *ab extra*, and drives a fiery chariot and four, making the horses feel the iron curb which holds them in. Shakespeare's poetry is characterless, that is, it does not reflect the individual Shakespeare; but John Milton himself is in every line of the Paradise Lost.[211]

While Emerson would have approved this passage from Coleridge's *Table Talk* provided that the phrase *the individual Shakespeare* was acceptably defined as not referring to the bias of his thought, which is reflected in his works, he would not have so easily approved the description, also in *Table Talk*, of the Creator's resting from his labors.[212] In a comparable passage Emerson had described the poet's soaring in his works to a "heaven of thought" and poising himself there "as if it were his natural element", then returning instantly to the ground where he "walks and plays and rolls himself in hearty frolic with his humble mates".[213] Both on the ground, however, and in a "heaven of thought", Shakespeare in his works continued to create; it is while creating that, "by his transcendent reach of thought", this poet "unites the extremes".[214] When, intermittently, according to Emerson, he ceased to create, it was not to rest, nor to play, but to engage in an activity that was more valuable than even creating was, although it often appeared to his contemporaries to be mere sport and good fellowship; this superior activity was listening, watching; it was, in fact, the passive receiving of the higher truth from the deity manifesting itself in him as instinct.

This higher truth included progressive elements which would change, by enlarging, the human outlook; it represented a certain aspect of the poet's age although the dominant aspect of that age was the traditional pattern of thought and feeling represented by Ben Jonson. When the poet turned from his act of receiving

---

[211] *Coleridge's Writings on Shakespeare*, ed. Terence Hawkes (New York, 1959), p. 92.
[212] *Ibid.*, p. 103.
[213] "Shakspear" (first lecture), *Early Lectures*, p. 300.
[214] "Shakspeare", *Works*, XI, 449-450.

the higher truth to the act of creating his works, both aspects of his age were fused in his poetry. They would not, in Emerson's view, have remained distinct entities as implied by Coleridge in *Table Talk*.[215] Like the universal and the particular, the traditional and the progressive, according to Emerson, were completely fused in the poet's work. Hence, he was the supreme representative of his age and, at the same time, supremely universal.

Such a failure to see Shakespeare truly in his historical relations would seem to account largely for Emerson's implying, in his letter to Margaret Fuller in 1838, that Coleridge, despite his "high criticism", had not "put Shakspeare at a true focal distance". The volume of *Literary Remains* which probably accompanied that letter had been published in 1836; it contained most of Coleridge's criticism of the poet, but many of its "good things" concerned with the order of his thoughts and "the essential quality of his mind" were ideas Emerson must have earlier found stated explicitly, or implied, in *Biographia Literaria, The Friend,* and *Table Talk.*

For example, Coleridge claimed here, as Emerson had found him implying in other works, that, because Shakespeare "followed the main march of the human affections", that is, perceived those "passions and faiths" which were "grounded in our common nature, and not in the mere accidents of ignorance or disease", he was "the morning star, the guide and the pioneer, of true philosophy".[216] Emphasizing the same idea, he declared, further: "He was not only a great poet, but a great philosopher", then presented as proof the characterizations of Richard III, Iago, and Falstaff, "men who reverse the order of things, who place intellect at the head, whereas it ought to follow, like Geometry, to prove and to confirm".[217]

Since he had already encountered such ideas before in those works of Coleridge he had read earlier, Emerson may have gained more of those insights he demanded of poet-critics from this volume's discussion of the general subject of Shakespeare

[215] *Coleridge's Writings on Shakespeare*, pp. 106-107.
[216] *Complete Works*, IV, 64.
[217] *Ibid.*, 66.

criticism. Certainly, the way of looking at that poet which prompted Emerson to declare, in his tercentenary address in 1864, that "the egotism of men is immense. It concealed Shakspeare for a century",[218] resulted from opinions and attitudes which resemble, at least superficially, those expressed or revealed by Coleridge in his attack on pedantic and vain critics of the poet in *Literary Remains*.[219] *Coleridge* would seem to have aimed his blow chiefly at those responsible for "every late voluminous edition of his works" rather than at the poet's earlier critics. His terms *mere instinct* and *child of nature*, moreover, do not denote, respectively, a manifestation of deity as experienced at an early stage of religious development and a person who is at that stage. But, despite these differences and the fact that his reasoning was not quite the same, he takes here a position in regard to the criticism which is close to Emerson's.

When his opinions are summarized, Coleridge's position would seem to be contained in the following: "The popular notion" that Shakespeare lacked learning and the powers of a philosopher were inaccurate; the belief, among others, that he did not recognize the value of his own genius was also inaccurate; a "feeling of pride" was the cause of these inaccuracies; and the classical tradition was the means by which they were dishonestly presented as truths. Although Emerson also believed that egotism had been the cause of these inaccuracies, he would not, in regard to the earlier critics, have been so inclined to condemn motives as Coleridge, at least in regard to the later ones, certainly was. For Emerson, their egotism was a kind of spiritual blindness caused, in part, by the classical tradition itself, but stemming also from other sources. Hence, the critics were able to praise the traditional elements in the poet's works, the "words" provided by his imagination when those "words" were familiar images, but they were blind to that which was progressive, the tendencies of the thoughts those "words" symbolized, tendencies traced by the poet's "Composition" in the unfolding of truth and therefore reflected in the organic form of his works. To be consistent,

[218] "Shakspeare", *Works*, XI, 451.
[219] *Complete Works*, IV, 50-51.

Coleridge should have condemned the critics for those moral failures which had impaired their "judgment"; instead, he would seem to have implied that their "judgment" was at least sound enough for them to recognize Shakespeare's vast superiority as a genius and for them to realize that what they were saying was not for truth's sake, but for their own aggrandizement. Emerson, on the other hand, meant that the egotism that "concealed Shakspeare for a century" had been more or less inevitable because the critics had had their powers of judging molded by other influences. The greater reasonableness of his position is obvious.

Despite these differences, they were both agreed that the cause of faulty criticism of Shakespeare had been some kind of pride. Similarly, they would seem to have been in general agreement that the ideal critic would possess powers of perception resembling those which were reflected most conspicuously in Shakespeare's works.

This meant, according to Emerson, that the ideal critic would be a poet. His distinctive qualities would therefore include the "childlike" religious and moral feelings described by Coleridge.[220] However, if Emerson's ideal critic were also an ideal poet, he would possess, in addition to these qualities characterizing a state of innocence, the deeper religious and moral feelings of the saint. In any case, whether such feelings resembled Shakespeare's "humanity", apparently existing without the deeper emotions, or whether they included both kinds as in the ideal poet, religious and moral feelings were necessary for producing that right tone which, for Emerson, was even more important than saying "good things" and which was described by Coleridge as "reverential".[221] But the reverential tone Emerson would seem to have demanded would possess a more purely religious quality with less of the national pride Coleridge required, for Shakespeare's kingdom stretched beyond all national boundaries.

Besides such feelings, the powers of perception of the ideal critic, in the opinion of both men, would include intellectual abilities resembling the poet's. Chief among these abilities, ac-

[220] *Ibid.*, 52.
[221] *Ibid.*

cording to Coleridge, would be the power of "judgment" because it was so conspicuous in the works of the poet himself. Indeed, his power of "judgment" would seem to have been identical with his "peculiar excellence" – his "method of thought"; it is "commensurate with his genius", for "his genius reveals itself in his judgment, as in its most exalted form". In fact, Coleridge declared, "to judge aright, and with distinct consciousness of the grounds of our judgment, concerning the works of Shakspeare, implies the power and the means of judging rightly of all other works of intellect, those of abstract science alone excepted".[222] For critics to judge the poet "rightly", furthermore, they must judge his works "disinterestedly", that is, without the prejudices inculcated by the "habits" and "the peculiarities of their education".[223] Coleridge's position, therefore, was that the critic should be concerned, first, with "the imperishable soul of intellect", "the spirit and substance of a work, something true in human nature itself, and independent of all circumstances", and, second, with that which enables him to "estimate genius and judgment" in the poet, "the mode of applying" "the spirit and substance", "the felicity with which the imperishable soul of intellect, shall have adapted itself to the age, the place, and the existing manners". The poet's "genius and judgment" should be estimated, therefore, according to the extent to which he has put first things first; his "error" would be "in reversing this, and holding up the mere circumstances as perpetual to the utter neglect of the power which can alone animate them". To "judge disinterestedly", with "true tolerance," consequently, the critic must himself be able to distinguish between the universal and the particular, that which is "independent of all circumstances", "something true in human nature itself", and that which results from "mere circumstances". To be able to make such distinctions, moveover, he must rely upon "some general rule, which, founded in reason, or the faculties common to all men, must therefore apply to each". This "general rule", or "criterion" for judging, according to Coleridge,

[222]   *Ibid.*, 52, 53.
[223]   *Ibid.*, 53.

should be the organic principle. When so judged, Shakespeare is seen to be nature's "chosen poet", "himself a nature humanized, a genial understanding directing self-consciously a power and an implicit wisdom deeper even than our consciousness". When not so judged, but by the rules designed to produce "mechanical regularity", he is seen to be either "the anomalous, the wild, the irregular, genius" of those commentators who are "(so they would tell you) almost idolatrous admirers", or "the drunken savage of that wretched socialist", Voltaire.[224] In other words, Coleridge's "true critic", superior to those Frenchmen who "attain to exquisite discrimination ... in their own literature",[225] will employ that same "general rule", founded in reason and nature, the organic principle, which governed Shakespeare's own method in thought and gave his works their organic form.

Emerson would also seem to have recognized the necessity for the ideal critic to judge by employing the organic principle; but, since he insisted that the ideal critic would be a poet, the manner in which this principle would be applied in criticism is more clearly implied than it is by Coleridge, who merely recommended that it be used as a criterion. For Emerson, the critic, like the poet, would have his powers of perception so co-ordinated that, in producing his critical works, he would be creating poetry in the organic form which reproduces the dialectical processes in nature. In other words, the critic's chief intellectual power would be, not what Coleridge called "judgment", but what Emerson called "imagination"; but this power would require the co-operation of its counterpart, Composition, which would perform the function of Coleridge's "judgment".

Emerson's "imagination" is a vision of all truth, experienced by the total mind in the act of creating, as it manifests itself in each of a succession of thoughts represented as a flowing of images. "As the bird alights on the bough, then plunges into the air again", he sang, "so the thoughts of God pause but for a moment in any form." [226] The flowing of thoughts in "high criti-

[224]   *Ibid.*, 54-56
[225]   *Ibid.*, 53.
[226]   "Poetry and Imagination", *Works*, VIII, 15.

cism" would reproduce this process.[227] Criticism could not reach this "poetic" level without "imagination", which "exists by sharing the ethereal currents"[228] and is "a very high sort of seeing, which does not come by study, but by the intellect being where and what it sees; by sharing the path or circuit of things through forms, and so making them translucid to others",[229] "the cardinal human power, the angel of earnest and believing ages".[230] Criticism's brow should not be "wrinkled by circumspection", because it is poetry; cheerfulness, Emerson claimed in his 1845 lecture on Shakespeare, is the "royal trait" "without which no man can be a poet, – for beauty is his aim".[231] It must be remembered, however, that when he says imagination does not "come by study" and that criticism's brow is not "wrinkled by circumspection", he is referring to those intermittent periods in which the poet is creating; the creative act itself requires neither circumspection nor study. That act produces images, or "words", which symbolize, or express, individual thoughts. Composition, on the other hand, is not creative; though indispensable in the making of a poem, it merely selects, arranges, gives organic form to the work; this function does require circumspection and study as well as the direct reception of truth from the deity during the periods that come between creative acts.

Because of his interest in this subject of criticism, and more specifically, of Shakespeare criticism, Emerson derived insights from his reading of Coleridge's *Literary Remains* which aided in the development of his own views. But he redefined terms and made distinctions that would better suit his own vision of truth. Hence, while both men saw the organic principle applied in the creation of criticism as well as poetry, there were significant differences in their views of the critic himself.

A similar disparity is seen in the respective ways they visualized the poet's creative power. For Coleridge, this power was "Imagination", a synthesizing faculty which only superficially

---

[227]   "The Editors to the Reader", *The Dial*, I (July, 1840), 3.
[228]   *Journals*, VII, 160 (1846).
[229]   "The Poet", *Works*, III, 26.
[230]   "The Man of Letters", *Works*, X, 243.
[231]   "Shakspeare; Or, The Poet", *Works*, IV, 215.

resembles what Emerson meant by that term.[232] In another passage in *Biographia Literaria*, he indicated that this power was also to be known as the "secondary Imagination", which he there contrasted with the "primary":

The Imagination then I consider either as primary, or secondary. The primary Imagination I hold to be the living power and prime agent of all human perception, and as a repetition in the finite mind of the eternal act of creation in the infinite *I AM*. The secondary Imagination I consider as an echo of the former, co-existing with the conscious will, yet still as identical with the primary in the *kind* of its agency, and differing only in *degree,* and in the *mode* of its operation. It dissolves, diffuses, dissipates, in order to re-create: or where this process is rendered impossible, yet still at all events it struggles to idealize and to unify. It is essentially vital, even as all objects (*as* objects) are essentially fixed and dead.[233]

Thus, Coleridge's poetic, or secondary, imagination, "that synthetic and magical power", "essentially vital", was itself the creative power of the poet.

For Emerson, the creative power was not what he called the "imagination", which he defined as "a second sight" that merely "dictates" the poetry,[234] providing "the Secretary for that Century or Nation", as he referred to the poet in his second lecture on Shakespeare, with the most appropriate terms. Furthermore, this process of dictation is a slow one; Shakespeare's "words" came to him, by means of the imagination, one by one; his works are "no rhapsodies cast forth at a heat but like all other truly great productions are the union of many parts each of which came solitary and slowly into the mind and did not at first attain its full expansion".[235]

[232] *Complete Works*, III, 374.
[233] *Ibid.*, 363-64.
[234] "Poetry and Imagination", *Works*, VIII, 19. *Cf. Journals*, VII, 160 (1846): "*Imagination.* There are two powers of the imagination, one, that of knowing the symbolic character of things and treating them as representative; and the other (Elizabeth Hoar thinks) is practically the tenaciousness of an image, cleaving unto it and letting it not go, and, by the treatment, demonstrating that this figment of thought is as palpable and objective to the poet as is the ground on which he stands, or the walls of houses about him. And this power appears in Dante and Shakspeare."
[235] "Shakspear" (second lecture), *Early Lectures*, p. 317.

Nor was the creative power the poet's Composition, which effected the unification of these many parts individually provided by the imagination to which it stood in the same relation as his humanity to his Common Sense. According to Emerson, Composition, "this instrument of Synthesis", "the most powerful secret of Nature's workmanship", "a law that lies at the foundation of literature",[236] is, despite this high praise, merely the instrument by which the "words" provided by the imagination are selected, ordered, arranged, so that the poem will have an organic form reflecting the unfolding of truth in the dialectrical pattern of natural processes. "The main is made up of many islands, the state of many men, the poem of many thoughts each of which in its turn filled the whole sky of the poet, was day and happiness to him." [237]

The creative power appears, however, when the poet's imagination and his Composition are functioning in harmony with one another; one, his imagination, consisting of his intellectual side geared for creative action; the other, his Composition, his sympathetic, formative power; the first representing the universal, centrifugal, masculine force; the second representing the universal, centripetal, feminine force. When these opposites are reconciled and therefore prepared for cooperative activity, the creative power appears in what Emerson called "intellect constructive", an aspect of the human "intellect" opposite to "intellect receptive" as imagination is opposite to Composition. This divine creative power, appearing in the human "intellect constructive", was evidently that "infinite invention" which Emerson found reflected in Shakespeare's works and which he claimed was the "concealed magnet of his attraction for us",[238] a divine, creative energy arising in "intellect" from the central "self" to utilize as instruments, and thereby enhance the power of, the poet's imagination and Composition.

Perhaps the most obvious effect it has upon those faculties is to accelerate their activity. It must work slowly at first because

[236] *Ibid.*, pp. 317-318.
[237] *Ibid.*, p. 318.
[238] "Shakspeare; Or, The Poet", *Works*, IV, 205-206.

of the resistance of the human material it has to work with; but, with the development of the will, which cooperates increasingly with the divine will, it works more and more swiftly, effecting a comparable change in the processes of thought, until it reaches its maximum speed on the level of imagination and Composition in the ideal poet. The "instinctive action never ceases in a healthy mind", Emerson declared, "but becomes richer and more frequent in its informations through all states of culture".[239] This acceleration is apparent in Shakespeare's works; when he came to express the thoughts he had received, his control over them suggested that he had been familiar with them for a thousand years.[240] But this acceleration in thought processes which occurs as a result of the stimulus given to creative activity by "intellect constructive" does not imply that the act itself will appear to have happened quickly; it implies merely that the poet will create works which seem to have taken a much longer time to be created. Although his works are "no rhapsodies cast forth at a heat but like all other truly great productions are the union of many parts each of which came solitary and slowly into the mind and did not at first attain its full expansion",[241] each of them is a world that appears to have required a millenium in the making.

Thus, according to Emerson's view of the creative power, it is the divine creative energy as it first appears in "intellect constructive". As such, it more nearly resembles Coleridge's "primary" than his "secondary Imagination" and thus conforms with the Emersonian belief that, in the act of creating, the poet not only reflects and represents the divine Creator, but is that aspect of the deity. Since Coleridge did not hold such a view, but regarded the poet's creative power as merely an "echo" of the divine, it would seem that here lies the fundamental difference between his approach to Shakespeare and Emerson's.

In his "higher criticism", however, Coleridge had gone further than any other English critic, Emerson believed, in attempting

---

[239] "Intellect", *Works*, II, 331.
[240] "Natural History of Intellect", *Works*, XII, 50.
[241] "Shakspear" (second lecture), *Early Lectures*, p. 317.

to "put Shakspeare at a true focal distance". His insights were
"only introductory", but the chief reason for their failure to satisfy
was that Coleridge did not share Emerson's vision of life; the
outlines of that vision were similar as it consisted of lines which,
for both men, formed a dialectical pattern of growth, but the
inner relations of the parts were significantly dissimilar because
of their respective views as to what those parts essentially consisted of.

Most pertinent to criticism, in Emerson's vision, was the divine
"intellect", the form in which the deity as Father and Knower
first rises from the central, universal "self" into the individual
human mind. As "the simple power anterior to all action or
construction", a "transparent essence" which "dissolves" everything "in its resistless menstruum",[242] it appears, then, as "instinct".[243] In its capacity as Knower, it brings knowledge in the
form of "intuition", which, as "a long logic", contains within
itself "the arithmetical or logical" principle which Emerson associated with the "understanding" and which, in his essay "Intellect", he called "the procession or proportionate unfolding of
the intuition".[244] As intuitive knowledge, divine "intellect" requires, for its appearance on any level of growth, the harmonious
activity of human thought and feeling; but it is always itself
objective, "void of affection", free of "the fog of good and evil
affections" which make it "hard for man to walk forward in a
straight line". Its growth, from one level to the next, is "spontaneous in every expansion", controlled by "the law of undula-
tion" [245] in both "the period of infancy" [246] and "the era of reflection".[247] Man, therefore, cannot determine the form and
movements of the waves of "intellect"; but, as "consciousness"
develops, he can decide when he will let those waves roll in. "We
do not determine what we will think. We only open our senses,

[242] "Intellect", *Works*, II, 326.
[243] *Ibid.*, 330.
[244] *Ibid.*, 329.
[245] *Ibid.*, 332.
[246] *Ibid.*, 327.
[247] *Ibid.*. 331.

clear away as we can all obstruction from the fact, and suffer the intellect to see." [248]

"Our thinking", Emerson claimed, "is a pious reception." [249] It is a reception, that is, of the divine "intellect" by the human "intellect", which also has two opposite aspects. The divine Knower is reflected in the human "intellect receptive", the Father in the human "intellect constructive". The divine "intellect" enters the human mind through the door provided by "intellect receptive", bringing as gifts the knowledge of truth bestowed by the divine Knower upon "intellect receptive" and creative power bestowed by the Father upon "intellect constructive", "which we popularly designate by the word Genius".[250] Thus, we are enabled to pass on to others the first gift, knowledge, by means of the second, the power of expression. The power thus given to "intellect constructive" permits that faculty to stimulate "imagination" and Composition by an inspiring spectacle of truth, shining through images whose beauty derives from their continuous flowing in endless transformation. "The ray of light", or truth, Emerson said, "passes invisible through space and only when it falls on an object is it seen." [251] That object is thus provided by "intellect constructive".

Although man decides when to open the door of the mind to the divine guest, he cannot determine the specific nature of the gifts he will receive. But, in bestowing them upon others, he is granted a measure of necessary control: "The thought of genius is spontaneous; but the power of picture or expression, in the most enriched and flowing nature, implies a mixture of will, a certain control over the spontaneous states, without which no production is possible." [252] This "mixture of will," then, is present in "intellect constructive". It permits that faculty to determine how it will make use of Composition in the selection of images and the consequent shaping of a poem, but it prevents "intellect constructive" from exercising a similar control over the produc-

---

[248] *Ibid.*, 328.
[249] *Ibid.*
[250] *Ibid.*, 334.
[251] *Ibid.*, 335.
[252] *Ibid.*, 336.

tion of images it presents to the "imagination". While the "power of picture or expression" is "a conversion of all nature into the rhetoric of thought, under the eye of judgment, with a strenuous exercise of choice", the "imaginative vocabulary" seems to be "spontaneous". "It does not flow from experience only or mainly, but from a richer source. Not by any conscious imitation of particular forms are the grand strokes of the painter executed, but by repairing to the fountain-head of all forms in his mind." [253] Dreams, according to Emerson, offer "some light on the fountain of this skill; for as soon as we let our will go and let the unconscious states ensue, see what cunning draughtsmen we are!" We then hold a "mystic pencil" in the hand.[254]

This "mixture of will" in the creative process is consistent with Emerson's view of Freedom and Fate. The specifically human will is controlled by Fate; hence the production of images that are presented to his "imagination" seems as "spontaneous" to the poet as the creations of the natural world. But, as the development of his consciousness results in his control of nature, so it results in his control, not of the creation of images, which represent eternal truths, but of the manner in which their flowing is to be reproduced by Composition in his poetry. Associated with the material world of nature, the universal masculine centrifugal tendency, and divine emanation, the specifically human will is strongest on the first level of development, but gradually weakens with the waning of the power of Fate as the universal feminine centripetal tendency, spurring moral evolution, grows stronger. Both wills, that of Fate and Freedom, are divine; but the first is conservative and "unconscious", the second progressive and "conscious". Shakespeare tends to represent the first, Milton the second.

The "mixture of will" consists, therefore, of two ingredients which correspond with the "two gifts" bestowed upon the poet by divine "intellect":

To genius must always go two gifts, the thought and the publication. The first is revelation, always a miracle, which no frequency of

253   Ibid.
254   Ibid., 337-38.

occurrence or incessant study can ever familiarize, but which must always leave the inquirer stupid with wonder. It is the advent of truth into the world, a form of thought now for the first time bursting into the universe, a child of the old eternal soul, a piece of genuine and immeasurable greatness. It seems, for the time, to inherit all that has yet existed and to dictate to the unborn. It affects every thought of man and goes to fashion every institution. But to make it available it needs a vehicle or art by which it is conveyed to men. To be communicable it must become picture or sensible object. We must learn the language of facts. The most wonderful inspirations die with their subject if he has no hand to paint them to the senses.[255]

This truth, when it is perceived by his imagination in a flowing of images, is the same truth the poet had received earlier: "We are stung by the desire for new thought; but when we receive a new thought it is only the old thought with a new face, and though we make it our own, we instantly crave another; we are not really enriched." Indeed, it was in us "before it was reflected to us from natural objects".[256] That is, we had already been given access to it by "intellect receptive" before we were given the opportunity by "intellect constructive" to see it, with our eye of imagination, beautifully represented by images. Moreover, truth was more fully and more accurately presented to us, or to the poet, by "intellect receptive" than by "intellect constructive", for its naked glory is somewhat concealed by a garment of dazzling images. Hence, the images spontaneously given to the poet's "imagination" to be used by that intellectual faculty as "words" are inferior as reflections of truth to the organic form of his poem, which results from the shaping power of his love as it appears in his Composition. His tone, produced by form, is more significant, therefore, than what he says.

As the "word" to the "spirit" and poetry to truth, the act of poetic creation is inferior to the act of passive reception of truth uncluttered by symbolic images. There is, Emerson declared, "somewhat more blessed and great in hearing than in speaking":

As long as I hear truth I am bathed by a beautiful element and am not conscious of any limits to my nature. The suggestions are

[255] *Ibid.*, 335.
[256] *Ibid.*, 341.

thousand-fold that I hear and see. The waters of the great deep have ingress and egress to the soul. But if I speak, I define, I confine and am less.[257]

Thus, the poet, in his higher moments, rises above his own level as a representative of the Sayer, the Interpreter of truth, and becomes the ideal scholar and lover of truth,[258] in other words, a representative of the Knower and of the first stage of a new cycle of development.

When the poet speaks, his tone, resulting from feeling, conveys truth more effectively than the "good things" he says which result from thought. Similarly, truth is conveyed to him more directly by "intellect receptive" than by "intellect constructive". When Emerson declared that Shakespeare's "point of praise" was "the pure poetic power",[259] he implied that truth came to him chiefly, not directly, but adorned by his "intellect constructive". However, when he tried to visualize the poet as "he looked at the Supreme Being in some lonely hour of fear or gratitude" and "forebore to say" what he heard,[260] Emerson was thinking of the more effective, though less conspicuous and characteristic, method employed by the poet in the reception of truth.

But, although Shakespeare was more creative than receptive, he was unsurpassed by other poets in both categories. It was his creative power which made him a representative of the Father, his ability to receive truth passively which made him a representative of the Father's counterpart, the Knower, or lover of truth.

Emerson believed, furthermore, that the passive receiving of thoughts from the divine "intellect" results, when a poet has received them, in a kind of fertilization followed by the birth of poetry. The human parent, in this process, tends to have either an "oviparous" or a "viviparous" mind.[261] Shakespeare's mind was primarily "viviparous":

Shakspeare. Some minds are viviparous; Every word is a poem. What

---

[257] *Ibid.*
[258] *Ibid.*
[259] *Journals*, X, 27 (April 24, 1864).
[260] *Ibid.*, IV, 332 (Oct. 20, 1837).
[261] "Natural History of Intellect", *Works*, XII, 18.

a fancy, what formativeness! All his thoughts are little men & women, complete to the hair.[262]

But he would seem to have been "oviparous", also, supremely capable of depositing thoughts that would begin to yield "sons" only in "the next age". Such fertility of mind reflects the "extremes" of thought as well as the distance lying between thought itself and the "higher truth" referred to in the following passage:

I dare not deal with this element in its pure essence. It is too rare for the wings of words. Yet I see that Intellect is a science of degrees, and that as man is conscious of the law of vegetable and animal nature, so he is aware of an Intellect which overhangs his consciousness like a sky, of degree above degree, of heaven within heaven.

Every just thinker has attempted to indicate these degrees, these steps on the heavenly stair, until he comes to light where language fails him. Above the thought is the higher truth, – truth as yet undomesticated and therefore unformulated.[263]

As "the mind is first only receptive",[264] afterwards "constructive", and as "the discerning intellect of the world is always much in advance of the creative",[265] so Shakespeare's mind was first receptive, then creative; and his passive receptivity to the divine mind that is "the creator of the world, and is ever creating"[266] is reflected in the attitude toward himself of those "sons" who have sprung from the eggs and seeds of thought deposited in his works. He was, indeed, chiefly creative. In fact, the "concealed magnet of his attraction for us", Emerson declared, is his creative power, that "affirmative force" found in those whose "*sex of mind*" is masculine, "the inventive or creative class of both men and women", of whom he is a supreme example.[267] But, as divine "intellect" has two aspects which are reflected in those of the human mind, "intellect receptive" and "intellect constructive", and the first member of the universal trinity is both Knower, lover of truth, and Father, creator, this poet's mind was, to an

[262]   MS of the Shakespeare reading, 1869. Houghton 211.4.
[263]   "Natural History of Intellect", *Works*, XII, 17.
[264]   *Ibid.*, 25.
[265]   "Intellect", *Works*, II, 338.
[266]   "Natural History of Intellect", *Works*, XII, 17.
[267]   "Power", *Works*, VI, 57-58.

unsurpassed extent, both passively receptive to truth and creative.

Shakespeare's magnetic, creative force may have drawn Emerson, as he claimed, to the poet's works; if so, such a response would seem to have resulted from the combination of strong religious feeling and a sincere belief that the works contained evidence of a divine manifestation of the Father. But, when Emerson attempted to render an "account" of the poet, he turned to the writings of biographers and critics for light that would illuminate chiefly that more truly significant aspect of this genius, his ability to receive the "higher truth", now manifested in "his immense and evergrowing influence" over his "sons", who comprise already a "kingdom of the intellect".[268] As critics, Goethe and Coleridge, Emerson found, had most to offer him; but they had not "put Shakspeare at a true focal distance". In fact, no critics or biographers had ever satisfied him, or ever would, unless they shared the same "angle of vision", which the vision itself would not permit.

Hence, claiming that he had to rely chiefly on his own insights, Emerson returned habitually to the works themselves for the light he sought. When he wrote in his journal in 1864 that he was "inquisitive of all possible knowledge concerning Shakspeare, and of all opinions", he felt it necessary to add: "Yet how few valuable criticisms, how few opinions I treasure! How few besides my own! And each thoughtful reader, doubtless, has the like experience." [269] This meant that the poet himself would always remain his own best critic as well as his own best biographer. No other could surpass him: "All criticism", Emerson declared earlier the same month, "is only a making of rules out of his beauties." [270] To approach the works with the usual critical attitudes, therefore, was sacrilegious. "Your criticism is profane", he announced. "Shakspeare by Shakspeare. The poet in his interlunation is a critic." [271] That poet-critic is essentially the Shakespeare in every heart.

[268] "Shakspear" (first lecture), *Early Lectures*, p. 288.
[269] *Journals*, X, 31 (April 24, 1864).
[270] *Ibid.*, 23 (April 8, 1864).
[271] *Works*, IV, 358, note 1 to p. 219.

II. BACON AS THE DOER

I

Emerson's vocabulary and tone, considered in relation to his habits of thought, indicate that, in his view of the English Renaissance, Francis Bacon was the central figure. With Shakespeare, who died before Bacon's fall from a position of power, and with Milton, who followed, he contributed to Emerson's image of the universal trinity as it was reflected in that age. As the second member of that triad, he manifested not only the opposition of tendencies that were united in the two poets, but also action that suggested the Doer and the "Double Consciousness" accompanying the Fall that occurs on the second stage of moral and religious growth.

While this study does not attempt to emphasize the development of Emerson's attitudes toward these three figures, or the extent to which they influenced him, it should be remembered that he sought his own reflection in each of them. What Emerson saw of himself in Bacon caused considerable "pain". Although the philosopher's "bias" was the opposite of his own dominant tendency toward "idealism", Bacon represented the level of the Fall and therefore the stage of moral development which, in relation to the whole of man's history, characterizes the entire human race. Hence, Emerson, the poet-preacher, was apparently reminded of his own painful conflicts when he contemplated the mind and career of the philosopher.

Vivian C. Hopkins, who has traced the development of Emerson's attitudes toward Bacon and shown the probable extent of his influence on Emerson's thought and style, points out that "Bacon's insistence on the importance of experimental science paved the way" for his reading in Cuvier, Lyell, and Laplace.[1] Indeed, in December, 1830, soon after the Baron de Gérando's *Histoire des Systèmes de Philosophie Comparée*[2] led him back to Bacon, Emerson wrote in his journal: "If anyone, denying Jesus, should bring me more truth, I cannot help receiving it also. . . . I am raised by the reception of a great principle to its height. And he who communicates, and applies, and embodies, a great principle for me, is my redeemer from the evil to which the want of it would have led me." Bacon, Emerson then declared, "showed the inanity of science not founded on observation. So he is the Restorer of science." Although he had not saved Emerson's life or estate, he had saved him from "one error", and to that degree was he "honorable" in Emerson's mind.[3] That "one

---

[1] Vivian C. Hopkins, "Emerson and Bacon", *American Literature*, XXIX (January, 1958), 417.

[2] "The four volumes of the Paris edition of 1822-1823 are still in Emerson's house, at Concord, and bear his signature." Rusk, ed., *Letters*, I, 291, note 3.

[3] *Journals*, II, 325-26 (Dec. 21, 1830), 330 (Oct. 27, 1830). Emerson owned and annotated Bacon's *Works, 10 vols.* (London, 1824), the edition hereafter referred to in this study. Emerson's *Letters* show that Bacon, one of his "Olympians", is "chiefly valued for other writings than the formal philosophical treatises". Rusk, ed., "Introduction", *Letters*, I, lvi. But Vivian C. Hopkins, who has carefully noted the extent of Emerson's reading of Bacon, states: "In 'Books,' Emerson listed the works of Bacon that the young scholar should read. *The Advancement of Learning*, the *Essays*, the *Novum Organum*, the *History of Henry VII*, and all the letters, especially those relating to the Essex affair (*Works*, C. Ed., VII, 207). While Emerson's reading in Bacon, like that of most Americans, was chiefly in the English works, he did pay this writer the rare attention of reading the Latin of the *Novum Organum* with some care, and that of the *De Augmentis* desultorily. The only works neglected which one might expect Emerson to find fruitful are the *New Atlantis* and the *De Sapientia Veterum*." *Op. cit.*, 421, note 69. "Certainly Emerson read earlier editions of the *Essays* and the *Novum Organum*. When he acquired the 1824 edition is not certain, but he must have had it in hand while working on the 1835 Lecture." *Ibid.*, 429, note 95. Miss Hopkins has appended to her article a list of the notations Emerson made, as a kind of index, in the backs of his volumes of Bacon's *Works*. He had read the English translation of *Novum Organum* by Peter Shaw (London, 1818), Rusk, ed., *Letters*, I, 446, note 52.

error" from which Bacon had saved him was, he implied, the failure to base beliefs on careful observations, to which his natural "bias" made him especially prone.

The influence of the philosopher's predominant concern with truth as it is manifested in the physical world provided a saving counterpoise to the preacher's tendency to overemphasize its spiritual aspects. Viewed, therefore, in relation to Emerson's "bias", this "Prince of philosophers" was his "redeemer". But they both had tendencies opposed to their natural "bias" and, consequently, unresolved conflicts. Hence, Bacon reflected the stage of development Emerson habitually felt that he was himself passing through while representing the masculine, rather than the feminine, side of the "platform".[4] This habit of viewing Bacon as a symbol of universal conflicts and of the "Double Consciousness" that characterizes the stage of "operation" in each cycle of growth seems to have had its inception in an early recognition of passages in the philosopher's writings that suggested the possibility of progressive development.

For example, Emerson, when he was seventeen years old, attempted to account for the excellence of the literary style of a passage in *Novum Organum*:

Speaking of bodies composed of two different species of things, he [Bacon] says: "but these instances may be reckoned of the singular or heteroclite kind, as being rare and extraordinary in the universe; yet for their dignity they ought to be separately placed and treated. For they excellently indicate the composition and structure of things; and suggest the cause of the number of ordinary species of the universe; and lead the understanding from that which is, to that which may be." There is nothing in this sentence which should cause it to be quoted more than another. It does not stand out from the rest; but it struck me accidentally as a very different sentence from those similarly constructed in ordinary writers. For instance, in the last three clauses (beginning "For they excellently") it is common to see an author construct a fine sentence in this way, with idle repe-

---

[4] Yet Emerson's friend Bronson Alcott saw him in 1838 as even closer to the type Bacon represented: " 'Men are uses, with him. Like Bacon, he slurs the affections. He loves his Ideals, and, because these have not actual life, condemns the men who live around him as unworthy.' " As quoted in Hopkins, *op. cit.*, 425.

titions of the same idea, embellished a little for the sake of shrouding the deception. In this, they all convey ideas determinate, but widely different and all beautiful and intelligent. – But, says Sterne, "the cant of criticism is the most provoking." [5]

Vivian C. Hopkins rightly states that "Bacon's first impression on Emerson was as a stylist and man of action".[6] But Emerson began early to think of the philosopher himself as representative of a "heteroclite" state of being "composed of two different species of things", physical and spiritual, of disunity in the middle stage of development. Admittedly perplexed because the passage had "struck" him, he tried to attribute his reaction to the superiority of Bacon's style, but he broke off, obviously dissatisfied with this explanation. Apparently, the real reason why he was "struck", which did not then occur to him, was that, even at the age of seventeen, he was reading for those "lustres" which he later described as intimations of "the author's author" that gave "the most pleasure in reading a book" and "a greater joy" than the author himself.[7] He could not continue his commentary on Bacon's style because he was chiefly concerned with the ideas the words suggested; these words, emitting "lustres" or "gleams", as if from the arcs of Bacon's circles,[8] gave intimations of the universality of that stage of development which Emerson was beginning to see manifested in him.

II

The lecture, "Lord Bacon", delivered on December 24, 1835,[9] is the chief source of information about Emersons's attitude to-

[5] *Journals*, I, 27-28.

[6] *Op. cit.*, 410.

[7] "Nominalist and Realist", *Works*, III, 233.

[8] "Men live, as it were, upon concentric circles, a king upon a little larger arc, a peasant upon a little less, but the most perfect proportion subsisting between the enjoyments and pains of one and of the other." *Journals*, II, 450 (1832). Emerson referred later to the "gleams" of great circles in Bacon's works and declared that "they astonish the understanding". *Ibid.*, III, 489-490 (June 10, 1835).

[9] This lecture is based mainly on the London, 1824 edition of Bacon's *Works*, which Emerson owned. The editors point out that it reflects the

ward the philosopher. As the seventh in the series on English literature, it followed immediately the two lectures on Shakespeare [10] and most clearly reveals that he tended to think of Bacon as representing the second stage of development and especially the side of that stage which was masculine rather than feminine, reflecting thought more than feeling, the "understanding" more than "sentiment". Hence, Emerson presented him here as an "Archangel", but with the "alien spirit" of Milton's "Archangel ruined". His imagery and tone throughout the lecture suggest strongly that Bacon reminded him of the Fall – he could hear in his *Essays* "the hiss of a snake amid the discourse of angels". Moreover, in accordance with the intention he had stated earlier, Emerson's purpose, as in his lectures on Shakespeare and on Milton, was more to inspire than to inform.[11] It was, indeed,

---

conflicts then unresolved in Emerson's own mind: "In the year of this lecture, he thought of Bacon's 'universal mind' as he endeavored to work out his own 'first philosophy' (*J*, III, 489), and Emerson here uses him to exhibit, somewhat unwittingly, most of the unresolved personal and philosophical issues with which he was struggling; the 'censure of Bacon' which he had wished to include in his British Plutarch (*J*, II, 504) turns out to contain its share of praise." *Early Lectures*, I. 320. "Lord Bacon" was Emerson's only lecture on the philosopher, but in 1869 he gave a "reading" entitled "Ben Jonson and Bacon" the manuscript of which is in the Houghton Library, Cambridge, Mass.

[10]   An alternate paragraph for the introduction shows that it was read at some time in series with the lecture on Luther. This alternate paragraph in the manuscript notes contains the following significant comparison: "We have considered Luther a scholar who by the predominance of a religious enthusiasm over a will of prodigious force introduced a great religious Revolution in modern times. Bacon is another Reformer of almost equal efficiency in far different sphere, who in his genius was in all points a contrast to Luther and acting very remotely on the multitude has established for himself a lasting influence in all studious minds and as far as every human being has an interest in the discovery of Truth." *Early Lectures*, I, 512-513. As a representative of the Doer, Bacon was a "Reformer", but he tended to remain on the side of the stage of conflict opposite to that of Luther and other preachers and "saints".

[11]   "Considered as a whole this lecture is one of the finest, most sensitive estimates of Bacon, in small compass, to be found in the first half of our nineteenth century. It reveals the wide, deep reading of years: not only in the better known works, the *Essays, The Advancement of Learning*, and the *Novum Organum*, but also in such minor writings as the early 'Brief Discourse Touching the Low Countries' and the 'Valerius

to "operate ... gracious motions upon the spirit" while he mourned as he censured him and spoke "as Christ" of his "good and evil" [12] to evoke a vision of deity as manifested in the moral character of "Lord Bacon".

Emerson referred to him in his introduction as one of those "divinities" before whom we make "that heartfelt, childlike obeisance which honors them and us", a "mighty orb" like "Plato or Dante or Milton", who are "antidotes to each other's excessive influence". Then he made the following significant comparison:

We have just now considered Shakspear the poet, whose mind was coextensive with nature. Bacon is another universal mind, one who to quite different ends exercised powers scarcely inferior, possessed an imagination as despotic as Shakespear's, which he yet employed rigorously as an instrument merely to illustrate and adorn the objects presented under the agency of the Understanding.[13]

In comments he made elsewhere on Shakespeare, Emerson claimed that the poet, "whose mind was coextensive with nature", had employed the intellectual faculty, "imagination", to entertain the public with the "objects", or truths, he had received from divine "intellect" through the "agency" of divine "instinct". The result was unified perception and organic art; "instinct" could function only when thought and feeling were in harmony. When the intellectual faculty that Emerson called "Common Sense" in speaking of Shakespeare is separated from feeling, it becomes, as a mode of perception characteristic of the masculine side of the second level of growth, the "Understanding". Hence, the "objects" Bacon used his "imagination" to "illustrate and adorn"

Terminus,' as well as the political speeches and letters concerning affairs of state. Although the lecture contains some of Emerson's finest writing, he did not print it – why, we may only conjecture: perhaps because the adverse criticism of a former god, however deeply felt, was too sharp for a published essay." Hopkins, *op. cit.*, p. 421. The writer notes that Bacon's authorship of the "Brief Discourse Touching the Low Countries" has been questioned.

[12] *Journals*, II, 503-504 (Aug. 12, 1832). Emerson's references to Christ indicate usually that he did not regard him as a manifestation of the Son but of the Spirit; he represented the "operation" of the Spirit as "Moral Sentiment" through preachers, like Emerson himself, on the feminine side of the second level of development.

[13] "Lord Bacon", *Early Lectures*, I, 321.

consisted of universal truths as presented by divine "intellect" through the "Understanding", a mode of perception that, when not balanced by feeling, produces distorted, one-sided views.

Giving the chief events of Bacon's life in a brief paragraph, Emerson said that "at nineteen he wrote a sketch of the state of Europe which both in style and matter indicates a mature mind", that in 1597 "he published the Essays", that in 1620 "he published the Novum Organon", and that in 1622 "he published his history of Henry VII".[14] The omission of the *Advancement* may have been an oversight. With the essays and the *Novum Organum*, it would seem to have contributed more than did the other works to Emerson's image of Bacon as a representative of a transitional era.

Emerson turned next to the subject which most concerned him, Bacon's character. Declaring that "by nature and by discipline" he was "a most accomplished man", that the "reverence of genius always followed him and while yet alive he was called Venerable Bacon", he quoted some of "the most decisive testimonies from his contemporaries" regarding his "rare eloquence" and his "singular weight of personal character".[15] He included a paragraph of praise from Francis Osborn's *Advice to a Son*,[16] another from Ben Jonson, and shorter commendations by Sir Walter Raleigh and James Howell. Then Emerson added: "But

[14]   *Ibid.*, 321-22.
[15]   The tenth and last lecture in this series, of which "Lord Bacon" was the seventh, was entitled "Modern Aspects of Letters" and included remarks on Dugald Stewart, the Scottish philosopher, "one of the most pleasing names in modern English literature", whose "true merit is that of an excellent Scholar and a lively and elegant Essayist", and whose "every page is enriched with quotations or allusions to his reading. They form a picture gallery in which we find originals or copies of all choice works of ancient and modern art". Referring to Stewart's work, *A General View of the Progress of Metaphysical, Ethical, and Political Philosophy* (Boston, 1822), Emerson said that its dissertations on the progress of ethical and metaphysical philosophy "are the most agreeable of his works and breathe the spirit of the gentleman and the scholar". *Early Lectures,* I, 374-75. The editors point out, pp. 323, 325, that Emerson could have found his quotations from Ben Jonson and Aubrey in this volume, pp. 244-45.
[16]   "Lord Bacon", *Early Lectures*, I, 322. See *Advice to a Son,* in *Works,* eighth edition (London, 1682). First Part, p. 151.

this shining picture has a sad reverse. He was a servile courtier, a low intriguer; he was an ungrateful friend."

This "censure" did not result chiefly, if at all, from the bribery charge:

It is well known that he was tried on the charge of Bribery and found guilty. This however is not a very grave charge against him. It was proved that in conformity with a dangerous custom he permitted his servants to receive presents from parties suing at his court. But he was not himself corrupt. And no sentence of his was ever reversed. His ruin was permitted by King James to save Buckingham on whom the national vengeance was ready to fall. James thrust in the Chancellor as a victim and forbade him to defend himself, promising to annul the sentence.

But Emerson did condemn Bacon for his "servility":

The grave charge against him is the servility of which his letters are too many proofs, the suing to the King, to the favorite, and to the favorite's favorite. Please recommend me. Your kind word for me with the king. Speak of me to him when Burleigh is by, that he may commend me also, and the suppleness of such an one as Bacon to such an one as Buckingham – who can remember without pain?

While he "certainly descended to some low shifts to hinder the prosperity of his rival", Sir Edward Coke, "the worst fact in his history is his servile obedience to Elizabeth who thrust Bacon forward in the prosecution of the Earl of Essex for treason." Although he "sought to excuse himself", he gave in eventually to the queen. Thus, according to Emerson, "did Bacon's love of preferment and fear of disgrace bend his sense of honor and friendship".[17]

[17]   *Ibid.*, 323-24. "This censure was not pronounced without careful study of the speeches and letters relating to Essex's and Bacon's trials. It merited special attention, because it presented the reverse side of the coin whose face would continue to shine untarnished for the mature as well as for the young Emerson: the idea that the scholar must take part in the action of his times. If so great a man as Bacon could fall, who could remain erect before the battering ram of corruption?" Hopkins, *op. cit.*, p. 423. "Both men were innovators, iconoclasts; yet both drew on the tradition whose abuses they sought to root out. The difference between their respective traditions comes into play in Emerson's adverse criticism; the American democrat must condemn Bacon the monarchist, the New England moralist cannot refrain from censure of the faithless friend." *Ibid.*, 429.

Such a "censure" is completely consistent with the view that Bacon, in his moral development, was at the level of the Fall, half-way between the "innocence" of Shakespeare and the inspiring "self-reliance" of Milton. Since Emerson was trying to speak "as Christ" of his "good and evil," he felt that Bacon's efforts to save Essex from his madness were insufficient: he should have remained loyal to the end to the friend who had helped him; he should have relied entirely upon the guidance of "instinct" and Moral Sentiment, which require "affection", or "sympathy", as well as "Common Sense". Thus Emerson condemned him as he would have condemned himself. Yet Bacon's behavior, he admitted, could be partially excused because his "education" and the "depraved politics of his times" exerted an influence still stronger than the new infusions of the Spirit as Moral Sentiment. His fall from power in the bribery case had been foreshadowed years before in his moral failure during the Essex trouble; both events reflected the fallen condition of his society. "Much palliation no doubt is to be found in his education and in the depraved politics of his times and in the hard necessity which threw such a prophet at the whim of so foolish and contemptible persons as Buckingham and King James." [18] It is more than likely that Emerson believed this "hard necessity" was the operation of the Spirit's law of compensation manifesting itself first in the moral Fall of "such a prophet" and the society he represented and then, years later, in that Fall's reflection in the ruin of the material conditions of his life.

Because of his habit of seeing himself in the subject he contemplated, Emerson would seem to have been sincere in claiming that he felt "pain" when he thought of the split, or "Double Consciousness", of this fallen angel:

It is with pain I recur to these deformities in the moral character of this highly endowed person; with pain; for I believe no man reads the works of Bacon without imbibing an affectionate veneration for their author. We owe to him sentiments so exalted; we see the deep thirst he had for all noble thoughts; we follow with toil the bold excursions of his masculine understanding, that we come to regard him

---

[18]   *Ibid.*, 325.

as an Archangel to whom the high office was committed of opening
the doors and palaces of knowledge to many generations. But his
works are coloured also with infusions of this alien spirit of courts
and contemptible selfishness. We are reminded of those cases of
Double Consciousness in which an individual is afflicted with intervals of insanity during which a totally different character is exhibited
from his own. The word King seems to be the fatal word that brings
back his madness for then the great Teacher makes an Asiatic pros-
tration, fawns and eats dust. His spirit of compliment is nauseous.[19]

There can be no doubt that Emerson's "pain" followed, first, an
attempt to identify himself with Bacon in his moral dilemma,
and, second, a recognition of what seemed to him to be the contrast between what the philosopher chose finally to do and what
Christ would have commanded. But it is important to remember
that such "pain" occurs only, according to Emerson's philosophy,
when morally significant action is viewed solely from the position,
or "angle of vision", of a "priest" like Christ. Seen from the
higher level of the Sayer, Bacon's behavior would have appeared
as the inevitable result of the way the deity was being manifested
in him, not as "evil", but as "good in the making". Individual
passages in Emerson's lectures reflect various points of view, but
they were usually designed to contribute to a synthesis which
would produce a total effect capable of inspiring the all-encom-
passing vision of a Sayer.

After this most severe "censure" of Bacon's "servility", therefore, Emerson passed quickly "to the blameless and exalted side
of his character", referring to him as "the Lawgiver of science and
the profound and vigorous thinker who has enlarged our knowledge in the powers of man, and so our confidence in them". He
quoted Aubrey and Ben Jonson on the "favorable parts of his
moral character".[20]

Like Shakespeare, "though in a different way", Bacon could
"claim the praise of Universality". The "most obvious trait" in
his genius was "the extent combined with the distinctness of his
vision". Indeed, his "expansive Eye opened to receive the whole
system, the whole inheritance of Man. He did not appreciate

[19]   *Ibid.*, 324-25.
[20]   *Ibid.*, 325-26.

only this or only that faculty, but all the divine energy that resides in him, and sought to make it all productive. None ever hoped more highly of what man could do." More significantly, he beheld the "sphere of life and power", and "he went over nature to make an inventory of man's kingdom. There in the great magazine of beings his genius finds room and verge enough." With no "favorite views" – he was no "system grinder" [21] – he limited the activity of his genius to the sphere of nature, "the great magazine of beings".[22]

Vivian C. Hopkins has shown clearly Bacon's influence on Emerson's thought and style. "Above all", she asserts, "reading Bacon drove home the message, underscored in 'The American Scholar,' that the thinker may not stay aloof from action." [23] Declaring that Bacon "conceived more highly than perhaps did any other of the office of the Literary Man", Emerson revealed by his tone his admiration for the idea that "the literary man should know the whole theory of all that was done in the world whether by nature or by men and this in no general and vague way but with sufficient particularity to make him if need be master of the practice also"; but he showed similarly his moral disapproval of Bacon's aiming "to make the Scholar not only equal to useful oversight and direction of business, but to outshoot the drudge in his own bow, and even to prove his practical talent by his ability for mischief also".[24] Yet this moral judgment does not imply a contradiction. While agreeing with Bacon that the scholar should possess all kinds of knowledge, even if "evil", Emerson would have denied that expediency is a greater aid to efficiency than the Moral Sentiment. "Humility", which was "properly the exaltation of the Spirit",[25] is "a great timesaver".[26]

[21] *Ibid.*, 326-27.
[22] "Emerson and Bacon", p. 412.
[23] "Lord Bacon", *Early Lectures*, I, 327-28.
[24] *Journals*, II, 300 (July 15, 1830).
[25] *Ibid.*, III, 516 (July 27, 1835).
[26] "Lord Bacon", *Early Lectures*, I, 329. Commenting on this passage, Miss Hopkins says: "Just here falls the dark shadow across the light of admiration: the fault in *architechtonike* which Emerson sees not only in *The Advancement* and the *Natural History*, but also in the *Essays*. Organic form, that *sine qua non* for the young American who has just been reading

Although he did not mention Milton in this passage, Emerson's tone indicated that his own attitude was expressed in *Areopagitica*: "He that can apprehend and consider vice with all her baits and seeming pleasures, and yet abstain, and yet distinguish, and yet prefer that which is truly better, he is the true warfaring Christian." Emerson fully agreed that "the thinker may not stay aloof from action", but the action itself, when no longer guided by the deity as "instinct", as was Shakespeare's, must be guided by the Spirit as Moral Sentiment and thus be dedicated to moral reform. The Fall occurs at the changing of the guard, when "instinct" as it functions on the first level retires and Moral Sentiment takes over. Turning to Bacon's "great literary labor", Emerson attempted to show how this Fall is reflected in the absence of organic unity in his works.

He began this part of his lecture with unqualified praise. "The Advancement of Learning is one of the principal books in the English language", he declared, "one on which the credit of the nation for wisdom mainly depends." As "a survey of the literature of the world, the Recorded Thinking of Man, to report its sufficiency and its defects", it is "the survey as of a superior being so commanding, so prescient". While its style is "an imperial mantle, stiff with gold and jewels", the sentences are "so dense with meaning that the attention is withdrawn from the general views to particular passages".[27] It is "one stream of sense and splendor".

The *Novum Organum*, Emerson continued, is "a new logic not to supply arguments for dispute but arts for the use of mankind, not to silence an academical antagonist but to subdue nature by experiment and inquiry", and the "Natural History" contains "observations on all parts of nature. Some of these observations are of greatest value. He anticipated by happy conjecture some great astronomical discoveries". However, some of

---

Coleridge's *Friend* with entire acceptance, is lacking. Bacon does not supply 'that highest perfection of literary works, an intrinsic unity, a method derived from the mind.' No one of Bacon's writings satisfies this requirement, so ably met by Milton's *Paradise Lost* and Shakespeare's *Hamlet*." *Op. cit.*, 422.

[27] "Lord Bacon", *Early Lectures*, I, 331.

them are "of no value and have exposed him to the derision of very inferior men, especially those investigations which were favorite speculations in his age".[28] Although he studied magic "with equal calmness" as those "parts of nature" which are "manifest", his speculations and proposed experiments on this class of acts "have no scientific value whatever; they are only material as they show his all-seeing curiosity".[29]

Emerson reserved his greatest praise for the *Essays*. "Few books ever written contain so much wisdom and will bear to be read so many times", and they are "clothed meantime in a style of so much splendor that imaginative persons find sufficient delight in the beauty of expression." But the *Essays* revealed most clearly, for Emerson, the moral defects in the man.

"They delight us", he said, "by the dignity of the sentiments whenever he surrenders himself to his genius." "And let us believe that the following sentence contains his own apology to himself for submitting to the mortifications of ambition. 'Power to do good is the true and lawful end of aspiring; for good thoughts though God accept them yet towards men are no better than good dreams except they be put in act, and that cannot be, without power and place, as the vantage and commanding ground.' "[30] But the "defects of this book stand in glaring contrast to its merits. Out breaks at intervals a mean cunning like the hiss of a snake amid the discourse of angels."[31] That "hiss of a snake" destroyed the organic unity of Bacon's angelic "discourse".

[28]   *Ibid.*, 332-33.
[29]   *Ibid.*, 333-34.
[30]   Bacon's sentence is in "On Great Place", *Works*, II, 276.
[31]   "Lord Bacon", *Early Lectures*, I, 334-35. "For Emerson, who saw in Francis Bacon one of the greatest spirits of all time, the repudiation of Essex constituted another Fall of Man. The lecturer sees evidence of this moral obliquity in the Essays, where it is a blot on the shining page. Undoubtedly under the influence of Gabriel Harvey's statement that Bacon had 'the eie of a viper,' Emerson says, of the Essays, 'Out breaks at intervals a mean cunning like the hiss of a snake amid the discourse of angels.' No commentator ever wrestled more valiantly than Emerson with the problem of Bacon's character. Certainly no one ever accused Waldo Emerson of a moral defect; but, just because his reading in Bacon penetrated his whole self, as well as his thought, he tried desperately to find some answer to the contradiction between the thinker and the man." Hopkins, *op. cit.*, 424-25.

Because the "infusions of this alien spirit of courts and contemptible selfishness" were in conflict with the infusions of Moral Sentiment, Bacon's works lacked the unity of Shakespeare's and Milton's:

If I may adventure a criticism upon Lord Bacon's writings, it would be to remark a fault not easily separable from so colossal undertakings. His works have not that highest perfection of literary works, an intrinsic Unity, a method derived from the Mind. If a comparison were to be instituted between the Instauration and the Epic of Milton or the Hamlet of Shakspear I think the preference must remain with these last as the production of higher faculties. They are the mind's own Creation and are perfect according to certain inward canons which the mind must always acknowledge. But Bacon's method is not within the work itself, but without. This might be expected in his Natural History but not in his elaborated compositions. Yet in his Essays it is the same. All his work lies along the ground, a vast unfinished city.

Because of the moral conflict, the creativity of Bacon's "intellect constructive" was hampered: "He did not arrange but unceasingly collect facts. His own Intellect often acts little on what he collects. . . . All his work is therefore somewhat fragmentary. The fire has hardly passed over it and given it fusion and a new order from his own mind. It is sand without lime." The "Composition" Emerson had referred to in his second lecture on Shakespeare, the feminine faculty that gives form to the presentation of truths, was lacking. Hence "the order is much of it quite mechanical . . . the order of a shop and not that of a tree or an animal where perfect assimilation has taken place and all the parts have a perfect unity".

While "so loose a method had this advantage, that it allowed of perpetual amendment and addition", and "every one of his works" was, consequently, "a gradual growth", it prevented Bacon from ever finishing a literary undertaking:

Three times he published the Essays with large additions. Twelve times he wrote over the Novum Organon, that is once every year from 1607. Many fragments remain to us among his works, by which we may see the manner in which all his works were written. Works of this sort which consist of detached observations and to which the mind has not imparted a system of its own, are never ended. Each

of Shakspear's dramas is perfect, hath an immortal integrity. To
make Bacon's works complete, he must live to the end of the
world.[32]

The "immortal integrity" of Shakespeare's works, and of "the
Epic of Milton", resulted from their authors' reliance on the
divine inspiration, whose source lies outside the world of nature
and time.

In concluding his lecture, which Emerson called "this hasty
retrospect of Bacon's achievement", he found that two reflections were "forced" on his mind. The first was a "new courage
and confidence in the powers of man at the sight of so great
works done under such great disadvantages by one scholar". The
second, the "other moral of his history", was "the insufficiency
we feel in his mighty faculties to varnish the errors of his life".

We are made sensible, in his example, of the impossibility of welding
together vice and genius. The first will stand out like a loathsome
excrescence in its old deformity, nor wit, nor eloquence, nor learning
will whiten ingratitude, or dignify meanness. There in the stream of
Time he rears his immortal front nor seems 'less than Archangel
ruined, and the excess of glory obscured,' dividing our sentiments
as we pass from point to point of his character, between the highest
admiration and the highest pity.

It is significant that Emerson chose to conclude with this image
of Milton's Satan.[33] As a figure that would suggest both the Fall
of Man and Bacon's "glory", it served more effectively his primary intention – to inspire moral and religious insights – than
could Pluto, whom Cudworth had described as the pagan god of
two worlds, earth and hell. This view of the "Prince of philos-

---

[32]   *Ibid.*, 335-36.
[33]   See Milton, *Paradise Lost*, I, 593-94. An early passage in Emerson's
journal that would seem, indubitably, to refer to Bacon, suggests that, for
years, he was in the habit of associating Bacon's fall with that of Milton's
Satan and of contrasting it with Milton's victory. After praising Milton
as "the sublimest bard of all", Emerson made the following assertion: "A
kindred genius born for the exaltation of mankind, who preceded the
poet, and who fell (alas for humanity!) into a snare and ruin for his
integrity, did yet contribute a mighty impulse to the cause of wisdom and
truth. And he also was no wise unconscious of the magnitude of the effort
and the power which supported him." This passage follows a quotation
from *Paradise Lost*. *Journals*, I, 237 (March 18, 1823).

ophers", as he described Bacon in an early journal, did not change, although Emerson's interest in him declined as he grew older.[34]

III

The two worlds of Emerson's Bacon were "materialism" and "idealism", but, like Pluto and Satan, the "Prince of philosophers" ruled chiefly in the lower. "Of the upper world of man's being", Emerson declared in his lecture on Milton, given earlier in 1835, Bacon's *Essays* "speak few and faint words".[35] Although Bacon had imbibed "that stray drop of nectar of idealism", he wrote in 1853, it produced little effect: "Bacon, rich with lustres

[34] The whole passage is worth quoting as evidence of the consistency of Emerson's view from the age of twenty: "My Lord Bacon, my trusty counsellor all the week, has six or seven choice essays for holy time. The aforesaid lord knew passing well what was in man, woman and child, what was in books, and what in palaces. This possessor of transcendent intellect was a mean slave to courts and a conniver at bribery. And now, perchance, if mental distinctions give place to moral ones at the end of life, now this intellectual giant, who has been the instructor of the world and must continue to be a teacher of mankind till the end of time, – has been forced to relinquish his pre-eminence, and in another world to crawl in the dust at the feet of those to whom his mounting spirit was once a sacred guide. One instant succeeding dissolution will perhaps satisfy us that there is no inconsistency in this. Till then, I should be loth to ascribe anything less than celestial state to the Prince of philosophers." *Journals*, I, 271-72. Later reading obviously convinced Emerson that Bacon could not be justly described as "a conniver at bribery", but he always condemned his "servility". Emerson's interest in both Shakespeare and Bacon declined; they were not, for him, "fixed stars" as, presumably, was Milton: "Once I took such delight in Montaigne that I thought I should not need any other book; before that, in Shakspeare; then in Plutarch; then in Plotinus; at one time in Bacon; afterwards in Goethe; even in Bettine; but now I turn the pages of either of them languidly, whilst I still cherish their genius." "Experience", *Works*, III, 55. This passage, written about 1840, was soon followed by another expressing also a decline of interest: "How great were once Lord Bacon's dimensions! he is now reduced almost to the middle height; and many another star has turned out to be a planet or an asteroid: only a few are the fixed stars which have no parallax, or none for us." "Lecture on the Times", *Works*, I, 267.
[35] "John Milton", *Early Lectures*, I, 149. Fourth in the lecture series entitled "Biography," it was probably given Feb. 19, 1835. The present text is that of the *North American Review*, July, 1838.

and powers stolen somehow from the upper world, and inevitably wonderful to men; but he has this plunder of ideas, or this degree of fine madness, to no purpose: he does nothing with it: it leads him nowhere; he is a poor mean fellow all the while. . . .".[36] In both these passages suggesting Pluto, Emerson contrasted Bacon with Milton.

The chapter, "Literature", in *English Traits,* published in 1856, shows Bacon's relationship to the two worlds, "materialism" and "idealism".[37] "Lord Bacon has the English duality." While his "materialism", as seen in his "centuries of observations on useful science, and his experiments", were perhaps "worth nothing", "he drinks of a diviner stream, and marks the influx of idealism into England".[38] This "influx" brought the growth which he represents:

Bacon, in the structure of his mind, held of the analogists, of the idealists, or (as we popularly say, naming from the best example) Platonists. Whoever discredits analogy and requires heaps of facts before any theories can be attempted, has no poetic power, and nothing original or beautiful will be produced by him. Locke is as surely the influx of decomposition and of prose, as Bacon and the Platonists of growth. The Platonic is the poetic tendency; the so-called scientific is the negative and poisonous.[39]

Attacking Macaulay's essay,[40] Emerson said: "He thinks it the distinctive merit of the Baconian philosophy in its triumph over the old Platonic, its disentangling the intellect from theories of the all-Fair and all-Good, and pinning it down to the making a better sick chair and a better wine-whey for an invalid; – this not ironically, but in good faith; – that, 'solid advantage,' as he

---

[36] *Journals,* VIII, 408 (1853).

[37] It should be remembered that Emerson's references to English writers reflect various points of view. Sometimes he contemplated them as representatives of tendencies within a single period, at other times in relation to the whole of British literary history. Similarly, he compiled lists of writers representing tendencies occurring in time or proceeding into or out of it. For example, two writers representing the same level of development in the process of transcending time would appear in these lists as if contemporaries although, historically, they belong to different periods.

[38] *Works,* V, 238.

[39] *Ibid.,* 239.

[40] "Lord Bacon", *Edinburgh Review,* 1837.

calls it, meaning always sensual benefit, is the only good." Thus, "denying morals and reducing the intellect to a sauce-pan", Macaulay "hides his skepticism under the English cant of practical". Bacon was not "only the sensualist his critic pretends". He had "imagination, the leisures of the spirit, and basked in an element of contemplation out of all modern English atmospheric gauges". Hence, he is "impressive to the imaginations of men and has become a potentate not to be ignored". He occupies his "high place" by "specific gravity or levity, not by any feat he did, or by any tutoring more or less of Newton, etc., but as an effect of the same cause which showed itself more pronounced afterwards in Hooke, Boyle and Halley." When this defense of his "idealism", provoked by Macaulay and based largely on Emerson's interpretation of the meaning of *prima philosophia*,[41] is placed next to his comments on the philosopher's "materialism", Bacon's relations with the upper and lower worlds become clear. For Emerson, he remained "this pivotal Lord Bacon".[42]

Rusk has shown that Coleridge most interested Emerson in those years when he "was developing most rapidly his peculiar mental bias". On November 16, 1826, he had borrowed the *Biographia Literaria* from the Harvard College library, and in 1829 and 1830 he was avidly reading *The Friend* and *The Aids to Reflection*.[43] These last two works, together with de Gérando's

---

[41] Reading de Gérando in 1830, Emerson seized on the idea of the "First Philosophy". This experience, that would seem to have marked a turning-point in his own personal and intellectual development, sent him back to Bacon. *Journals*, II, 330-32 (Oct. 27, 1830). "Emerson really grasped Bacon's definition of the term to mean a statement of the principles that hold true in all sciences, morals, and mechanic arts; but, where Bacon considered 'prima philosophia' merely a groundwork laid down so that empirical investigation might proceed, Emerson elevated the term to the highest place in his scheme of values, deeming it worthy of a life 'to announce the laws of the First Philosophy.'" Hopkins, *op. cit.*, 414. See Bacon's *Advancement of Learning*, Bk. II, *Works*, I, 95-96, 100-101.

[42] *Journals*, VIII, 492 (1854).

[43] *Letters*, I, xxxvi, Rusk, ed.; 286, note 99. "All three volumes of the 1818 edition of *The Friend* are in Emerson's library at the Antiquarian House in Concord." *Ibid.*, 291, note 2. Emerson wrote his brothers William and Edward, Jan. 4, 1830, Boston, that he was reading, besides de Gérando, *The Friend* "with great interest" and *Aids to Reflection* "with yet deeper". *Ibid.*, 291.

Histoire, renewed his interest in Bacon. Coleridge in his comments would seem to have contributed more to Emerson's view of the philosopher than the author of the *Histoire.*

Marsh, in his "Preliminary Essay" to *Aids to Reflection,* had probably prepared Emerson to seek "lustres" in Coleridge's references to Bacon:

I can not but add, as a matter of simple justice to the question, that however our prevailing system of philosophizing may have appealed to the authority of Lord Bacon, it needs but a candid examination of his writings, especially the first part of his *Novum Organum,* to be convinced that such an appeal is without grounds; and that in fact the fundamental principles of his philosophy are the same with those taught in this work. The great distinction especially, between the understanding and the reason, is fully and clearly recognized; and as a philosopher he would be far more properly associated with Plato, or even Aristotle, than with the modern philosophers, who have miscalled their systems by his name. For further remarks on this point, the reader is requested to refer to the notes.[44]

Emerson's habit of viewing historical development as a dialectical process reflecting a divine trinity owes much to Coleridge, who, in *The Friend,* declared:

Such is the inherent dignity of human nature, that there belong to it sublimities of virtues which all men may attain, and which no man can transcend: and though this be not true in any equal degree of intellectual power, yet in the persons of Plato, Demosthenes, and Homer, and in those of Shakspeare, Milton, and Lord Bacon, were enshrined as much of the divinity of intellect as the inhabitants of this planet can hope will ever take up its abode among them.

After making this assertion, Coleridge showed its relevance to the belief in "a progress in the species towards unattainable perfection", which "neither is nor can be like that of a Roman road in a right line", but is "more justly compared to that of a river,

---

[44] James Marsh, "Preliminary Essay", in Shedd, ed., *The Complete Works of Samuel Taylor Coleridge,* I, 102. Marsh's essay appeared first in his edition of Coleridge's *Aids to Reflection* (Burlington, 1829). In "James Marsh and the Vermont Transcendentalists", *Philosophical Review,* Vol. 34, pp. 28-50 (January, 1925), Marjorie H. Nicolson has demonstrated the pervasive influence of Marsh on the early development of American transcendentalism.

which, both in its smaller reaches and larger turnings, is frequently forced back towards its fountains by objects which can not otherwise be eluded or overcome".[45] In the same work, Coleridge referred to Bacon's "courtly, – alas! his servile, prostitute, and mendicant – ambition".[46] More significantly, he attempted to show the essential identity of Plato's and Bacon's philosophies: "They are radically one and the same system; – in that, namely, which is of universal and imperishable worth, the science of method, and the grounds and conditions of the science of method".[47] This argument, largely based on his misleading identification of Bacon's "dry light" with the Coleridgean "Reason" and on his coupling of "Heraclitus and Plato, among the ancients, and among the moderns, Bacon and Stewart (rightly understood)",[48] had James Marsh's indorsement; it was apparently sufficient to convince Emerson of Bacon's "idealism".

The chief cause of Emerson's admiration of Bacon was to a large extent responsible for the archetypal image taking form in his mind. In his 1835 lecture, he said: "This last sentence contains the theory of his life and labors as a philosopher: 'There should not be anything in being and action which should not be drawn and collected into contemplation and doctrine.' It is not an occasional expression but his settled creed."[49] Bacon's "settled creed" evoked in Emerson's mind the dynamic image of a superhuman archetype, the Knower passing beyond the stage of poetic creativity represented by Shakespeare and becoming, in the process, a Doer:

This happy constitution of mind, this Universal Curiosity determined undoubtedly his election of his literary task. He would not dedicate his faculties to the elucidation of the principles of law, though his law tracts are highly commended. He would not found a sect in moral, or intellectual philosophy, though familiar with these inquiries; nor in natural nor in political science; but he would put his

---

[45] Complete Works, II, 362.
[46] Ibid., 441.
[47] Ibid., 442.
[48] Ibid., 444-45. See Advancement of Learning, Bk. I, Works, I, 9; Bk. II, Works, I, 131; "Friendship," Works, II, 318. Hopkins, op. cit., 420-21, note 66. Emerson, Works, V, 380-81, editor's note 1 to p. 241.
[49] See Advancement of Learning, Works, I, 200.

Atlantean hands to heave the whole globe of the Sciences from their rest, expose all the gulfs and continents of error, and with creative hand remodel and reform the whole. In the execution of his plan there is almost no subject of human knowledge, especially none of human action, whereto he has not directed some attention and some experiment in the manner of one who was in earnest by acting to learn the facts.[50]

Emerson's image of Shakespeare suggested the first member of the trinity with the Father, or creative, aspect already dominant over the Knower. In Bacon, the masculine, centrifugal tendency toward action, manifested in Shakespeare as poetic creativity, reached its culmination. While the love of truth that distinguished the Knower was reflected in Bacon's "Universal Curiosity", his masculine tendency became increasingly dominant as he approached the limits of its power.

It would seem that, according to Emerson's view of the English Renaissance, Bacon's "Atlantean hands" did "heave the whole globe of the Sciences from their rest", that his "creative hand" did most to "remodel and reform the whole", but that his inevitable Fall came with the breaking of the link that joined his centrifugal and centripetal sides; overextending himself in the direction of worldly action, he lost contact for awhile with the contemplative life. After foundering in those waters where the Spirit as Moral Sentiment begins the turning of the tide, Bacon had been sufficiently goaded by pain to effect colossal reforms as a Doer. Milton would represent for Emerson the return of the waters to their source as the position of the Knower again became dominant at the dawn of a new age.

III. MILTON AS THE SAYER

While Emerson, in 1845, chose Shakespeare as the representative of the poet in "Representative Men", he used Milton for the same purpose in his first organized series of lectures, that on biography, in 1835.[1] In that lecture, "John Milton", published in the July, 1838 *North American Review*, and elsewhere in his writings, he showed that he was less concerned with the biographers and critics of Milton than with those of Shakespeare. The obvious reason for this was that he found Milton, as a man, easier to understand because his works had revealed clearly that his life and the condition of his "soul" were nearer the ideal to which Emerson himself aspired[2] than were the life and the condition

---

[1] "Introduction", *Early Lectures*, I, xix. These lectures, six in all, were delivered before the Society for the Diffusion of Useful Knowledge at the Masonic Temple (Boston, beginning Jan. 29, 1835). *Ibid.*, 93. "John Milton", fourth in the series, was given, probably, on Thursday evening, Feb. 19. In July, 1838, it was published, with revisions that would seem not to have altered its essential meaning, in the *North American Review*. As such, it was published in *Works*, XII, 245-279, and in *Early Lectures*, I, 144-163. Although Emerson's working notes are with his lecture manuscripts in the Houghton Library, the original manuscript is missing. After *Early Lectures* went to press in 1959, however, a printer's copy of what seems to have been the original, containing Emerson's alterations for publication as well as printer's marks, was discovered in the Houghton Library among the papers of John Gorham Palfrey, editor of the *North American Review* between 1835 and 1843. The editors of *Early Lectures* could therefore include among their textual notes information derived from the Palfrey manuscript which would aid in the reconstruction of the original text. *Ibid.*, 442-43.

[2] " 'Emerson had the same lofty aim as Milton, "to raise the idea of man;" he had "the power *to inspire*" in a preeminent degree. If ever a man communicated those *vibrations* he speaks of as characteristic of

of soul of the world's "best poet". In other words, the image of
Milton he had derived from his works, though comparatively
meager in its accumulation of significant details, was less obscured
by mystery than was the image of Shakespeare he had derived
from all sources of information. Emerson's words often suggest
that he regarded the level of his own spiritual development as
both above Shakespeare's and below Milton's. It would seem
that he had found it more difficult, in trying to assess Shakespeare's character and mind, to look backward, as it were, and
recapture the innocence that had enabled the divine "instinct"
to speak in his works, and to reconcile his having to look backward with his religious feelings as he contemplated the poet's
achievements, than, in evaluating Milton's character and mind,
to look forward and upward in the direction toward which he
hoped he was naturally moving. The light that inspired Emerson
as he endeavored to grow toward its source would seem to have
shone through and illuminated Milton's figure on the path ahead.
When Emerson asked himself, in 1838, "And what can you say
for Milton, the King of song in the last ages?" his answer came
quickly and confidently, without any puzzled regrets, in words
referring to a representative of the ideal poet and, therefore, of
the Sayer and Son: "Milton the heroic, the continuator of the
series of the Bards, the Representative of the Immortal Band
with fillet and harp, and soul all melody." [3] As Matthiessen has

---

Milton, it was Emerson. In elevation, purity, nobility of nature, he is
worthy to stand with the great poet and patriot, who began, like him, as
a schoolmaster, and ended as the teacher in a school-house which had
for its walls the horizons of every region where English is spoken.' "
Oliver Wendell Holmes, *Ralph Waldo Emerson*, 1885, as quoted in
Works, XII, 459, editor's note.
[3] *Journals*, IV, 395 (Feb. 16, 1838). Emerson was then preparing his
Milton lecture for publication in the *North American Review*. The difficulties this task apparently gave him would seem to have been chiefly
literary; they were not difficulties of interpretation and character evalua-
tion like those Shakespeare had presented. He was trying to give freshness
to truths that had been stated before, at least in his lecture, and that he
knew would be regarded by many as obvious. "The suds toss furiously in
our wash bowl", he wrote to his brother a few days earlier. "I promised
Dr. Palfrey one of my old biographical lectures for the N.A. Review &
now I am furbishing up my Milton." "To William Emerson, Concord,

pointed out, it was "no less characteristic of him than it was of Dr. Channing to feel a special veneration for Milton, who still remained the archetype of the poet for New England." [4] It was, therefore, far easier for Emerson to render an "account" of Milton in terms consistent with his own philosophical views than of Shakespeare, who, though the "best poet" of all, could not represent the ideal. When he turned to Milton's biographers and critics for information and inspiring insights, it was not with the same feeling of need for enlightenment on a vexing problem concerning religious and moral truth.

The first part of this chapter will attempt to show Emerson's view of the poet as it is revealed in his references to those who have written about him; it will indicate, at the same time, the extent of his knowledge of the biographers and critics. The second part will clarify his view of Milton as it is revealed elsewhere, especially in his lecture on the poet. Both parts should demon-

---

February 12 and 13, 1838", *Letters*, II, 108. On the day of his journal entry, he wrote to his wife: "I have begun to Miltonize a little this morn'g, for if I remember the copy slip said, when I learned to write K, *Keep your promises*; & the memory of the good Dean of Cambridge has begun to be odious to me my sin to him ward is grown so great." "To Lidian Emerson, Concord, February 16, 1838." *Letters*, II, 111. The "good Dean of Cambridge" was Palfrey, editor of the *North American Review*, in which the article at last appeared the following July (XLVII, 56-73). His difficulties are more clearly revealed, however, in a letter written in March: ". . . but I used all the time I got in vamping up an old *dead* paper that more than a year since I had promised Dr. Palfrey & with all my chemistry & chirography I cannot make it alive. I will promise no more: & yet is the pale horse not to amble till July." "To Frederic Henry Hedge, March 27 and 30, 1838", *Letters*, II, 122. Emerson's dissatisfaction with the results of this labor is indicated in the following, written more than eight years later: "In answer to your inquiry respecting the N. A. Review; – I did write an article on Milton & one on Michel Angelo, in that Journal; the former in the Number for July, 1838; and the latter, in I know not what Number, but within a year, I should think, of the other. I have written nothing else in the N. A. R. I am not very eager to recall either of these papers to notice, – which I have never seen since they were printed, and which were printed only to oblige the editor. I had rather not have them printed with my name." "To John Chapman, Boston, October 30, 1846", *Letters*, III, 359. "Michel Angelo Buonaroti" appeared in January, 1837.

[4] F. O. Matthiessen, *American Renaissance: Art and Expression in the Age of Emerson and Whitman* (Oxford University Press, 1941), p. 103.

strate that Emerson saw in him a representative of the Son, the third member of his trinity. In 1852, he wrote in his journal:

'T is said that the age ends with the poet or successful man who knots up into himself the genius or idea of his nation; and that when the Jews have at last flowered perfectly into Jesus, there is the end of the nation.[5]

Milton, the poet who ended the age of the English Renaissance, represented a similar flowering. Viewed from Emerson's "angle of vision", he symbolized the Effect by reflecting the light streaming through the Operation from the Cause. He thus inspired others to see that each cycle of moral growth begins and ends in eternity.

I

Even in childhood, Emerson knew something about Milton and felt his influence. In 1815, when he was only twelve years old and a freshman at Harvard, he wrote to his brother William: "This afternoon I began to read Johnson's lives of the Poets and have read Cowley, Denham, and began Milton: I like it very much for Johnson intersperses it with his own wit." [6] While this passage indicates some knowledge, it may be assumed that even earlier, through the guidance of his aunt and other elders,[7] he had been introduced to Milton and taught to regard him as a poet to be revered. Years later, when he composed his 1835 lecture, Emerson's subject was a man who had long been an ideal, a source of inspiration, a large part of whose poetry and prose he had read and reread since early youth.[8]

---

[5]   *Journals*, VIII, 345 (1852).
[6]   "To William Emerson, Boston, June 2 and 3, 1815", *Letters*, I, 10.
[7]   In "Mary Moody Emerson", *Works*, X, 402, 411, Emerson referred to his aunt's devotion to Milton and *Paradise Lost*.
[8]   Emerson's early interest in Milton's character is indicated in a letter to his brother William in 1818: "Consider too the character of Milton as Johnson gives it, at the conclusion of his life 'Milton was born for all that was great & arduous; Difficulty retired at his touch.' Do not know that I have the words exactly it is the sense however." "To William Emerson, Waltham, Massachusetts, May 19, 1818", *Letters*, I, 61. The last sentence of Johnson's essay reads as follows: "His great works were per-

His attitude toward Milton the man, like his attitude toward Shakespeare, was greatly affected by his own religious and moral thought and feeling. Both poets revealed to Emerson manifestations of deity; hence, his most significant reactions to them were

formed under discountenance, and in blindness, but difficulties vanished at his touch; he was born for whatever is arduous; and his work is not the greatest of heroic poems, only because it is not the first." *Lives of the English Poets* (London, 1925), I, 114. In Emerson's journals and notebooks for 1820-1822, he referred to or quoted from Milton's "Il Penseroso", "Comus", "Paradise Lost", and "Samson Agonistes"; and the "Reason of Church Government Urged Against Prelaty", "An Apology for Smectymnuus", and "Areopagitica". Under the date Nov. 2, 1820, Emerson wrote: "What a grand man was Milton! so marked by nature for the great Epic Poet that was to bear up the name of these latter times." Then, after referring to " 'Reason of church government urged against Prelaty' written while young", he quoted at some length from the biographical section at the beginning of the Second Book of that work, as he had quoted also at some length from the same section under the date "September, 1820", and declared that here Milton's spirit is "already communing with itself & stretching out into its colossal proportions & yearning for the destiny he was appointed to fulfil." *The Journals and Miscellaneous Notebooks of Ralph Waldo Emerson*, ed. William H. Gilman, George P. Clark, Alfred R. Ferguson, Merrell R. Davis (Harvard University Press, 1960), I, 41-42, 373-74. Referring, in 1823, to this section of the same prose work, Emerson said he could not "conceive of any man of sense" reading these passages "without his heart warming to the touch of noble sentiments; and his faith in God and in the eternity of virtue and of truth being steadfastly confirmed. Nothing of human composition", he added, "is so akin to inspiration." *Journals*, I, 241-42. These references to the biographical passages in "Reason of Church Government" are significant because they indicate how early in life Emerson saw Milton as a representative of the ideal poet who could inspire moral and religious growth. He recorded that, by the end of 1824, he had read the life of Milton by Charles Symmons and one volume of Milton's prose (*The Prose Works*, with life, by Charles Symmons, 7 vols., London, 1806). *The Journals and Miscellaneous Notebooks*, I, 397, 399; Rusk, *Life*, 92, 578. But he, or his mother, had borrowed earlier, in 1818, from the Boston Library Society, the first two volumes of the revised variorum edition of Henry J. Todd's *The Poetical Works of John Milton, with notes of various authors*, 7 vols. (London, 1809), (including Todd's account of Milton's life and writings). Cameron, *Emerson the Essayist*, II, 154, 180. Early in his life Emerson would thus seem to have been exposed to the best editions of Milton's prose and poetry besides various volumes containing selections of his work. In preparing his lecture on the poet, he reviewed the prose works and took notes on the recently published biography by Joseph Ivimey, *John Milton: His Life and Times . . .* (New York, 1833). *Early Lectures*, I, 144-45, 390.

in some way religious experiences. But, while Shakespeare's brain and the manifestation in his works of the divine "intellect" had caused sublime wonder and awe, Milton's heart and his power to inspire religious and moral sentiments had kindled "a love and emulation".

Believing that true critics should be similarly inspired by Milton's power, Emerson found that the poet's own contemporaries had not been. He was not "seen" by them, but "valued most as a scholar".[9] His "poem", that is, his greatest poetry and, by implication, his real stature as a poet, was ignored.[10] Furthermore, Emerson found, the generations that followed, until recently, were also deficient in appreciation. Even Dryden, Addison, and Johnson, though "able", were "unsympathizing critics" because of their not responding to his influence with sufficiently Miltonic feelings of "love and emulation". The criticism of these earlier writers was only a "general and vague acknowledgment of his genius"; they were deficient in the "intimate knowledge and delight" that only his spirit can convey.[11]

True inspiration, Emerson believed, would bring the right tone,[12] which the work of these critics had evidently lacked. But he found an "altered tone" in more recent criticism, that which had appeared after the discovery of Milton's treatise "On the Christian Doctrine" in 1823.[13] Like that of Shakespeare, it would seem, this "new criticism" of Milton "indicated a change in the public taste, and a change which the poet himself might claim to have wrought".[14] A "great Poet", he wrote chiefly "for the gods" and future readers. Hence, like Shakespeare, he, too, had his progeny in a "new race."[15] Growing up "in the taste and

---

[9]   *Journals*, III, 414 (Dec. 27, 1834).
[10] "John Milton", *Early Lectures*, I, 146.
[11] *Ibid.*, 148.
[12] "Whatever language the bard uses, the secret of tone is at the heart of the poem. Every great master is such by this power, ... The true inspiration always brings it." "Preface", *Parnassus*, x. For Emerson, the true critic was a poet.
[13] "John Milton", *Early Lectures*, I, 145.
[14] *Ibid.*, 146.
[15] "I now speak of men of talent – for genius makes its own law and does not write down to any one's comprehension. Thus Milton sang a

spirit of the work" would seem to have given this "new race" of writers "the utmost advantage for seeing intimately its power and beauty" because such a nurture had developed in them a state of religious and moral feeling which had enabled them to be truly inspired; [16] the "altered tone" resulting from that inspiration had apparently expressed the "world's reverence" in which "this man has steadily risen" by his own "innate worth".[17] Thus, Milton's best critics, according to Emerson, have but recently appeared; only a "new race", his progeny, could have struck the new tone distinguishing their criticism and indicating their ability to respond to that force which he possessed before "all men in literary history, and so (shall we not say?) of all men": "the power *to inspire*".[18]

While Shakespeare's salient power was his "imagination", Milton's was this "power *to inspire*", which apparently represented, for Emerson, the distinguishing mark of the true poet. Hence, the best critics would be those who could be inspired by this power as it manifested itself in those with an intellectual bias like Shakespeare's or a moral bias like Milton's; they could neither appreciate nor estimate its force unless they had felt in themselves its effect.

"Inspiration" itself, Emerson believed, is the deity. "It is this Instinct", he declared, "whose normal state is passive, at last put in action." [19] In other words, "inspiration" is the divine "instinct" when its activity has been accelerated. The divine "intellect", the creator of the natural world, is sluggish when, as "instinct", it first enters the mind through the passive, human "intellect receptive". Its creative activity is then speeded up in the active, human "intellect constructive". As a result, the deity

---

song to the music of his own ear and he knew that England held not another ear, and might not for a century, which should hear its rhythms. The great Poet writes for the gods, ..." Kronman, ed., "Prospects", in "Three Unpublished Lectures", 103.
[16] "John Milton", *Early Lectures*, I, 148.
[17] *Ibid.*
[18] *Ibid.*
[19] "Natural History of Intellect", *Works*, XII, 68.

as "inspiration" can create worlds in art which "instinct" could not complete in the short period of a human lifetime.

"Inspiration" would seem to be, furthermore, the divine Son, uniting opposite aspects of deity as they are revealed in nature: "intellect receptive", then, is the Knower; "intellect constructive" is the Doer; "inspiration", reconciling their opposite functions and completing their work, is the Sayer. It is, therefore, most fully represented in the true poet; and it completes the circle symbolizing the cyclical movement of deity in the created universe, the process of emanation and evolution: "A fuller inspiration should cause the point to flow and become a line, should bend the line and complete the circle." [20]

Hence, it corresponds with motion, love, beauty: the final impulse of the universal wave as it attempts simultaneously to flood every human mind. "Inspiration", Emerson said, "is vital and continuous. It is also a public or universal light, and not particular." [21] While truth is perceived by the human "imagination" as a succession of symbolic images given form by Composition, "intellect receptive" passively receives the truth itself, "intellect constructive" presents it to the "imagination" clothed in images, and "inspiration" is the power – like that of a projecting machine in our day – which changes the images continuously and, in so doing, determines the ends they serve, the directions of the flowing, the speed at which truth will thus be unfolded. What inspiration produces, therefore, is always a surprise, always new.[22] Besides this "newness", which characterizes organic growth in nature and art, and for which "inspiration", on both divine and human levels, is responsible, "inspiration's" power of accelerating all activity to some end produces in the mind intimations of that which is to come. That is, the "newness" makes itself felt first in the poet's mind and is then reflected in his work.[23] Because of this "secret augury", the true poet is not only a philosopher, but also a prophet; he not only sees truth, but sees that

---

[20]   "Inspiration", *Works*, VIII, 273.
[21]   "Natural History of Intellect", *Works*, XII, 70.
[22]   *Ibid.*, 72.
[23]   "Inspiration", *Works*, VIII, 271.

toward which truth in its present form is tending. Since the
tendency of all action is ever toward some ultimate end which
is good, the true poet, because he has intimations of that end,
must be cheerful; his poem must be exhilarating;[24] and the
process of completing, which writing the poem consists of, must
also be a process of perfecting, of creating a world more perfect
than our own would appear to us to be when viewed without
his perception of a beneficent tendency. Hence, he is a "per-
fecter".[25] Poetry, therefore, "perfects" the movement of the wave,
whose initial motions usually, in real life, are the only ones seen;
it must consist of "something old and something new": the water
of truth, "as old as the rock", which instructs, and the foam, as
new as the changing images whose beauty delights us; yet both
water and foam consist of the same element which, in all its
motions, tends toward some ultimate, good end.

In describing the divine power that produces these motions
and determines their direction, "inspiration", Emerson employed
such figures as light,[26] yeast, wine, fire,[27] and electricity.[28] He
compared the inspired poet to lightning rods[29] and mountains,

[24] "The Poet", *Works*, III, 12.
[25] "Poetry and Imagination", *Works*, VIII, 38-40.
[26] "Natural History of Intellect", *Works*, XII, 70: "It is also a public or
universal light, and not particular."
[27] "Inspiration", *Works*, VIII, 271: "Inspiration is like yeast"; "Natural
History of Intellect", *Works*, XII, 69: "Where is the yeast that will leaven
this lump? Where the wine that will warm and open these silent lips?
Where the fire that will light this combustible pile? That force or flame
is alone to be considered; 't is indifferent on what it is fed." The terms
lump, silent lips, and *combustible pile* all refer to "instinct".
[28] "Inspiration", *Works*, VIII, 273: "A fuller inspiration should cause
the point to flow and become a line, should bend the line and complete
the circle. To-day the electric machine will not work, no spark will pass;
then presently the world is all a cat's back, all sparkle and shock. Sometimes there is no sea-fire, and again the sea is aglow to the horizon"; *ibid.,*
274: "But where is the Franklin with kite or rod for this fluid?" It is
obvious that Emerson associated the power of "this fluid" also with that
of water. As a representative of the Sayer and Son, Milton would suggest
Neptune, whose relation to Jupiter and Pluto, "high and neather Jove",
is referred to in the opening lines of *Comus*, one of the poems Emerson
most highly valued because of its "power *to inspire*".
[29] *Ibid.,*; "Europe and European Books", *Works*, XII, 366: "The poet,
like the electric rod, must reach from a point nearer the sky than all

especially volcanoes.[30] It was apparently not very difficult for him to find such analogies in nature and thus to see in concrete terms how the poet receives divine "inspiration": it arises in the central "self" as fire in a volcano might seem to begin at the center of the earth, then passes upward with ever increasing pressure and speed through the mountain's cone-shaped core to cause finally an eruption at the top which creates an entirely new landscape.

But, while Emerson claimed also to know something about the conditions necessary for its reception, he could not so easily see how this fire of "inspiration" functioned in the act of creation itself – that was a divine mystery –[31] and how this "river of electricity" that flows through the poet, the conducting rod, is communicated "from one to another" – that made, he said, "the

---

surrounding objects, down to the earth, and into the dark wet soil, or neither is of use. The poet must not only converse with pure thought, but he must demonstrate it almost to the senses. His words must be spheres and cubes, to be seen and smelled and handled. His fable must be a good story, and its meaning must hold as pure truth"; "The Poet", *Works*, III, 40: "Doubt not, O poet, but persist. Say 'It is in me, and shall out.' Stand there, balked and dumb, stuttering and stammering, hissed and hooted, stand and strive, until at last rage draw out of thee that *dream*-power which every night shows thee is thine own; a power transcending all limit and privacy, and by virtue of which a man is the conductor of the whole river of electricity."

[30] *Journals*, V, 179 (1839): "The volcano has its analogies in him. He is in the chain of magnetic, electric, geologic, meteorologic phenomena, and so he comes to live in nature and extend his being through all: then is true science"; *ibid.*, VI, 401 (1843): "Mountains are great poets, and one glance at this fine cliff scene undoes a great deal of prose, and re-instates us wronged men in our rights"; "Poetry and Imagination", *Works*, VIII, 10: "The poet knows the missing link by the joy it gives. The poet gives us the eminent experiences only, – a god stepping from peak to peak, nor planting his foot but on a mountain."

[31] "Of the *modus* of inspiration we have no knowledge. But in the experience of meditative men there is a certain agreement as to the conditions of reception. Plato, in his seventh Epistle, notes that the perception is only accomplished by long familiarity with the objects of intellect, and a life according to the things themselves. 'Then a light, as if leaping from a fire, will on a sudden be enkindled in the soul, and will then itself nourish itself.' He said again, 'The man who is his own master knocks in vain at the doors of poetry.'" "Inspiration", *Works*, VIII, 274.

perpetual problem of education".[32] He believed, however, that Milton possessed this power of communicating it to others, that is, "the power *to inspire*", beyond all men and that his best critics would be most able to receive the divine electricity that had flowed through him.

One of the most notable of that inspired group of recent writers seems to have been Dr. Ellery Channing, whose "piety and wisdom had such weight that, in Boston, the popular idea of religion was whatever this eminent divine held"; [33] "the powerful influence" of his "genius and character" had given the most recent, and apparently the most effective "shocks" to the "popular religion of our fathers".[34] This "star of the American Church", "one of those men who vindicate the power of the American race to produce greatness", whose "printed writings are almost a history of the times", had produced two papers, one on Milton and the other on Napoleon, which, according to Emerson, were "the first specimens in this country" of "large criticism". Hence, he attributed to them "much importance".[35]

But he was obviously not much impressed by what the writers before Johnson had said about Milton. While he quoted Aubrey and Wood on such matters as his physical appearance and demeanor,[36] Emerson merely indicated that he was familiar with "the

[32] "Inspiration", *Works*, VIII, 274: "But where is the Franklin with kite or rod for this fluid? – a Franklin who can draw off electricity from Jove himself, and convey it into the arts of life, inspire men, take them off their feet, withdraw them from the life of trifles and gain and comfort, and make the world transparent, so that they can read the symbols of Nature?" "Natural History of Intellect", *Works*, XII, 75: "It must be owned that what we call Inspiration is coy and capricious; we must lose many days to gain one; and in order to win infallible verdicts from the inner mind, we must indulge and humor it in every way, and not too exactly task and harness it. Also its communication from one to another follows its own law, and refuses our intrusion. It is one, it belongs to all: yet how to impart it? This makes the perpetual problem of education "
[33] "The Superlative", *Works*, X, 166-67.
[34] "Life and Letters in New England", *Works*, X, 329-330.
[35] *Ibid.*, 339-340.
[36] For example, the following: "Wood, his political opponent, relates, that 'his deportment was affable, his gait erect and manly, bespeaking courage and undauntedness.' Aubrey adds a sharp trait, that 'he pronounced the letter R very hard, a certain sign of a satirical genius.'" "John Milton", *Early Lectures*, I, 151.

general and vague acknowledgment of his genius" [37] by Dryden, who had, he declared elsewhere, a "frivolous style of thought" [38] and "no permanent interest".[39] Moreover, "Addison's heart was in the right place and his influence has been undoubtedly beneficent",[40] but his essays on Milton apparently lacked "the power *to inspire*" Emerson.

Among these earlier writers, the only one whose treatment of the poet he was inclined to admire was Dr. Johnson.[41] Especially

---

[37]   *Ibid.*, 148.

[38]   "Chaucer", *Early Lectures*, I, 274.

[39]   "Ethical Writers", *Early Lectures*, I, 357. Emerson agreed with Dryden's statement in his "Essay on Satire" that Milton "runs into a flat of thought, sometimes for a hundred lines together, but it is when he is got into a track of Scripture". *Milton Criticism*, ed. James Thorpe, 1950, p. 338. In his lecture, he said: "Milton, the controvertist, has lost his popularity long ago: and if we skip the pages of 'Paradise Lost' where 'God the Father argues like a school divine,' so did the next age to his own." *Early Lectures*, I, 148. See Alexander Pope, "The First Epistle of the Second Book of Horace", line 102. Included in Emerson's working notes is the following: "Paradise Lost is not all Real. His Comus is. The defects of Paradise Lost are the fictitious part. The Reason of Ch. Gov & Areopagitica, are better poems than whole books of P. L." *Early Lectures*, I, 450. In a letter to his brother William in 1841 appears an echo of Dryden's "Lines Printed Under the Engraved Portrait of Milton": "The force of candor could no farther go I am strongly tempted to say, Yea. such an appetite I have to these things." "To William Emerson, Concord, March 30, 1841", *Letters*, II, 390. Dryden's poem may have helped to strengthen Emerson's tendency to view Milton as the representative of a final stage of development and the reconciliation of opposite tendencies:

> "Three poets, in three distant ages born,
> Greece, Italy, and England did adorn.
> The first in loftiness of thought surpass'd,
> The next in majesty, in both the last:
> The force of Nature could no farther go;
> To make a third, she join'd the former two."
>
>   (*Milton Criticism*, p. 337).

But this tendency may have been indebted also to Selvaggi's Latin epigram – "Let Greece boast of Maeonides and Rome of Maro; England boasts of Milton, the peer of both" – and the concluding lines of Samuel Barrow's Latin poem "On the Paradise Lost of John Milton, Consummate Poet" – "Yield, ye writers of Rome, yield, ye writers of Greece, and all that Fame whether modern or ancient has celebrated. Whoso shall read this poem will think that Homer sang only of frogs, Vergil only of gnats."

[40]   "Ethical Writers", *Early Lectures*, I, 366.

[41]   Emerson's opinion of Dr. Johnson is clearly indicated in the following: "The pride of ethical writers in later times was Dr. Samuel Johnson, who

impressive was the conclusion to his life of Milton.[42] But, as Emerson implied in his lecture on the poet, even this passage was but "the general and vague acknowledgment of his genius" by an "able, but unsympathizing" critic.

Although he did not refer to Coleridge in this lecture, it may be assumed that he valued the observations of that writer beyond those of any predecessor; his "true merit", Emerson claimed, "undoubtedly is not that of a philosopher or of a poet but a critic"; his *Biographia Literaria* is "undoubtedly the best body of criticism in the English language".[43] Praising *Areopagitica*, in his lecture, as "the most splendid" of Milton's prose works, Emerson said, in a passage indebted to Coleridge, that it is "valuable in history as an argument addressed to a government to produce a practical end, and plainly presupposes a very peculiar state of society".[44] In his working notes for his lecture, he added: "Mr. Coleridge adduces evidence of the same fact." [45] Emerson was referring perhaps to a passage in his own copy of *Literary Remains*.[46]

---

more than any other of the English authors impresses us by the peculiarities of his personal character. A man whom it is always a refreshment to remember because with whatever faults and whatever mountainous prejudices encumbered he was a man of principle and therefore had the inexhaustible resources of principle and the power which always attends it to inspire respect into men of every degree and every character. He is always accompanied by something of the majesty proper to virtue. His intellect is not very subtle nor do his observations indicate very profound philosophy yet always is his sense so vigorous and his sympathy with virtue so perfect, and moreover so deeply does he stamp every sentence with his own mode of thought that the faults of his learning and the limits of his own speculation have not diminished his fame or influence." "Ethical Writers", *Early Lectures*, I, 366.

[42] "Ethical Writers", *Early Lectures*, I, 366-67. Emerson's edition of Johnson was *Works* (London, 1806).

[43] "Modern Aspects of Letters", *Early Lectures*, I, 378-79.

[44] "John Milton", *Early Lectures*, I, 147.

[45] Notes for lecture on Milton, 1835. Houghton 194.6. The editors of *Early Lectures* have not included this statement among the working notes they printed as "not for the most part in either lecture or journal". *Op. cit.*, I, 499. Remarks on Milton had appeared in Coleridge's lecture given Feb. 27, 1818, and published in 1836 in *Literary Remains*.

[46] Emerson may have had access to this lecture in some periodical while writing his own lecture on Milton in 1835. He had certainly read it when

There Coleridge had described the author of *Paradise Lost* as
"the representative of the combined excellence" of the "characters of the great men" that distinguished the two periods preceding its production, the first period beginning with the accession of Elizabeth and ending with the death of James I, "the
other comprehending the reign of Charles and the brief glories
of the Republic". While he admitted that the first period was
superior to the second in the universality of achievement of its
geniuses which, in Elizabeth's court, could be paralleled only by
"Greece in her brightest moment", he praised the second for
being superior in "moral grandeur", "with which the low intrigues,
Machiavellic maxims, and selfish and servile ambition of the
former, stand in painful contrast".[47]

Milton had acquired his education in "the close of the former
period, and during the bloom of the latter". When he produced
Paradise Lost, according to Coleridge, he "combined the excellence of both".[48] The "conditions under which such a work was
in fact producible at all", Coleridge found, were "in the character
of the times" and in Milton's own character. The "foundations
of his mind" were laid in the first period, its "superstructure" in
the second. Thus, while the first period was congenial to his
mind as one of "profound erudition and individual genius", the
second, "no less favorable to it by a sternness of discipline and
a show of self-control", "acted on him" and "modified his
studies" by a "characteristic controversial spirit".[49] These statements, inspiring Emerson, must have contributed greatly to his
view of Milton as a representative of the ideal poet, the Sayer,
the reconciler of opposite tendencies, the third and final stage
of a cycle of growth.

But an essay that appeared several years after Coleridge gave

his lecture was revised for publication in the *North American Review*,
July, 1838, and given the form in which we now find it. On May 30,
1837, he received from Margaret Fuller his own copy of *Literary Remains*, which he had lent her and which he apparently returned to her on
Nov. 9, 1838. *Letters*, II, 77-78, 173.

[47] *Complete Works*, IV, 298.
[48] *Ibid.*, 299.
[49] *Ibid.*, 299-300.

his lecture and that Emerson presumably had read earlier, Dr. Channing's "Remarks on the Character and Writings of John Milton," [50] was surely regarded by him as at least equally significant. This essay and one on Napoleon, also by "our bishop",[51] were, he declared, "the first specimens in this country of that large criticism which in England had given power and fame to the Edinburgh Review".[52] Published in 1826, Channing's essay was evidently among the most outstanding works possessing the significant "altered tone" [53] of criticism after the discovery of *De Doctrina,* and it had emphasized what Emerson later proclaimed as Milton's greatest gift, the divine "power *to inspire*".

It is obvious that Channing wished to present this poet as more truly god-like than a saint, as a kind of incarnation of deity. In Milton's salutation to his readers in *De Doctrina,* Channing said, this "sainted spirit" spoke in the "style of an Apostle".[54] He was "in truth the sublimest of men" and "always moves with a conscious energy".[55] He "lived in light"; past and future, heaven, hell, and paradise were "open to him".[56] His "sphere", according to Channing, was "only inferior to that of angels": "Milton we should rank among seraphs." [57]

Emerson, however, was probably most impressed by Channing's emphasizing his Christlike power to inspire. After declaring, in his lecture on the poet, that it is "the prerogative of this great man to stand at this hour foremost of all men in literary history, and so (shall we not say?) of all men, in the power *to inspire*", Emerson added: "Virtue goes out of him into others." [58] Channing had used the same Biblical term originally applied to

---

[50] *The Works of William E. Channing* (Boston, 1841-1843), I, 3-68. This essay appeared in the *Christian Examiner* in 1826.
[51] *Works*, X, 576, editor's note 1 to page 340.
[52] "Life and Letters in New England", *Works*, X, 339.
[53] "John Milton", *Early Lectures*, I, 145.
[54] *Op. cit.*, I, 4.
[55] *Ibid.*, 12.
[56] *Ibid.*, 36.
[57] *Ibid.*, 37.
[58] "John Milton", *Early Lectures*, I, 148. A little further on, Emerson said: "The man of Lord Chesterfield is unworthy to touch his garment's hem." *Ibid.*, 150.

Christ: "A 'virtue goes out'" from him.[59] But Milton's power to inspire, according to Channing, would kindle only "congenial spirits"; it would merely dazzle "common readers".[60]

We venerate him as a man of genius, but still more as a man of magnanimity and Christian virtue, who regarded genius and poetry as sacred gifts, imparted to him, not to amuse men or to build a reputation, but that he might quicken and call forth what was great and divine in his fellow-creatures, and might secure the only true fame, the admiration of minds which his writings were to kindle and exalt.[61]

Reading this, Emerson must have recalled Shakespeare, who used his sacred gifts "to amuse men", and Bacon, who used his, at times, "to build a reputation".

But, although Channing had shown why Milton should be venerated as holy, if not divine, Emerson regarded him, not as the ideal Sayer, but as his representative in an earlier age:

How much one person sways us, we have so few. The presence or absence of Milton will very sensibly affect the result of human history: the presence or absence of Jesus, how greatly! Well, tomorrow a new man may be born, not indebted like Milton to the Old, and more entirely dedicated than he to the New, yet clothed like him with beauty.[62]

However, Milton's "merit" was "so near to the modern mind as to be still alive and life-giving". Although "the new and temporary renown of the poet is silent again", Emerson said, "he has gained, in this age, some increase of permanent praise." [63] That praise would eventually be further increased by future critics more capable of receiving his inspiration and therefore of appreciating the extent to which he revealed, in his life and works, what he represented in the world.

[59]   *Op. cit.*, 30-31.
[60]   *Ibid.*, 21-22.
[61]   *Ibid.*, 39-40.
[62]   *Journals*, VI, 141 (Dec. 18, 1841).
[63]   "John Milton", *Early Lectures*, I, 145.

II

Emerson's early journals and letters show how deeply the poet had affected him as a young man before he presented the fruits of inspiration in the lecture he delivered in 1835. It was Milton's character that had chiefly inspired him; and the passages in the works he had most admired were those which revealed his nobility and the irresistible attractiveness of virtue itself.

A week before his fifteenth birthday he quoted approvingly, in a letter to his brother William, a passage from the conclusion of Dr. Johnson's life of the poet.[64] Later, he noted that "Milton's Masque of Comus contains the finest strains which Milton ever wrote".[65] In 1822, at the age of nineteen, he took a summer walking tour with his brother and "lounged on the grass, with Bacon's Essays, or Milton, for hours".[66] The following March he wrote in his journal that he could not "conceive of any man of sense" who would read the first part of the second book of the *Reason of Church Government* "without his heart warming to the touch of noble sentiments; and his faith in God and in the eternity of virtue and of truth being steadfastly confirmed". He added, significantly, "Nothing of human composition is so akin to inspiration." [67]

As he approached his twenty-first birthday, the following winter and spring, Emerson's mind turned frequently to Milton when he wished to evaluate and to increase his own moral strength. On February 17, 1824, for example, he recorded an item he had gotten from Dr. Johnson: " 'Milton was very frugal of his praise.' " After the quotation, he appended the comment: "A man is not more known by the company he keeps." [68] Three days later, he wrote: "None that can understand Milton's *Comus* can read it without warming to the holy emotions it panegyrizes. I would freely give all I ever hoped to be, even when my air-

---

[64] "To William Emerson, Waltham, Massachusetts, May 19, 1818", *Letters*, I, 61.
[65] *The Journals and Miscellaneous Notebooks*, I, 298 (1821).
[66] "To Mary Moody Emerson, Boston, June 10, 1822", *Letters*, I, 115.
[67] *Journals*, I, 241-42 (March 18, 1823).
[68] *Ibid.*, 340 (Feb. 17, 1824).

blown hopes were brilliant and glorious, – not as now – to have given down that sweet strain to posterity to do good in a golden way".[69] Then, in a passage introduced by the words "I am beginning my professional studies. In a month I shall be legally a man",[70] Emerson expressed privately the desire "to love virtue for her own sake. I would have my pen so guided as was Milton's when a deep and enthusiastic love of goodness and of God dictated the *Comus* to the bard, or that prose rhapsody in the Third Book of Prelaty".[71] Indeed, it might also be said that, when he began his formal preparation for the ministry in the Spring of 1824, Emerson found the source of his greatest inspiration in the moral, religious example of John Milton and of his admirers such as Aunt Mary Moody Emerson, Dr. Channing, and Edward Everett.

When, eight years later, he went up to the White Mountains after announcing to his congregation his inability to share their view of the Communion rite, Emerson was obviously seeking a refuge in solitude for the further development of what he believed to be the best method of seeing. He wrote then in his journal: "Here, among the mountains, the pinions of thought should be strong, and one should see the errors of men from a calmer height of love and wisdom." [72] This "calmer height of love and wisdom" provided the best way of seeing, a mode of perception represented by Milton and all true poets.

Some months before, in February, 1832, Emerson had quoted Castelli's saying that Galileo's darkened eye had seen "more than all of those who are gone" and had "opened the eyes of all who are to come", and he had added the brief, emphatic comment: "So the eye of Milton." [73] This superiority of vision had resulted not only from the union of head and heart, but from the dominance of the heart in that union. The summer before Emerson went up to the mountains, he had recorded "Shaftesbury's maxim, That wisdom comes more from the heart than the head" and had

---

[69]   *Ibid.*, 345 (Feb. 20, 1824).
[70]   *Ibid.*, 360 (April 18, 1824).
[71]   *Ibid.*, 364.
[72]   *Ibid.*, II, 492 (July 6, 1832).
[73]   *Ibid.*, 466-67 (Feb. 20, 1832).

himself declared that "the moral sense is the proper keeper of
the doors of knowledge" and that the "point of view is of more
importance than the sharpness of sight".[74] To develop further,
in his own great crisis, this truly poetic "point of view", Emerson
sought in mountain solitude "a calmer height of love and wisdom".

The view he hoped to obtain from this "calmer height" would
be superior to the "half-views of half-men" like Shakespeare,
Swedenborg,[75] Voltaire, "who forsook good, aiming at truth, and
grew up half, or less than half, a man", and "many a religionist"
who "hurts the cause of religion by the opposite error".[76] In
March, 1831, he had not only written that "Milton, Burke, and
Webster get most of their wisdom from the heart",[77] but had
implied that Milton's verse, in contrast with Shakespeare's, indicated the dominance of the passive "intellect receptive" over
the active "intellect constructive": "The moment you describe
Milton's verse you use words implying, not creation, but increased perception, second-sight knowledge of what *is*, beyond
the ken of others. Yet these are prophecy...."[78] Indeed, Milton
was, for Emerson, a more highly developed man than Shakespeare because he was more inclined to receive divine truth than
to express it by means of his creative power. "Bacon, Shakespeare,
Caesar, Scipio, Cicero, Burke, Chatham, Franklin, – none of
them will bear examination or furnish the type of a *Man*",[79]
Emerson wrote later that summer when he sought the mountain
heights; but Milton, because of the vision produced by this "increased perception, second-sight knowledge of what *is*, beyond
the ken of others", was, especially in this period of severe trial,

[74]   *Ibid.*, 399 (July 6, 1831).
[75]   "Shakspeare; Or, The Poet", *Works*, IV, 219.
[76]   *Journals*, II, 363 (March 4, 1831).
[77]   *Ibid.*, 362.
[78]   *Ibid.*, 364. The omitted portion is not included in the text.
[79]   *Ibid.*, 505 (Aug. 12, 1832). Emerson's "type of a *Man*" reflects "this
Archetype of Man" that Milton described in his Latin poem "On the
Platonic Idea as Understood by Aristotle". *Cf. Journals*, III, 409 (Dec.
23, 1834): "Out of these fragmentary, lob-sided mortals shall the heaven
unite Phidias, Demosthenes, Shakspear, Newton, Napoleon, Bacon and
Saint John in one person."

an inspiring representative of the most highly developed mode of perception.[80]

This crucial period in Emerson's life seems to have effected a change in his attitude toward Milton: a deeper appreciation of what he found inspiring in his works and a growing impatience with passages that displeased him. On February 1, 1832, he wrote to a cousin of his wife's: "For poetry read Milton. If the *Paradise Lost* tires you, it is so stately, try the Minor Poems. *Comus*, if the mythology does not make it sound strange, is a beautiful poem and makes one holy to read it." [81] *Paradise Lost* was again slighted in an observation he made in May; compared with "the science of astronomy", it could not "elevate and astonish like Herschel or Somerville".[82]

During Emerson's voyage to Europe, the following winter, he claimed he could remember nearly all of *Lycidas*, and he referred to the story of Isis and Osiris that Milton had employed in *Areopagitica*.[83] Still at sea, two weeks later, he wrote: "Yet I comforted myself at midnight with *Lycidas*. What marble beauty in that classic pastoral. I should like well to see an analysis of

---

[80] See *ibid.*, 514-15 (Sept. 17, 1832): "Socrates believed in man's moral nature and knew and declared the fact that virtue was the supreme beauty. He was capable therefore of enthusiasm. Jesus Christ existed for it. He is its Voice to the world. Phocion felt it, recognized it, but was a man of action, true in act to this conviction; Luther, More, Fox, Milton, Burke, every great man, every one with whose character the idea of stability presents itself, had this faith. The true men are ever following an invisible Leader, and have left the responsibleness of their acts with God. But the artificial men have assumed their own bonds and can fall back on nothing greater than their finite fortunes; ... empirics with expedients for a few years, reputation instead of character, and fortune instead of wisdom. The true men stand by and let reason argue for them." The omitted portion is not included in the text. Burke is given a place in this list because of his faith in the moral sentiment. He was, therefore, not an "artificial" man, but one of the "true men" who are "ever following an Invisible Leader". Depite this faith, which made him a "true" rather than an "artificial" man, he could not "furnish the type of a *Man*" because of an insufficient development of the perception provided by the "head".

[81] *Journals*, II, 462. Letter to Miss Elizabeth Tucker, Feb. 1, 1832. See Rusk, *Letters*, I, 345.

[82] *Journals*, II, 487 (May 19, 1832).

[83] *Ibid.*, III, 3 (At sea, Jan. 2, 1833).

the pleasure it gives. That were criticism for the gods." [84] On Emerson's return voyage, Milton was again a source of moral strength. "I kept Sunday", he wrote, "with Milton and a Presbyterian magazine. Milton says, if ever any was ravished with moral beauty, he is the man." [85] Commenting on this thought the following day, Emerson revealed a significant aspect of his own moral and religious life:

Milton describes himself in his letter to Diodati as enamoured of moral perfection. He did not love it more than I. That which I cannot yet declare has been my angel from childhood until now. It has separated me from men. It has watered my pillow, it has driven sleep from my bed. It has tortured me for my guilt. It has inspired me with hope. It cannot be defeated by my defeats. It cannot be questioned, though all the martyrs apostatize. It is always the glory that shall be revealed; it is the "open secret" of the universe; and it is only the feebleness and dust of the observer that make it future, the whole is now potentially in the botom of his heart. It is the soul of religion. Keeping my eye on this, I understand all heroism, the history of loyalty and of martyrdom and of bigotry, the heat of the Methodist, the nonconformity of the Dissenter, the patience of the Quaker. [86]

Soon after his return, Emerson declared he was certain that "by going much alone a man will get more of a noble courage in thought and word than from all the wisdom that is in books". He then added: "He will come to hear God speak as audibly through his own lips as ever He did by the mouth of Moses or Isaiah or Milton." [87]

During the following year, when Emerson was attempting to find the right vocation without a church, he recalled Milton's example with even greater frequency. He quoted the "Sonnet On His Blindness" while expressing a view that he found then especially consoling:

If nobody wants us in the world, are we not excused from action & may we not blameless use the philosophy which teaches that by all events the individual is made wiser & that this may be an ultimate

[84]   *Ibid.*, 19 (Jan. 16, 1833).
[85]   *Ibid.*, 205 (At sea, Sept. 16, 1833).
[86]   *Ibid.*, 208-209 (Sept. 17, 1833).
[87]   *Ibid.*, 222 (Oct. 21, 1833).

object in the benevolence of the creator. "Thousands at his bidding speed They also serve who only stand & wait".[88]

In defending his own type of religion, Emerson quoted something Milton had said about Christ that would have made him condemned as a "free-thinker" in the vicinity of Boston:

A religion of forms is not for me. I honor the Methodists who find, like St. John, all Christianity in one word, Love. To the parishes in my neighborhood Milton would seem a freethinker when he says, "They [the Jews] thought it too much licence to follow the charming pipe of him who founded and proclaimed liberty and relief to all distresses." [89]

But Emerson found that Milton's learning "wrecked his originality": "Milton was too learned, though I hate to say it. It wrecked his originality. He was more indebted to the Hebrew than even to the Greek. Wordsworth is a more original poet than he." [90] On the same day, he declared that "There is nothing in Wordsworth so vicious in sentiment as Milton's account of God's chariots, etc., standing harnessed for great days" and added: "We republicans cannot relish Watts' or Milton's royal imagery." [91] He noted later that the poet's errors, in his battles for the right, were those that inevitably beset the "surface" level of awareness: "The idea is deep and pervades the whole mass of men and institutions involved, but that which makes the surface is the names of certain men and other accidents. Even the divine Milton recurs with bitterness to tippet and surplice, etc." [92] Yet, despite the "vicious" sentiment of the poet's "royal imagery" and other errors, Emerson listed Milton among those names that are "seeds" – "The sentiment which, like Milton's, comes down to

<hr/>

[88] "To William Emerson, Boston, January 18, 1834", *Letters*, I, 405.
[89] *Journals*, III, 284-85 (April 27, 1834).
[90] *Ibid.*, 328 (Aug. 17, 1834). *Cf. Ibid.*, IV, 92 (1836): "We come to Milton; learning threatened to make him giddy, but he was wise by ancient laws and clave to the piety and principle of his times. A whole new world of science and reflective thought has since opened which he knew not."
[91] *Ibid.*, III, 329 (August 17, 1834). Emerson would seem to be referring specifically to the description given in *Paradise Lost*, Book VII, lines 192-209.
[92] *Journals*, III, 366-67 (Nov. 19, 1834).

new generations is that which was no sham or half sentiment to Milton himself, but the utterance of his inmost self." [93] He included him also among "the most devout persons": those who are "the freest of their tongues in speaking of the Deity", "whose words are an offence to the pursed mouths which make formal prayers", and who, "beyond the word", are "free-thinkers also".[94]

In the middle of December, 1834, as Emerson indicated in a letter to his brother William,[95] he was planning the lecture on Milton he would give that winter. His journal entries, during the ensuing weeks, reveal both an intensified effort to put Milton "at a true focal distance" [96] and a continuing tendency to regard him as a representative of the moral ideal. In a significant passage on December 17, he referred to the superiority of "generosity of sentiment" to "genius" in human development and, with a quotation from *Paradise Lost* describing Raphael as he first appeared to Adam, presented an image of rebirth that he could have applied to Milton:

If it has so pleased God, it is very easy for you to surpass your fellows in genius; but surpass them in generosity of sentiment; see not their meanness, whilst your eyes are fixed on everlasting virtues; being royal, being divine, in your sentiment: "this shall be another morn risen on mid-noon." This shall be your own, – O no; God forbid! not your own, but a vast accession of the Divinity into your trembling clay.[97]

Referring, on December 19, to one function of those poets who represent the Sayer, Emerson chose another image borrowed from *Paradise Lost*: "The maker of a sentence, like the other

[93]   *Ibid.*, 351-52 (Oct. 29, 1834).
[94]   *Ibid.*, 378-79 (Dec. 2, 1834).
[95]   "For me I have got no farther in my selection of heads for my Lecture than to nominate four Luther Michel Angelo Milton George Fox. Many others gay dreadful or venerable uplift their brows out of the sea of generations but none yet have I dared to call mine." "To William Emerson, Concord, December 16 and 18, 1834", *Letters*, I, 428.
[96]   *Letters*, II, 173. Emerson wrote to Margaret Fuller on November 9, 1838, that it will be a great day for any mind "when it has come to put Shakspeare at a true focal distance".
[97]   *Journals*, III, 394 (Dec. 17, 1834). See *Paradise Lost*, Book V, lines 308-311.

artist, launches out into the infinite and builds a road into Chaos and old Night, and is followed by those who hear him with something of wild, creative delight." [98] For the combined function of perceiving and reporting divine truth, Emerson chose, a few days later, an image combining echoes of Bacon's *Essays* and *New Atlantis*, on the one hand, and Milton's description of Uriel, on the other:

It is a manifest interest which comes home to my bosom and every man's bosom, that there should be on every tower Watchers set to observe and report of every new ray of light, in what quarter soever of heaven it should appear, and their report should be eagerly and reverently received. There is no offence done, certainly, to the community in distinctly stating the claims of this office. [99]

Then, as if remembering Satan's bowing low before Uriel "As to superior Spirits is wont in Heav'n, Where honour due and reverence none neglects", Emerson referred to the "free-thinker" Milton as, like "every great man", reverent and loyal to "the institutions and orders of a state": "Throughout his being is he loyal. Such was Luther, Milton, Burke; each might be called an aristocrat, though by position the champion of the people." [100] Under the same date, December 27, he stated his position in regard to Christianity as he saw it and cited Milton, who "apprehended its nature", as authority:

It taught, it teaches the eternal opposition of the world to the truth, and introduced the absolute authority of the spiritual law. Milton apprehended its nature when he said, "For who is there almost that measures wisdom by simplicity, strength by suffering, dignity by lowliness?" [101]

After describing what he called the "Idea" of a man as "his genius, or his nature, or his turn of mind", Emerson quoted Milton on the "guiding Genius" of the ancients [102] and declared

[98] *Journals*, III, 395. See *Paradise Lost*, Book I, line 544; Book II, lines 1024-1030.
[99] *Journals*, III, 406-407 (Dec. 22, 1834). See *Paradise Lost*, Book III, lines 708-721.
[100] *Journals*, III, 414 (Dec. 27, 1834). See *Paradise Lost*, Book III, lines 736-38.
[101] *Journals*, III, 415-416 (Dec. 27, 1834).
[102] *Ibid.*, 417 (Dec. 27, 1834).

later that this poet drank deeply of Greek fountains, that "in an age and assembly of fierce fanatics, he drew as freely from these resources and with just acknowledgement, as from those known and honored by his party: – 'His soul was like a star and dwelt apart' ".[103] Referring to Milton's "class of men", that included "Socrates, St. Paul, Antoninus, Luther", he noted their effect: "We recognize with delight a strict likeness between their noblest impulses and our own. We are tried in their trial. By our cordial approval we conquer in their victory. We participate in their act by our thorough understanding of it." [104] A few days before delivering his lecture, Emerson praised "that word of Milton in his letter to Diodati excusing his friend for not writing to him": " 'for though you have not written, your probity writes to me in your stead' ",[105] and he commented on his beneficent influence as a nature poet: "If Milton, if Burns, if Bryant, is in the world, we have more tolerance, and more love for the changing sky, the mist, the rain, the bleak, overcast day, the indescribable sunrise and the immortal stars." [106] But this passage does not imply that Milton was significant chiefly as a nature poet. He transcended the limitations of those who could sing merely of the beauties of the physical world. He was most significant as an inspirer of love for the beauties of moral truth. Hence, Emerson's lecture would be primarily a "commentary on the character of John Milton".[107]

In his introduction, he remarked on the history of the poet's reputation, noting that, in his lifetime, he was "little, or not at all, known as a poet, but obtained great respect from his contemporaries as an accomplished scholar, and a formidable controvertist" and that "his prose writings, especially the 'Defence of the English People,' seem to have been read with avidity". Though "earnest, spiritual, rich with allusion, sparkling with in-

[103]   Ibid., 419-420 (Dec. 28, 1834). Wordsworth's line, from "London, 1802", was slightly changed by Emerson: "The soul was like a Star, and dwelt apart; . . ."
[104]   Journals, III, 441 (Jan. 13, 1835).
[105]   Ibid., 449 (Feb. 14, 1835).
[106]   Ibid., 449 (Feb. 16, 1835).
[107]   "John Milton", Early Lectures, I, 163.

numerable ornaments", these "remarkable compositions" failed
as "writings designed to gain a practical point": "There is no
attempt to conciliate, – no mediate, no preparatory course suggested, – but, peremptory and impassioned, he demands, on the
instant, an ideal justice.' [108] Rhetorically, they "must also suffer
some deduction. They have no perfectness". While they are
"wonderful for the truth, the learning, the subtilty and pomp of
the language", Emerson declared, "the whole is sacrificed to the
particular"; "he has never *integrated* the parts of the argument
in his mind".[109] The "worst of his works" is the "Defence of the
People of England"; it is saved only by "its general aim, and a
few elevated passages". "The lover of his genius will always
regret, that he should not have taken counsel of his own lofty
heart at this, as at other times, and have written from the deep
convictions of love and right, which are the foundations of civil
liberty." [110] Emerson added, however, that "when he comes to
speak of the reason of the thing, then he always recovers himself. The voice of the mob is silent, and Milton speaks." His
peroration, "in which he implores his countrymen to refute this
adversary by their great deeds, is in a just spirit." But the "most
splendid of his prose works" is his *Areopagitica*: "Is is, as Luther
said of one of Melancthon's writings, 'alive, hath hands and feet,
– and not like Erasmus's sentences, which were made, not grown.'
The weight of the thought is equalled by the vivacity of the expression, and it cheers as well as teaches." [111] However, times
have changed, and we have lost all interest in Milton "as the
redoubted disputant of a sect". By "his own innate worth this
man has steadily risen in the world's reverence, and occupies a
more imposing place in the mind of men at this hour than ever
before". Now he stands before all men in "the power *to inspire*".[112]

Hence, Emerson claimed, "we think no man can be named,
whose mind still acts on the cultivated intellect of England and

---

[108] *Ibid.*, 146.
[109] *Ibid.*
[110] *Ibid.*, 147.
[111] *Ibid.*
[112] *Ibid.*, 148.

America with an energy comparable to that of Milton". "Shakspeare is a voice merely; who and what he was that sang, that sings, we know not. Milton stands erect, commanding, still visible as a man among men, and reads the laws of the moral sentiment to the newborn race." [113] His "purely spiritual" influence "makes us jealous for his fame as for that of a near friend. He is identified in the mind with all select and holy images, with the supreme interests of the human race".

Because of what he has thus come to represent in our minds, we can now see with "more precision" that "no man in these later ages, and few men ever, possessed so great a conception of the manly character". According to Emerson, "the office of every great man" is "to raise the idea of Man in the minds of his contemporaries and of posterity, – to draw after nature a life of man, exhibiting such a composition of grace, of strength, and of virtue, as poet had not described nor hero lived". Milton has discharged this office better than any other great man. "Human nature in these ages is indebted to him for its best portrait." [114] Bacon, who wrote "much and with prodigious ability on this science, shrinks and falters before the absolute and uncourtly Puritan". While Shakespeare is "a voice merely", Bacon's essays reveal "an ambitious and profound calculator, – a great man of the vulgar sort. Of the upper world of man's being they speak few and faint words." [115] That "upper world of man's being" Milton represented by his own character; he was thus able to alert us to its reflection in his works. The "idea of a purer existence than any he saw around him, to be realized in the life and conversation of men, inspired every act and every writing of John Milton".[116] This "idea of a purer existence" is seen in his statement of the object of education and in his description of what is required of the true poet.[117] It is reflected in the noblest outline of a "wise and

[113]   *Ibid.*, 149.
[114]   *Ibid.*
[115]   *Ibid.*
[116]   *Ibid.*, 150.
[117]   *Ibid.*, See "Of Education", ed. Symmons, *The Prose Works*, I, 277; "An Apology for Smectymnuus", ed. Symmons, *The Prose Works*, I, 224. "He defined the object of education to be, 'to fit a man to perform justly,

external education" in all literature, that which appears in his "Letter to Samuel Hartlib". This outline shows us the skeleton of the ideal man as he saw him. "The muscles, the nerves, and the flesh, with which this skeleton is to be filled up and covered, exist in his works and must be sought there." [118] But, Emerson implied, we could not easily find "so great a conception of the manly character" in the poet's works without the inspiration we receive from his own character.

Emerson described next the "singular advantages' that helped Milton to delineate his "heroic image of man". "Perfections of body and of mind are attributed to him by his biographers"; they suggest the "ideal" portraits in legend and myth.[119] Without these "singular advantages", apparently, Milton could not have produced, in his work, the "heroic image of man" that was somehow a reflection of himself.

He had, indeed, "the senses of a Greek" – a "quick" eye and "acute" ear – which he "naturally received" with "a love of nature, and a rare susceptibility to impressions from external beauty". These qualities would seem to resemble what Emerson, in praising Shakespeare, called "Common Sense" and "humanity". They apparently suggested to Emerson the presence of "instinct", for they were accompanied by a rhythmic alternation of periods of creativeness corresponding with the changes of the seasons:

In the midst of London, he seems, like the creatures of the field and the forest, to have been tuned in concord with the order of the world; for, he believed, his poetic vein only flowed from the autumnal to the vernal equinox; and, in his essay on Education, he doubts whether, in the fine days of spring, any study can be accomplished by young men.[120]

This "sensibility to impressions from beauty needs no proof from

---

skilfully, and magnanimously all the offices, both private and public, of peace and war.' He declared, that 'he who would aspire to write well hereafter in laudable things, ought himself to be a true poem; that is, a composition and pattern of the best and honorablest things, not presuming to sing high praises of heroic men or famous cities, unless he have in himself the experience and the practice of all that which is praiseworthy.' "

[118]   "John Milton", *Early Lectures*, I, 150.

[119]   *Ibid.*

[120]   *Ibid.*, 151.

his history; it shines through every page", and it is seen in the effect produced by the "form and the voice of Leonora Baroni", who seems to have "captivated him in Rome".

Besides these "senses of a Greek" and corresponding love of "external beauty", Milton possessed a "power of language" that rivals Shakespeare's. First, "his address and his conversation were worthy of his fame".[121] Then, too, he acquired "a profound skill in all the treasures of the Latin, Greek, Hebrew, and Italian tongues", and his foreign travel "contributed to forge and polish that great weapon of which he acquired such extraordinary mastery, – his power of language". But, more importantly, he surpassed all writers as a benefactor of the English tongue: "No individual writer has been an equal benefactor of the English tongue by showing its capabilities." [122] While his mind seemed "to have no thought or emotion which refused to be recorded",[123] he was obviously, for Emerson, more representative of the Sayer, the true poet, than was Shakespeare, because he was more "conscious". Milton, Emerson declared, was "conscious of possessing this intellectual voice, penetrating through ages, and propelling its melodious undulations forward through the coming world", and "he knew also, that this mastery of language was a secondary power, and he respected the mysterious source whence it had its spring; namely, clear conceptions, and a devoted heart".[124]

This "consciousness", springing from the combination of "clear conceptions" and "a devoted heart", reflected, Emerson implied, the stage of Redemption. In Milton, "humanity rights itself":

But, as basis or fountain of his rare physical and intellectual accomplishments, the man Milton was just and devout. He is rightly dear to mankind, because in him, – among so many perverse and partial men of genius, – in him humanity rights itself; the old eternal goodness finds a home in his breast, and for once shows itself beautiful. And his virtues are so graceful, that they seem rather talents than labors. Among so many contrivances as the world has seen to

121   *Ibid.*
122   *Ibid.*, 152.
123   *Ibid.*, 153.
124   *Ibid.*

make holiness ugly, in Milton, at least, it was so pure a flame, that the foremost impression his character makes, is that of elegance.[125]

The "foremost impression his character makes" is "that of elegance". Milton represented, therefore, a union of the best qualities of such "half-men" as Swedenborg the saint and Shakespeare the player. These qualities were united in him, not conflicting as in Bacon, and he did not "grope in graves" nor "trifle".[126]

Indeed, Milton represented also, for Emerson, a union of classic and of Christian virtues. His classic virtue would seem to have stemmed from a fundamental "humanity" resembling Shakespeare's moral feelings; however, in Milton, the "humanity" had grown into a "magnanimity", or "native honor", which manifested itself in his praise of chastity, his amusements, and his "antique heroism".[127] This classic virtue was combined with his "genius of the Christian sanctity", expressed by Milton more truly than it was by most prophets and saints because he better understood "what is peculiar in the Christian ethics": its emphasizing chiefly humility.[128] According to Emerson, the poet's "own perception of the doctrine of humility" was provided by the divine "sentiment", obedience to which made him deserving of "the apostrophe of Wordsworth" which concludes with the words "and yet thy heart The lowliest duties on itself did lay".[129] In other words, Milton saw clearly the truth of "the doctrine of humility" because "he felt the heats of that 'love' which 'esteems no office mean'". This "religious sentiment warmed his writings and conduct with the highest affection of faith". Hence, "for the first time since many ages, the invocations of the Eternal Spirit

---

[125] *Ibid.*, 154.
[126] "Shakspeare; Or, The Poet", *Works*, IV, 219.
[127] "John Milton", *Early Lectures*, I, 155-56. In "Modern Literature", *Works*, XII, 321, Emerson attributed to Wordsworth "that property common to all great poets, a wisdom of humanity, which is superior to any talents which they exert. It is the wisest part of Shakespeare and of Milton. For they are poets by the free course which they allow to the informing soul, which through their eyes beholdeth again and blesseth the things which it hath made. The soul is superior to its knowledge, wiser than any of its works."
[128] *Ibid.*, 156.
[129] *Ibid.*, 156-57. See Wordsworth's sonnet "London, 1802".

in the commencement of his books, are not poetic forms, but are
thoughts". They are still read, therefore, with delight. They imply
a "divine leading" by the "sentiment", which is the "Eternal
Spirit". His views, furthermore, of "choice of profession, and
choice in marriage", Emerson declared, "equally expect" such a
"divine leading". Thus, he united in himself a classic "magnanimity" and a Christian "humility" which comprised the chief
and most distinctive virtues of both traditions.

Milton, therefore, was "chosen, by the felicity of his nature
and of his breeding, for the clear perception of all that is graceful
and all that is great in man". He was "gentle, learned, delicately
bred in all the elegancy of art and learning". But he was "not
less happy in his times". He was born in a period unsurpassed
in "the general activity of mind". However, it was a period of
conflict, of "the agitated years, when the discontents of the
English Puritans were fast drawing to a head against the tyranny
of the Stuarts", when "questions that involve all social and personal rights were hasting to be decided by the sword, and were
searched by eyes to which the love of freedom, civil and religious,
lent new illumination". Milton was then "set down in England in
the stern, almost fanatic, society of the Puritans". Yet the fact
that it was a period of conflict proved to be advantageous, for
"the part he took, the zeal of his fellowship, make us acquainted
with the greatness of his spirit, as in tranquil times we could not
have known it".[130]

In fact, Emerson seems to imply that Milton represented a
union of the best tendencies of both sides; though "the flower of
elegancy", he threw himself on "the side of humanity . . . unlearned and unadorned. His muse was brave and humane, as well
as sweet." [131] That "humanity, which warms his pages, begins as
it should at home": he felt "the dear love of native land and
native language". Hence, "he preferred his own English, so man-
like he was, to the Latin, which contained all the treasures of his
memory", and "he meditated writing a poem on the settlement
of Britain", "a history of England was one of the three main

[130]   *Ibid.*, 157-58.
[131]   *Ibid.*, 158.

tasks which he proposed to himself", he "studied with care the character of his countrymen, and once in the 'History,' and once again in the 'Reason of Church Government,' he has recorded his judgment of the English genius". However, though "drawn into the great controversies of the times, in them he is never lost in a party". He was distinguished from them by his "private opinions and private conscience". Thus, while he represented historically a union of the best tendencies of both sides, Emerson saw him as transcending, by his humble obedience to the "divine leading", the limitations of each. As a true poet, or "reconciler", he was therefore a "synthesis", representing the high water mark of divine manifestation in his age.

That high water mark was the love that distinguished Milton. It saved him from being "lost in a party": "That which drew him to the party was his love of liberty, ideal liberty; this therefore he could not sacrifice to any party." Hence, he was truly "an apostle of freedom". What he desired was "the liberty of the wise man". He "pushed", therefore, "as far as any in that democratic age", his ideas of civil and ecclesiastical liberty; the tracts he wrote on these topics, as well as those on literary and domestic liberty, are, "for the most part", Emerson claimed, "as fresh and pertinent today, as they were then". True to the "divine leading", this "philanthropist" utilized the opportunities provided by the historical situation "to blow his trumpet for human rights". While his tracts were "all varied applications of one principle, the liberty of the wise man", they were marked by his search for "absolute truth, not accommodating truth". Therefore, "his opinions on all subjects are formed for man as he ought to be, for a nation of Miltons". The "most devout man of his time", he was, "throughout all his actions and opinions", "a consistent spiritualist, or believer in the omnipotence of spiritual laws".[132]

---

[132]   *Ibid.*, 159-160. In his notes for this lecture, Emerson wrote: "Milton belongs to the race of Bards & Prophets a class of men always continued in a line in history as Levites or true priests & in some fortunate ages immediately intelligible to the people; generally, believed to speak a high speculative & quite impracticable truth, & requiring that some mild two-edged Aaron less wise than the seer more good than the people should go between them & the man who had seen the face of God. Milton sought

At this point in his lecture, Emerson attempted to illuminate the symbolic aspects of the image he was invoking in the minds of his audience. "Was there not a fitness in the undertaking of such a person", he asked, "to write a poem on the subject of Adam, the first man?" "By his sympathy with all nature; by the proportion of his powers; by great knowledge, and by religion, he would reascend to the height from which our nature is supposed to have descended. From a just knowledge of what man should be, he described what he was." [133] When we are "fairly in Eden", Emerson declared, "Adam and Milton are often difficult to be separated." [134] Milton's Adam, representing Emerson's ideal if not the poet's, exemplifies the perfect fusion of superior physical and spiritual qualities and, in doing so, suggests a new and higher species. He is a "divine creature" whose soul is "excellent as his form", and "the tone of his thought and passion is as healthful, as even, and as vigorous, as befits the new and perfect model of a race of gods". Significantly, it was not only his character, but also his perception of this "purer ideal of humanity" that made Milton, who "would reascend to the height from which our nature is supposed to have descended", a symbol of Redemption and rebirth, the completing of a lower cycle of human development and the beginning of another on a higher plane.

This perception, Emerson claimed, "modifies his poetic genius". It makes him more than just a great poet:

The man is paramount to the poet. His fancy is never transcendent, extravagant; but, as Bacon's imagination was said to be "the noblest that ever contented itself to minister to the understanding," so Milton's ministers to character. Milton's sublimest song, bursting into heaven with its peal of melodious thunder, is the voice of Milton still ... The creations of Shakspeare are cast into the world of

only absolute truth not accommodating truth, no compromise." Houghton 194.6. Similarly, he likened Milton to Jeremiah: "The tragic part is his knowledge that he was alone. Like Jeremiah he says Wo is me my mother that thou hast borne me a man of strife. he feels the sad condition of Vision. that unhappy handful of men whose misfortune it is to have understanding." *Ibid.* See also *Early Lectures,* I, 450, note.

[133] *Ibid.*, 160.
[134] *Ibid.*, 161.

thought, to no farther end than to delight. Their intrinsic beauty is their excuse for being. Milton, fired "with dearest charity to infuse the knowledge of good things into others," tasked his giant imagination, and exhausted the stores of his intellect, for an end beyond, namely, to teach.[135]

While Emerson referred often to Shakespeare's great brain, it was Milton's heart that impressed him: "His own conviction it is, which gives such authority to his strain. Its reality is its force. If out of the heart it came, to the heart it must go." In thus representing the type of the true poet, the Sayer, Milton manifested the restoration of a harmonious relationship between the heart and the brain, but a relationship superior to that existing before the Fall because in him the heart was dominant.[136]

Concluding his lecture, Emerson called Milton "an angelic soul" who suffered "more keenly than others from the unavoidable evils of human life". He was "a man whom labor or danger never deterred from whatever efforts a love of the supreme interests of man prompted". His "angelic devotion" in "a revolutionary age" – with "the bravery, the purity, the temperance, the toil, the independence" – led him, "in his writings and in his life, to carry out the life of man to new heights of spiritual grace and dignity, without any abatement of its strength." All men are consequently the beneficiaries of his love.[137]

Emerson's view of Milton would seem not to have materially changed after he gave this lecture in 1835. He continued to

---

[135] *Ibid.*, 160-62. The quotation " 'with dearest charity to infuse the knowledge of good things into others' " is a paraphrase of a passage from Milton's "Apology for Smectymnuus". See Symmons, ed., *The Prose Works of John Milton*, I, 268.

[136] "To Elizabeth Palmer Peabody, Concord, August 3, 1835", *Letters*, I, 450. See *Paradise Regained*, I, 171-72. "The two attributes of wisdom & goodness always face & always approach each other. Each when perfect becomes the other. Yet to the moral nature belongs sovereignty, & so we have an instinctive faith that to it all things shall be added, that the moral nature being righted, the circulations of the Universe take effect thro' the man as a member in its place, & so he learns sciences after a natural or divine way. A good deed conspires with all nature, as 'the hand sang with the voice' in the angels' concert, but there's a kind of falsehood in the enunciation of a chemical or astronomical law by an unprincipled savant."

[137] *Op. cit.*, 162-63.

praise the poet's character in similar terms, and he retained, so far as the works were concerned, similar reservations. Later, for example, he employed in *English Traits* an image that, in view of his conviction that Milton's character was superior to Shakespeare's, suggests escalators moving in opposite directions as symbols of the "two histories": Milton was "the stair or high table-land to let down the English genius from the summits of Shakspeare".[138] Milton thus continued to represent, for Emerson, an evolution of character proceeding simultaneously with a decline of creative genius.

This decline in Milton's age accompanied an increased dependence on the past which, according to Emerson, was reflected in the poet's bookishness. Milton was "the most literary man in literature".[139] He was, indeed, "too literary".[140] But, Emerson insisted, "The poet should rejoice if he has taught us to despise his song; if he has so moved us as to lift us, – and to open the eye of the intellect to see farther and better." If he has done so, then "perhaps Homer and Milton will be tin pans yet".[141] Grateful for the inspiration the poet had given him, Emerson could easily excuse the fact that "learning threatened to make him giddy", for "he was wise by ancient laws and clave to the piety and principle of his times. A whole new world of science and reflective thought has since opened which he knew not." [142] In other words, as a symbol of the Sayer, he was, through his learning, too much indebted to the "Old"; but his effect on history is like that of Jesus, and he was clothed with beauty.[143] Indeed, while his works did not sufficiently reflect the beautiful "newness" of each fresh appearance of eternal truth to the ideal poet-priest, because they were usually draped in the old garments that the living truth had long since cast off, "Lycidas" and "Comus", at least, were notable exceptions: they were "made of pure po-

[138] "Literature", *Works*, V, 244. *English Traits* was published in 1856.
[139] *Journals*, VI, 369 (March 23, 1843).
[140] "The Poet", *Works*, III, 38.
[141] "Poetry and Imagination", *Works*, VIII, 68.
[142] *Journals*, IV, 92 (Sept. 23, 1836).
[143] *Ibid.*, VI, 141 (Dec. 18, 1841).

etry".[144] "Lycidas", in fact, was "a copy from the poet's mind printed out in the book, notwithstanding all the mechanical difficulties, as clear and wild as it had shone at first in the sky of his own thought".[145]

These two poems, therefore, were the clearest reflections of Milton's "self-reliance". They best revealed the "highest merit" of his character: "Familiar as the voice of the mind is to each, the highest merit we ascribe to Moses, Plato and Milton is that they set at naught books and traditions, and spoke not what man, but what *they* thought." [146] This "self-reliance", the complete reliance on God, the inner "self", depends on humility. "In the Christian graces", Emerson insisted, "humility stands highest of all, in the form of the Madonna; and in life, this is the secret of the wise." [147] While "properly the exaltation of the Spirit",[148] it is "a sentiment of our insignificance when the benefit of the universe is considered." [149] In his lecture he had said of Milton: "Few men could be cited who have so well understood what is peculiar in the Christian ethics, and the precise aid it has brought to men" – the fact that it lays "its chief stress on humility". That "true greatness is a perfect humility" is a "revelation" of Christianity "which Milton well understood". It gives, Emerson had declared, "an inexhaustible truth to all his compositions. His firm grasp of this truth is his weapon against the prelates." Moreover, his "own perception of the doctrine of humility" is revealed, not only in his writings, but in his life: "He laid on himself the lowliest duties." "He felt the heats of that 'love' which 'esteems no office mean.' " [150]

Emerson continued, therefore, to associate humility and its counterpart, "self-reliance", with Milton's character. He wrote,

[144] "Preface", *Parnassus*, p. vii.
[145] *Journals*, III, 571 (Nov. 14, 1835).
[146] "Self-Reliance', *Works*, II, 45.
[147] "Works and Days", *Works*, VII, 176.
[148] *Journals*, II, 300 (July 15, 1830).
[149] "Character", *Works*, X, 93.
[150] "John Milton", *Early Lectures*, I, 156-57. Emerson had just quoted from Wordsworth's "London, 1802": "and yet thy heart The lowliest duties on herself did lay", substituting "itself" for the "herself" in the original poem.

not long after he gave his lecture: "The mystery of Humility is treated of by Jesus, by Dante, by Chaucer in his Griselda, by Milton and by Sampson Reed." [151] In August, 1836, he wrote: "Humility characterises the highest class of genius, Homer, Milton, Shakspear. We expect flashes of thought, but this is highest yet; The sorrows of Adam and Eve." [152] Yet it would seem that, for Emerson, while Shakespeare's works contain more "flashes of thought" than do Milton's, they reveal less humility – the "exaltation of the Spirit", "a sentiment of our insignificance when the benefit of the universe is considered."

Though giving "an inexhaustible truth" to all Milton's compositions, this Christian virtue was specifically represented by the poet not only in his description of the "sorrows of Adam and Eve", but also in his portrayal of Eve as a symbol of humility in "the form of the Madonna":

We men have no right to say it, but the omnipotence of Eve is in humility. The instincts of mankind have drawn the Virgin Mother
> "Created beings all in lowliness
> Surpassing, as in height above them all."
This is the Divine Person whom Dante and Milton saw in vision. This is the victory of Griselda, her supreme humility. And it is when love has reached this height that all our pretty rhetoric begins to have meaning. When we see that, it adds to the soul a new soul, it is honey in the mouth, music in the ear and balsam in the heart.[153]

In Shakespeare, love had not "reached this height".

This moral difference between the two great poets is apparent, in their works, in their treatment of symbols. While Shakespeare "saw the splendor of meaning that plays over the visible world; knew that a tree had another use than for apples, and corn another than for meal, and the ball of the earth, than for tillage and roads", he merely "employed them as colors to compose his picture". Resting in their beauty, as Emerson described it, he "never took the step which seemed inevitable to such genius,

---

[151]   *Journals*, III, 496 (June 26, 1835). Sampson Reed (1800-80), a Swedenborgian, wrote *Observations on the Growth of the Mind* (1826), an essay that greatly impressed the young Emerson.
[152]   *Ibid.*, IV, 83 (Aug. 29, 1836).
[153]   "Woman", *Works*, XI, 413.

namely to explore the virtue which resides in these symbols and imparts this power." Instead, "he converted the elements which waited on his command, into entertainments. He was master of the revels to mankind." [154] Shakespeare had had sufficient humility for him to receive divine truth, but not enough to receive it in the form of Moral Sentiment; since the Spirit had not been exalted over the "instinct" on his level of moral and religious growth, he had not been impelled "to explore the virtue which resides in these symbols and imparts this power". Milton, on the other hand, was no "master of the revels". He did not rest in the beauty of "the elements which waited on his command" to convert them into entertainments, but "took the step" and explored the virtue they symbolized. Yet, though "heartily enamoured" of those "sweet thoughts" they suggested, he knew that "this correspondence of things to thoughts is far deeper" than he could penetrate, "defying adequate expression; that it is elemental, or in the core of things".[155] With such profound reverence for the religious truths variously symbolized in the physical world, Milton drew his readers into "the new & delicious atmosphere of Genius, the Benefactor".[156] He made others his beneficiaries. From that "celestial region of Milton and Angels", he spoke.[157]

His "grace of humility", therefore, was apparently similar to that of "George Fox, Behmen, Scougal, the Mahometan Saint Rabia, and the Hindoos", who have "the art to cheapen the world thereby". But such experts on the subject as Emerson himself lack it:

Jesus was grand where he stood, and let Rome and London dance after Nazareth. But the thinkers or litterateurs of humility are not humble. Thus Alcott, Thoreau, and I know the use and superiority of it, but I cannot praise our practice.[158]

Since "genius takes its rise out of the Mountains of Rectitude" and "all beauty and power, which men covet, are born out of

[154] "Shakspeare; Or, The Poet", *Works*, IV, 217.
[155] "Poetry and Imagination", *Works*, VIII, 29.
[156] "To Mary Moody Emerson, London, June 22, 1848", *Letters*, IV, 90.
[157] *Journals*, VI, 223 (July 12, 1842).
[158] *Ibid.*, X, 19 (April, 1864).

that Humility egg which they disdain",[159] Milton's beauty and his
"power *to inspire*" were thus born in his assumption of those
"lowliest duties" whose value had escaped the notice of the
"master of the revels to mankind".

Hence, although Milton was "the stair or high table-land to
let down the English genius from the summits of Shakspeare",
he was like the man Emerson described in the following passage:
"A man in the view of absolute goodness, adores, with total
humility. Every step so downward, is a step upward. The man
who renounces himself, comes to himself." [160] Because of this
kind of humility, which was different from Shakespeare's, Milton
represented a higher synthesis of opposites.

Referring to "classes of men", Emerson saw him as a synthesis
of those intellectual qualities that made Shakespeare primarily
a "man of the world" and of those moral feelings that made men
like Swedenborg saints. Milton outsainted the saints because he
was also "of the world": "What a saint is Milton! How grateful
we are to the man of the world who obeys the morale, as in
humility, and in the obligation to serve mankind." [161] He revealed
that the deity as "intellect" and as "moral sentiment" "in the
last analysis can never be separated".[162] But, early in life, Emerson had seen that this synthesis Milton represented was like
Shakespeare's because it included powers of perception derived
from worldly experience:

It would seem as if abundant erudition, foreign travel, and gymnastic
exercises must be annexed to his awful imagination and fervent piety
to finish Milton. That the boisterous childhood, careless of criticism
and poetry, the association of vulgar and unclean companions, were
necessary to balance the towering spirit of Shakspeare, and that Mr.
Wordsworth has failed of pleasing by being too much a *poet*.[163]

[159]   *Ibid.*, VIII, 14 (1849).
[160]   "An Address" (Delivered before the Divinity School), *Works*, I, 122.
[161]   *Journals*, X, 154 (July 2, 1866). *Cf. Journals*, VII, 478 (1848):
"Carlyle is mixed up with the politics of the day, earth-son Antaeus.
Milton mixes with politics, but from the ideal side."
[162]   "Greatness", *Works*, VIII, 302.
[163]   *Journals*, II, 106 (Letter to Miss Emerson, Cambridge, June 30, 1826).
See *Letters*, I, 169.

The worldly element in Milton, however, was obviously of a higher moral order, and this fact, paradoxically, made him less of a *poet* than Shakespeare. His "Humility egg", in giving birth to "beauty and power", had produced the knowledge that "this correspondence of things to thoughts is far deeper" than he could penetrate, "defying adequate expression; that it is elemental, or in the core of things". Milton's "intellect receptive", therefore, had achieved dominance over his "intellect constructive". As a true poet, or Sayer, he was more concerned with the passive acceptance of divine truths than with their inevitably inadequate enunciation in his art.

Although both Shakespeare and Milton, according to this view, could receive truths and create new forms to express them because their humility permitted the unification of thought and feeling necessary for the infusions of deity, Milton's unity was of a higher order: it revealed more effectively the oneness of the divine trinity. Hence, Emerson tended to describe Milton, more frequently than Shakespeare, in the terms of a synthesis. He saw him, for example, as representing a synthesis of the "two classes of poets":

There are two classes of poets, – the poets by education and practice, these we respect; and poets by nature, these we love. Pope is the best type of the one class: he had all the advantage that taste and wit could give him, but never rose to grandeur or to pathos. Milton had all its advantages, but was also poet born. Chaucer, Shakspeare, Jonson (despite all the pedantic lumber he dragged with him), Herbert, Herrick, Collins, Burns, – of the other.[164]

Similarly, more than ten years after his lecture on the poet, Emerson again described Milton as a synthesis, but this time of three, not two elements: native English stock, Greek and Hebrew influences:

Criticism is in its infancy. The anatomy of genius it has not unfolded. Milton in the egg, it has not found. Milton is a good apple on that tree of England. It would be impossible, by any chemistry we know, to compound that apple otherwise: it required all the tree; and out of a thousand of apples, good and bad, this specimen apple is at

[164] "Preface", *Parnassus*, p.iv.

last procured. That is: We have a well-knit, hairy, industrious Saxon race, Londoners intent on their trade, steeped in their politics; wars of the Roses; voyages and trade to the Low Countries, to Spain, to Lepanto, to Virginia, and Guiana – all bright with use and strong with success. Out of this valid stock choose the validest boy, and in the flower of this strength open to him the whole Dorian and Attic beauty and the proceeding ripeness of the same in Italy. Give him the very best of this Classic beverage. He shall travel to Florence and Rome in his early manhood: he shall see the country and the works of Dante, Angelo, and Raffaelle. Well, on the man to whose unpalled taste this delicious fountain is opened, add the fury and concentration of the Hebraic genius, through the hereditary and already culminated Puritanism, – and you have Milton, a creation impossible before or again; and all whose graces and whose majesties involve this wonderful combination; – quite in the course of things once, but not iterated. The drill of the regiment, the violence of the pirate and smuggler, the cunning and thrift of the haberdasher's counter, the generosity of the Norman earl, are all essential to the result.[165]

It is significant that "Milton in the egg" was produced by seeds of bad as well as good English apples. Good and bad are erroneously perceived as essentially distinct and in conflict only on our second level of development, that of the Fall. Milton represented for Emerson the third level, Redemption, where the tendencies whose apparent opposition in time produced Bacon's "double consciousness" are seen united once again in eternity.

---

[165] *Journals*, VII, 213-14 (June 27, 1846).

CONCLUSION

1

Dr. Oliver Wendell Holmes, in his life of Emerson,[1] likened the quotations in his works to "the miraculous draught of fishes". "He believed in quotation, and borrowed from everybody and every book. Not in any stealthy or shamefaced way, but proudly, as a king borrows from one of his attendants the coin that bears his own image and superscription."[2] Holmes found "a key to Emerson's workshop" in his essay "Quotation and Originality".[3] That essay is indeed such a key; it both illuminates Emerson's method of borrowing and attempts to explain, if not to justify, large indebtedness to others in terms consistent with his philosophy. It is the chief source of Emerson's ideas on this subject.

His epigraph to the essay indicates clearly his philosophical approach:

Old and new put their stamp to everything in Nature. The snowflake that is now falling is marked by both. The present moment gives the

[1] *Ralph Waldo Emerson*, 1885.
[2] As quoted in Emerson, *Works*, VIII, 403, editor's note 1 to p. 203. Holmes counted "the named references, chiefly to authors, and found them to be three thousand three hundred and ninety-three, relating to eight hundred and sixty-eight different individuals. He also gives a list of those to whom there are twenty or more references." *Ibid.* These figures would be considerably enlarged by Emerson's borrowings in works to which Holmes did not have access.
[3] *Ibid.* "This essay was read as the second lecture in a course given at Freeman Place Chapel in Boston in March, 1859, following 'The Law of Success' and preceding 'Clubs.' Mr. Emerson seems to have made few changes in it." *Ibid.*, 398, editor's note.

motion and the color of the flake, Antiquity its form and properties. All things wear a lustre which is the gift of the present, and a tarnish of time.[4]

When truth appears in a flux, the "old", wearing "a tarnish of time", is its "form and properties", the "new", wearing a "lustre" bestowed by the present, is its "motion and the color". The "lustres" Emerson sought in his reading were glimpses of ancient truths from the wholly new and unique position of his "angle of vision". Viewed from his own position, therefore, these opposites, the "old" and the "new", corresponded with the universal masculine and feminine principles, centrifugence and centripetence, thought and feeling, "Imagination" and "Composition", "words" and tone. The newness of old "words" resulted from tone.

In the essay itself, Emerson claimed that "there is no pure originality. All minds quote. Old and new make the warp and woof of every moment. There is no thread that is not a twist of these two strands."[5] The history of philosophy reveals "this perpetual circle":

The highest statement of new philosophy complacently caps itself with some prophetic maxim from the oldest learning. There is something mortifying in this perpetual circle. This extreme economy argues a very small capital of invention. The stream of affection flows broad and strong; the practical activity is a river of supply; but the dearth of design accuses the penury of intellect. How few thoughts![6]

In literature, "the debt is immense to past thought. None escapes it. The originals are not original. There is limitation, model and suggestion, to the very archangels, if we knew their history." If you read Tasso, "you think of Virgil; read Virgil, and you think of Homer; and Milton forces you to reflect how narrow are the limits of human invention." Similarly, "Hegel preexists in Proclus, and, long before, in Heraclitus and Parmenides". And "Swedenborg, Behmen, Spinoza, will appear original to uninstructed and to thoughtless persons: Their originality will disappear to such as

---

[4] "Quotation and Originality", *Works*, VIII, 175.
[5] *Ibid.*, 178.
[6] *Ibid.*, 179.

are either well read or thoughtful; for scholars will recognize their dogmas as reappearing in men of a similar intellectual elevation throughout history." [7] While in "romantic literature examples of this vamping abound", [8] it would seem "that only the first men were well alive, and the existing generation is invalided and degenerate", but a "more subtle and severe criticism might suggest that some dislocation has befallen the race; that men are off their centre; that multitudes of men do not live with nature, but behold it as exiles". Thus Emerson's habits of mind led him to view this subject as a reflection of the "faithful" and "poetic" history of humanity. As opposed to "self-reliance", indebtedness characterizes the "romantic" period, the Fall. "Quotation confesses inferiority." [9]

Yet, for the fallen "exiles" it serves a useful purpose: "In literature, quotation is good only when the writer whom I follow goes my way, and, being better mounted than I, gives me a cast, as we say; but if I like the gay equipage so well as to go out of my road, I had better have gone afoot." [10] Coleridge had given Emerson himself such a "cast":

Original power is usually accompanied with assimilating power, and we value in Coleridge his excellent knowledge and quotations perhaps as much, possibly more, than his original suggestions. If an author gives us just distinctions, inspiring lessons, or imaginative poetry, it is not so important to us whose they are. If we are fired and guided by these, we know him as a benefactor, and shall return to him as long as he serves us so well. [11]

"Genius borrows nobly." A certain "valor" in a writer's tone may indicate his "consciousness that truth is the property of no individual, but is the treasure of all men. And inasmuch as any writer has ascended to a just view of man's condition, he has adopted this tone." It is heard in Bacon's line: " 'I take all knowledge to be my province.' " "In so far as the receiver's aim is on

7   *Ibid.*, 180-81.
8   *Ibid.*, 186.
9   *Ibid.*, 187-88.
10 *Ibid.*, 189.
11 *Ibid.*, 190-91.

life, and not on literature, will be his indifference to the source." [12]

Emerson sought, in his own writings, to attain originality chiefly in his tone; its cause was the uniqueness of his "angle of vision":

Truth is always present: it only needs to lift the iron lids of the mind's eye to read its oracles. But the moment there is the purpose of display, the fraud is exposed. In fact, it is as difficult to appropriate the thoughts of others, as it is to invent. Always some steep transition, some sudden alteration of temperature, or of point of view, betrays the foreign interpolation. [13]

Originality of tone, he believed, may be attained by selection – "the use and relevancy of the sentence" – and by emphasis: "As the journals say, 'the italics are ours.' " [14]

The whole subject of "quotation and originality", moreover, illustrates the "organic principle". Since "all things are in flux", it is

... inevitable that you are indebted to the past. You are fed and formed by it. The old forest is decomposed for the composition of the new forest ... So it is in thought. Our knowledge is the amassed thought and experience of innumerable minds: our language, our science, our religion, our opinions, our fancies we inherited.

But "there remains the indefeasible persistency of the individual to be himself. One leaf, one blade of grass, one meridian, does not resemble another. Every mind is different; and the more it is unfolded, the more pronounced is that difference." [15]

Hence, Emerson claimed, "To all that can be said of the preponderance of the Past, the single word Genius is a sufficient reply. The divine resides in the new. The divine never quotes, but is, and creates. The profound apprehension of the Present is Genius, which makes the Past forgotten." Believing "its faintest presentiment against the testimony of all history",

---

[12] *Ibid.*, 191-92.
[13] *Ibid.*, 193.
[14] *Ibid.*, 194.
[15] *Ibid.*, 200-201. This idea is consistent with Emerson's belief that Milton's individuality in his life and works was far more pronounced than Shakespeare's; he represented a higher development.

"Genius" "knows that facts are not ultimates, but that a state of mind is the ancestor of everything". While Originality is "being, being one's self, and reporting accurately what we see and are", "Genius" is characterized by the following:

Genius is in the first instance, sensibility, the capacity of receiving just impressions from the external world, and the power of coordinating these after the laws of thought. It implies Will, or original force, for their right distribution and expression. If to this the sentiment of piety be added, if the thinker feels that the thought most strictly his own is not his own, and recognizes the perpetual suggestion of the Supreme Intellect, the oldest thoughts become new and fertile whilst he speaks them.[16]

Emerson expressed his dislike of the poet's choosing "an antique or far-fetched subject for his muse, as if he avowed want of insight. The great deal always with the nearest." [17]

In his concluding paragraph, he reiterated: "We cannot overstate our debt to the Past, but the moment has the supreme claim. The Past is for us; but the sole terms on which it can become ours are its subordination to the Present." He warned: "We must not tamper with the organic motion of the soul." And he concluded with a final organic image: "This vast memory is only raw material. The divine gift is ever the instant life, which receives and uses and creates, and can well bury the old in the omnipotency with which Nature decomposes all her harvest for recomposition." [18]

Thus Emerson expressed his own views on the subject of "quotation and originality". He was aware of the tradition he was following by natural inclination and choice, and the "valor" in the tone of many of his vatic pronouncements proceeded largely from that awareness. But it is obvious from this essay alone that he regarded his great indebtedness to the past as a reflection of the Fall. His statements on the subject were therefore in keeping with his philosophy, his habits of thought and feeling; they reveal a wise, not a "foolish consistency".

[16]   *Ibid.*, 201-202.
[17]   *Ibid.*, 203.
[18]   *Ibid.*, 204.

II

Emerson's evaluations of the characters of Shakespeare, Bacon, and Milton show that his thoughts, conveyed by "words", were undeniably Coleridgean. As this study has shown, he produced "just distinctions, inspiring lessons", and often created "imaginative poetry", but his criticism contained little that was truly original. Yet his statements possess a quality that is unique. This quality, which Emerson would call "tone", has demonstrated its power to inspire: especially during the years before the Civil War it fortified the morale, enriched the religious experience, stimulated the moral thinking and feeling, and excited the imagination of multitudes of listeners and readers of all classes; and, despite the changes of a century, this "tone" reverberates still. While this study, concerned chiefly with his ideas, has not attempted to show the originality of this quality in his works, it is obvious in the many quotations that have been presented; it is that which is distinctly Emersonian in his statement of old "truths". He succeeded to a remarkable degree in doing what he had attempted to do.

This achievement was noted by the elder Henry James. "A spare New Englander came to New York to lecture; and the tone and spirit of the man, still more than what he said, bespoke a *spiritual* authority beyond the reach of scribes." [19] Thus Austin Warren has described the effect Emerson made on James in the Spring of 1842. James presented his view in his lecture on Emerson, composed about 1868 and read a few times to private audiences:

I shall have ill succeeded in my task, if I fail to convince you that Mr. Emerson's authority to the imagination consists, not in his ideas, not in his intellect, not in his culture, not in his science, but all simply in himself, in the form of his natural personality. There are scores of men of more advanced ideas than Mr. Emerson, of subtler apprehension, of broader knowledge, of deeper culture; but I know of none who is half so interesting in himself, none whose nature

[19]   Austin Warren, *The Elder Henry James* (New York, 1934), p. 41. Emerson referred to this first meeting with James in *Journals*, VI, 163 (March 18, 1842).

exhibits half so clear and sheer a reconciliation of infinite and finite.[20]

James would seem, moreover, to have had intimations of the source of this unique quality in Emerson, a source that Emerson himself would have approved: an "angle of vision" on the feminine side of awareness, like that of prophets and saints, producing a mode of perception in the process of becoming that of a true poet, in which the feminine predominated. Attempting to explain Emerson's "magic", James, in his lecture, declared: "I often found myself, in fact, thinking: if this man were only a woman, I should be sure to fall in love with him." [21] In the sketch of Emerson that William James published in his father's *Literary Remains* appears the following statement:

I found in fact, before I had been with him a week, that the immense superiority I ascribed to him was altogether personal or practical – by no means intellectual; that it came to him by birth or genius like a woman's beauty or charm of manners; that no other account was to be given of it in truth than that Emerson himself was an unsexed woman, a veritable fruit of almighty power in the sphere of our *nature*.[22]

Whether or not one can agree with the elder Henry James as to the manner in which Emerson's "immense superiority" "came to him," one has to admit that his moral and religious background and experience – the Puritan and Unitarian New England heritage, the early battles with poverty and disease, deaths, the atmosphere of plain living and high thinking in Boston and Concord, the lifelong daily need of spiritual support in facing a variety of family, social, and professional problems, the moments of inspiration that seemed heaven-sent – certainly helped to produce the unique Emersonian tone; a combination of many elements, it included disdain as well as reverence, both playfulness and complete sincerity.

Like Coleridge, he was conscious of a divine mystery when he approached the subject of Shakespeare; his attitude partook

[20]   Henry James, "Emerson", *Atlantic Monthly*, XCIV (Dec., 1904), 744.
[21]   *Ibid.*, 740.
[22]   Henry James, *Literary Remains* (Boston, 1885), pp. 296-297. This sketch was written not long after Emerson's death.

of the reverential awe of Goethe and succeeding Romantic critics; he saw that the "divine" poet "worked his miracle with his imagination – imagination which is an originating and not a decorative faculty".[23] Emerson's view of Bacon was also largely Coleridge's; but his enthusiasm for what he took to be the "First Philosophy" was often stronger than the feeling that Bacon was his "Redeemer" from the evil of not basing science on observation. Although he saw him as a "Reformer" of a type opposite to Luther's, he venerated him for his "idealism", and he shared the dominant opinion of his age that Bacon's chief claim to greatness was as a philosopher; modern scholarship has shown that he is more rightly extolled as "the herald of the industrial revolution", "the reformer of the material conditions of human life".[24] Emerson's largely reverential treatment of Milton, furthermore, reflected the early nineteenth-century tendency to admire his poetic technique and ignore his thought and the somewhat later tendency to praise him "more for his private nobility and exemplary life than for his public virtue".[25] He was markedly influenced by the contemporary practice of pairing Milton with Shakespeare as, in Coleridge's phrase, "the two glory-smitten summits of the poetic mountain", and contrasting them as opposites, viewing Shakespeare as the objective poet who lost himself in his characters and Milton as the subjective poet who, even in his highest flights, remained Milton still.[26] Coleridge was certainly his source for the relationship between Milton's career and the three stages of the English Renaissance, and he would seem to have been the first to inspire Emerson's vision of a dialectical pattern of growth reflecting the trinity.[27] The "Germans" and the Hindus served

[23]   Augustus Ralli, *A History of Shakespearian Criticism* (London, 1932), I, 142.
[24]   See Benjamin Farrington, *Francis Bacon: Philosopher of Industrial Science* (London, 1951), 176.
[25]   See James Thorpe, ed., "Introduction", *Milton Criticism* (New York, 1950), pp. 11-12.
[26]   James Graham Nelson, *The Sublime Puritan; Milton and the Victorians* (University of Wisconsin Press, 1963), pp. 15-16.
[27]   See Richard P. Adams, "Emerson and the Organic Metaphor", in Charles Feidelson, Jr., and Paul Brodtkorb, Jr., ed., *Interpretations of American Literature* (Oxford University Press, 1959), p. 148.

chiefly to confirm the truth of the Neo-Platonic ideas Emerson had found expressed in Coleridge and seventeenth-century English writers.

According to Matthiessen, Cudworth's *True Intellectual System of the Universe,* "one of his earliest enthusiasms", probably gave Emerson as an undergraduate his first introduction to Plato. It remained for him "a magazine of quotations".

Where Emerson felt really at home was with the "English transcendental genius," and, in the sentence where he uses that phrase, his examples are not his contemporaries but, once again, Herbert, Henry More, Donne, and Browne. The literature of that age was peculiarly his own tradition, since it gave expression to spiritual aspirations of which the settlement and early life of New England had been another manifestation.[28]

If Emerson needed justification for seeking "lustres" in Coleridge and such seventeenth-century Platonists as Cudworth and Henry More, it was enthusiastically provided by James Marsh, who was recognized by Coleridge as his principal disciple in America and who, even before 1821, was an enthusiastic student of the Cambridge Platonists.[29]

Marjorie H. Nicolson has shown clearly that Marsh, who organized the University of Vermont, in 1826, on Coleridgean principles, created there an institution that "has a right to be considered the home of American Transcendentalism".[30] When Marsh edited Coleridge's *Aids to Reflection* at Burlington, Vermont, in 1829, and published it with his "Preliminary Essay", he put into the hands of Emerson, Parker, Alcott, and their group the book that Perry Miller has described as having "the greatest single importance in the formation of their minds." [31] His religious orthodoxy was probably no more appealing to Emerson than was Coleridge's, but his defence of the Coleridgean distinction be-

---

[28] F. O. Matthiessen, *American Renaissance: Art and Expression in the Age of Emerson and Whitman* (Oxford University Press, 1941), pp. 104-105.
[29] Marjorie H. Nicolson, "James Marsh and the Vermont Transcendentalists", *Philosophical Review*, Vol. 34 (Jan., 1925), 30.
[30] *Ibid.,* 36.
[31] Perry Miller, ed., *The Transcendentalists,* p. 34.

tween the "Reason" and the "Understanding" and his insistence that the "New Movement in Germany" was just a revival of Cambridge Platonism convincingly showed the young transcendentalists the seventeenth-century sources of their tradition. Marsh was himself both an "American Coleridge" and a "later Cambridge Platonist".[32]

In evaluating the moral and religious development of Shakespeare, Bacon, and Milton, Emerson remained faithful to an idea described by Ernst Cassirer as "the core of English Neoplatonism" and "the basic thought" in the theology of Plotinus: " 'Never would the eye have seen the sun unless first it had assumed its form; likewise, the soul could never see beauty, unless she herself first became beautiful.' " [33] While he felt obliged to speak as Christ, Emerson tried earnestly to make himself morally capable of receiving a vision of truth and its beauty so that he could put these writers at a "true focal distance" and compare, in the life and work of each of them, the "form" of the "eye" reflected there with the "form" of the "sun" as he devoutly beheld it from his own "angle of vision".

---

[32] Nicolson, *op. cit.*, 34, 49. "When W. G. T. Shedd, in 1853, published the first complete American edition of Coleridge, he was merely completing the work which the Coleridges had planned that Marsh should do, and which Shedd himself began as Marsh's pupil." *Ibid.*, 30.
[33] Plotinus, "Of Beauty", *Ennead I*, Book VI, chaps. 8-9. As quoted in Ernst Cassirer, *The Platonic Renaissance in England*, trans. James P. Pettegrove (University of Texas Press, 1953), p. 28.

BIBLIOGRAPHY

Adams, Richard P., "Emerson and the Organic Metaphor", in Charles Feidelson, Jr., and Paul Brodtkorb, Jr., ed. *Interpretations of American Literature* (Oxford University Press, 1959).

Anderson, F. H., *The Philosophy of Francis Bacon* (University of Chicago Press, 1948).

Arvin, Newton, "The House of Pain: Emerson and the Tragic Sense", *The Hudson Review*, XII (Spring, 1959), 37-53.

Bacon, Francis, *The Works of Francis Bacon*, 10 vols. (London, W. Baynes and Son, 1824).

Beach, Joseph W., *The Concept of Nature in Nineteenth-Century English Poetry* (New York, MacMillan, 1936).

Blair, Walter, and Faust, Clarence, "Emerson's Literary Method", *Modern Philology*, XLII (1944), 79-95.

Blau, Joseph L., *Men and Movements in American Philosophy* (New York, Prentiss-Hall, 1952).

Brett, R. L., *The Third Earl of Shaftesbury: A Study in Eighteenth Century Literary Theory* (New York, Hutchinson's University Library, 1951).

Brittin, Norman A., "Emerson and the Metaphysical Poets", *American Literature*, VIII (March, 1936), 1-21.

Brown, Stuart Gerry, "Emerson's Platonism", *New England Quarterly*, XVIII (1945), 325-345.

Cabot, James, *A Memoir of Ralph Waldo Emerson*, 2 vols. (Boston, Houghton, Mifflin, 1887).

Cameron, Kenneth W., *Emerson the Essayist*, 2 vols. (Raleigh, N.C., Thistle Press, 1945).

——, *Emerson's Early Reading List (1819-1824)* (New York, Public Library, 1951).

——, *Ralph Waldo Emerson's Reading* (Raleigh, N.C., Thistle Press, 1941).

——, "Emerson, Thomas Campbell, and Bacon's Definition of Poetry", *Emerson Society Quarterly*, No. 14 (First quarter, 1959), pp. 48-56.

——, "Coleridge and the Genesis of Emerson's Uriel", *Philological Quarterly*, Vol. 30 (April, 1951), 212-217.

Caponigri, A. Robert, "Brownson and Emerson: Nature and History", *New England Quarterly*, XVIII (Sept., 1945), 368-390.

Cassirer, Ernst, *The Platonic Renaissance in England,* Translated by James P. Pettegrove (University of Texas Press, 1953).

Channing, William E., *The Works of William E. Channing,* 6 vols. (Boston, J. Munroe, 1841-1843).

Clark, Harry Hayden, "Emerson and Science", *Philological Quarterly,* X (July, 1931), 225-260.

Coleridge, Samuel Taylor, *The Complete Works of Samuel Taylor Coleridge.* Edited by W. G. T. Shedd, 7 vols. (New York, Harper & Bros., 1853).

——, *Coleridge's Writings on Shakespeare.* Edited by Terence Hawkes (New York, G. P. Putnam's Sons, 1959).

——, *Coleridge on the Seventeenth Century.* Edited by Roberta Florence Brinkley (Duke University Press, 1955).

Collingwood, R. G., *The Idea of Nature* (Oxford University Press, 1945).

——, *The Idea of History* (Oxford University Press, 1946).

Cudworth, Ralph, *The True Intellectual System of the Universe.* Translated by John Harrison, 3 vols. (London, Thomas Tegg, 1845).

Davis, Merrell R., "Emerson's 'Reason' and the Scottish Philosophers", *New England Quarterly,* XVII (1944), 209-228.

Dewey, John, "James Marsh and American Philosophy", *Journal of the History of Ideas,* Vol. 2 (1941), 131-150.

Dryden, John, *Essays of John Dryden.* Edited by W. P. Ker, 2 vols. (Oxford, Clarendon Press, 1900).

Emerson, Ralph Waldo, *The Complete Works of Ralph Waldo Emerson.* Edited by Edward Waldo Emerson, 12 vols. (Boston, Houghton, Mifflin, 1903-1904).

——, *Journals of Ralph Waldo Emerson.* Edited by Edward Waldo Emerson and Waldo Emerson Forbes, 10 vols. (Boston, Houghton, Mifflin, 1909-1914).

——, *The Letters of Ralph Waldo Emerson.* Edited by Ralph L. Rusk, 6 vols. (Columbia University Press, 1939).

——, *The Early Lectures of Ralph Waldo Emerson.* Edited by Stephen E. Whicher and Robert E. Spiller, Vol. I (Harvard University Press, 1959).

——, *The Journals and Miscellaneous Notebooks of Ralph Waldo Emerson.* Edited by William H. Gilman, George P. Clark, Alfred R. Ferguson, Merrell R. Davis, Vol. I (Harvard University Press, 1960).

——, "Preface", in *Parnassus.* Edited by Ralph Waldo Emerson (Boston, James R. Osgood, 1875).

——, "Three Unpublished Lectures of Ralph Waldo Emerson", edited by Jeanne Kronman, in *New England Quarterly,* XIX (March, 1946), 98-110.

——, "Early Letters of Emerson", edited by Mary S. Withington, in *The Century,* XXVI (July, 1883), 454-58.

——, "The Editors to the Reader", in *The Dial,* I (July, 1840), 1-4.

——, Lecture manuscripts at Houghton Library, 194.1-214.3.

Falk, Robert P., "Emerson and Shakespeare", *PMLA,* LVI (1941), 532-43.

Farrington, Benjamin, *Francis Bacon: Philosopher of Industrial Science* (London, Lawrence and Wishart, 1951).

Feidelson, Charles, *Symbolism and American Literature* (Chicago University Press, 1953).

Feuer, Lewis, "James Marsh and the Conservative Transcendentalist Philosophy", *New England Quarterly*, XXXI (March, 1958), 3-31.

Foerster, Norman, *American Criticism: A Study in Literary Theory from Poe to the Present* (Boston, Houghton, Mifflin, 1928).

Foster, Charles Howell, "Emerson as American Scripture", *The New England Quarterly*, XVI (March, 1943), 91-105.

Goethe, Johann Wolfgang, *Goethe on Shakespeare, being Selections from Carlyle's translation of Wilhelm Meister* (London, De La More Press, 1904).

——, "Shakespeare ad Infinitum". Translated by Randolph S. Bourne. In *Goethe's Literary Essays*. Edited by J. E. Spingarn (New York, Harcourt, Brace, 1921).

Gray, H. D. *Emerson: A Statement of New England Transcendentalism as Expressed in the Philosophy of its Chief Exponent* (Stanford University, 1917).

Harris, William T., "The Dialectic Unity in Emerson's Prose", *Journal of Speculative Philosophy*, XVIII (April, 1884), 195-202.

——, "Ralph Waldo Emerson", *Atlantic*, L (Aug., 1882), 238-252.

Harrison, John S., *The Teachers of Emerson* (New York, Sturgis and Walton, 1910).

Hopkins, Vivian C., "Emerson and Cudworth: Plastic Nature and Transcendental Art", *American Literature*, Vol. 23 (March, 1951), pp. 80-98.

——, "Emerson and Bacon", *American Literature*, Vol. 29 (Jan., 1958), pp. 408-430.

——, *Spires of Form: A Study of Emerson's Aesthetic Theory* (Harvard University Press, 1951).

Ivimey, Joseph, *John Milton: His Life and Times, Religious and Political Opinions* (New York, 1833).

James, Henry, "Emerson", *Atlantic Monthly*, XCIV (Dec., 1904), 740-745.

——, *Literary Remains*. Edited by William James (Boston, J. R. Osgood, 1885).

Jameson, Thomas Hugh, *Francis Bacon: Criticism and the Modern World* (New York, F. A. Praeger, 1954).

Kloeckner, Alfred J., "Intellect and Moral Sentiment in Emerson's Opinions of 'The Meaner Kinds' of Men", *American Literature*, Vol. 30 (Nov., 1958), 322-338.

Lemmi, Charles W., *The Classic Deities in Bacon: A Study in Mythological Symbolism* (The Johns Hopkins Press, 1933).

Lovejoy, Arthur O., "Coleridge and Kant's Two Worlds", in *Essays in the History of Ideas* (The Johns Hopkins Press, 1948).

——, "The Dialectic of Bruno and Spinoza," in *The University of California Publications in Philosophy*, Vol. 1 (1904), pp. 141-174.

——, *The Great Chain of Being: A Study of the History of an Idea* (Harvard University Press, 1953).

——, *The Reason, the Understanding, and Time* (The Johns Hopkins Press, 1961).

——, "Kant and the English Platonists", in *Essays Philosophical and Psychological in Honor of William James, by his colleagues at Columbia University* (1908), pp. 265-302.

Marks, Alfred H., "Whitman's Triadic Imagery", *American Literature,* Vol. 23 (March, 1951), 99-126.

Marsh, James, *Remains, with a Memoir of his Life* (Boston, 1843).

——, "Preliminary Essay", in Samuel Taylor Coleridge, *Aids to Reflection,* Edited by James Marsh (Burlington, Vermont, C. Goodrich, 1829).

Matthiessen, F. O., *American Renaissance: Art and Expression in the Age of Emerson and Whitman* (Oxford University Press, 1941).

McCormick, John O., "Emerson's Theory of Human Greatness", *New England Quarterly,* Vol. 26 (Sept., 1953), 291-314.

Metz, Rudolf, "Bacon's Part in the Intellectual Movement of his Time", in *Seventeenth Century Studies Presented to Sir Herbert Grierson* (Oxford, 1938), pp. 21-32.

Miller, Perry, "Edwards to Emerson", *New England Quarterly,* XIII (1940), 589-617.

——, (ed.), *The Transcendentalists* (Harvard University Press, 1950).

Milton, John, *The Poetical Works of John Milton,* 7 vols. Edited by Henry J. Todd (London, 1809).

——, *The Prose Works.* Edited by Charles Symmons. 7 vols. (London, 1806).

Muirhead, John H., *Coleridge as Philosopher* (New York, The Humanities Press, 1930).

Nelson, James Graham, *The Sublime Puritan; Milton and the Victorians* (University of Wisconsin Press, 1963).

Nicoloff, Philip L., *Emerson on Race and History; An Examination of "English Traits"* (Columbia University Press, 1961).

Nicolson, Marjorie H., "James Marsh and the Vermont Transcendentalists", *Philosophical Review,* Vol. 34 (Jan. 1925), pp. 28-50.

——, *The Breaking of the Circle.* Revised edition (Columbia University Press, 1960).

——, *Mountain Gloom and Mountain Glory: The Development of the Aesthetics of the Infinite* (Cornell University Press, 1959).

——, "Christ's College and the Latitude-Men", *Modern Philology,* XXVII (Aug., 1929), 35-53.

——, "The Spirit World of Milton and More", *Studies in Philology,* XXII (Oct., 1923), 433-452.

Paul, Sherman, *Emerson's Angle of Vision* (Harvard University Press, 1952).

Perry, Thomas A., "Emerson, the Historical Frame, and Shakespeare", *Modern Language Quarterly,* Vol. 9 (Dec., 1948), 440-447.

Pettigrew, Richard C., "Emerson and Milton", *American Literature,* III (March, 1931), 45-59.

Pochmann, Henry A., *German Culture in America: Philosophical and Literary Influences, 1600-1900* (University of Wisconsin Press, 1957).

Pollitt, Joe Donald, "Ralph Waldo Emerson's Debt to John Milton", *Marshall Review,* III (Dec., 1939), 13-21.

Proclus, Diadochus, *The Six Books of Proclus,* Translated by Thomas Taylor. 2 vols. (London, A. J. Valpy, 1816).

Ralli, Augustus, *A History of Shakespearean Criticism,* 2 vols. (Oxford University Press, 1932).

Roberts, J. Russell, "Emerson's Debt to the Seventeenth Century", *American Literature,* Vol. 21 (Nov., 1949), 298-310.

Rusk, Ralph L., *The Life of Ralph Waldo Emerson* (New York, Charles Scribner's Sons, 1949).

Schlegel, August Wilhelm, *A Course of Lectures on Dramatic Art and Literature.* Translated by John Black, revised by A. J. W. Morrison (London, Henry G. Bohn, 1861).

Schneider, Herbert W., *A History of American Philosophy* (Columbia University Press, 1946).

Shakespeare, William, *The Plays and Poems of William Shakespeare.* Edited by James Boswell, 21 vols. (London, F. C. and J. Rivington, 1821).

——, *Mr. William Shakespeares Comedies, Histories & Tragedies.* Facsimile edition of the First Folio. Edited by Helge Kökeritz (Yale University Press, 1954).

——, *The Dramatic Works of William Shakespeare.* Edited by Isaac Reed. 12 vols. (London, 1820).

Silver, Mildred, "Emerson and the Idea of Progress", *American Literature,* XII (1940), 1-19.

Smith, D. Nicholl (ed.), *Shakespeare Criticism* (Oxford University Press, 1916).

Stephen, Leslie, "Emerson", in *Studies of a Biographer,* Vol. IV (London, Duckworth, 1902), pp. 130-167.

Stovall, Floyd(ed.), *The Development of American Literary Criticism* (University of North Carolina Press, 1955).

Strauch, Carl F., "Emerson's Sacred Science", *PMLA,* LXXIII (June, 1958), 237-250.

Thompson, Frank T., "Emerson's Indebtedness to Coleridge", *Studies in Philology,* XXIII (1926), 55-76.

Thorpe, James (ed.), *Milton Criticism: Selections from Four Centuries* (Rinehart, 1950).

Very, Jones, *Essays and Poems.* Edited by Ralph Waldo Emerson. (Boston, Charles C. Little and James Brown, 1839).

Warren, Austin, *The Elder Henry James* (New York, Macmillan, 1934).

Wellek, René, "Emerson and German Philosophy", *New England Quarterly,* XVI (March, 1943), 41-62.

Wells, Ronald V., *Three Christian Transcendentalists: James Marsh, Caleb Sprague Henry, Frederic Henry Hedge* (Columbia University Press, 1943).

Whicher, Stephen E., *Freedom and Fate: An Inner Life of Ralph Waldo Emerson* (University of Pennsylvania Press, 1953).

Whipple, Edwin P., "Some Recollections of Ralph Waldo Emerson", *Harper's New Monthly Magazine,* Vol. 65 (Sept., 1882), 576-587.

Williams, Mentor L., " 'Why Nature Loves the Number Five': Emerson Toys with the Occult", in *Papers of the Michigan Academy of Science, Arts, and Letters,* XXX (1944), 639-649.

Winters, Yvor, *Maule's Curse: Seven Studies in the History of American Obscurantism* (Norfolk, Conn., New Directions, 1938).

INDEX

STUDIES IN ENGLISH LITERATURE

Out:

MOUTON & CO. — PUBLISHERS — THE HAGUE